Rabbit Production

FIFTH EDITION

with chapters co-authored by

Steven D. Lukefahr

Oregon State University Rabbit Research Center

James I. McNitt

Bunda College of Agriculture, Malawi

THE INTERSTATE
PRINTERS & PUBLISHERS, INC.

Danville, Illinois

Rabbit Production

by

Peter R. Cheeke

Director of Research
Oregon State University Rabbit Research Center

Nephi M. Patton

Director
Oregon State University Rabbit Research Center

George S. Templeton

Former Director
U.S. Rabbit Experiment Station

Library of Congress Catalog Card No. 81-84394

ISBN 0-8134-2222-1

Dedicated to
the members and friends of the
Oregon State University
Rabbit Research Center program.

Preface

Interest in the rabbit as a meat-producing animal is widespread and increasing. Recognition that rabbits efficiently convert high roughage diets into high quality meat has stimulated interest in their production in North America, Europe, and tropical developing countries in Africa and the Caribbean region. The energy shortage in the United States has stimulated interest in self-sufficiency and home food production. Rabbits are ideally suited to small-scale production, even in cities. Thus the future of the rabbit industry looks bright.

Rabbit production techniques, and knowledge of rabbit nutrition, genetics, and diseases, lag behind the situation with other domestic species. Nevertheless, in the 1970's, significant rabbit research programs in the United States and Europe contributed much new knowledge concerning rabbit production. With these advances, it is appropriate that Templeton's book *Domestic Rabbit Production* be revised and updated. We have undertaken this task enthusiastically. We know that with the rapidly expanding research activities taking place, further revisions will be needed in the future as new knowledge is developed.

We are donating our royalties from the sale of this book to the research program of the Oregon State University Rabbit Research Center. Thus the users of this book will be contributing directly to the expansion of research on rabbit production.

We thank several individuals at the Rabbit Research Center for their help in preparing this volume. To Grace Hayes we owe special thanks for her efforts in typing the manuscript. Steven D. Lukefahr reviewed the entire text, and also co-authored the genetics chapter. David J. Harris provided many of the photographs used in the book, including those in the color section, and reviewed portions of the text. Dr. James I. McNitt of Bunda College of Agriculture, Malawi, reviewed the entire text and wrote much of the chapter on reproductive physiology.

We also thank numerous rabbit raisers who sent photographs for use in the book. We extend our sincere appreciation and thanks to all the supporters of the OSU Rabbit Research Center, who have made it possible for us to engage in rabbit research.

PETER R. CHEEKE
NEPHI M. PATTON

Table of Contents

1

Introduction

Rabbit production is developing into a significant agricultural enterprise in the US, and is relatively important in several European countries such as France and Italy, where rabbit is regarded as a gourmet meat. In addition to being raised commercially for meat and fur, rabbits are also produced in large numbers for laboratory use. They are particularly useful in certain types of medical research. Many people in the US raise rabbits for show purposes, for the pleasure and challenge of breeding animals that possess traits that best exemplify the standards of a particular breed. Others keep rabbits simply as pets. Regardless of one's motivation for keeping rabbits, information on nutrition, diseases, breeding, and management is useful for attaining an end product of healthy, well nourished animals.

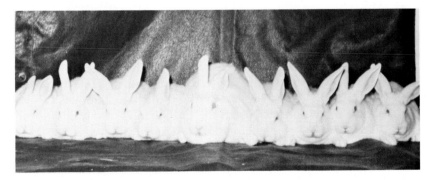

Fig. 1-1. A productive doe and her litter. Because of their high reproductive capacity and high growth rate, rabbits are among the most productive of domestic livestock. (Courtesy of *The Journal of Applied Rabbit Research*)

HISTORY, TAXONOMY, AND DOMESTICATION
OF THE RABBIT

All the domestic breeds of rabbits are descendants of the European wild rabbit, *Oryctolagus cuniculus*. Rabbits were originally classified as rodents, but are now placed in a separate order, the Lagomorphs. Lagomorphs have two more incisor teeth than rodents (six instead of four). The Lagomorphs are divided into two major families: pikas, and rabbits and hares. Pikas, or rock rabbits, are common inhabitants of mountainous areas. Hares differ from rabbits in that they are born fully haired, with their eyes open, and can run within a few minutes of birth. They have long legs and take long leaps or bounds when running. They are born in the open without a well defined nest. Hares have the scientific name *Lepus* (e.g., *Lepus europaeus*—European hare; *Lepus californicus*—black tailed jack rabbit). The two main genera of rabbits are the true rabbits *(Oryctolagus)* and the cottontail rabbits *(Sylvilagus)*. *Oryctolagus cuniculus* includes the European wild rabbit and its domesticated descendants, which are all the breeds of domestic rabbits. *Sylvilagus* includes a number of North American cottontails, including the Eastern, Desert, Marsh, and Brush cottontail rabbits. Cottontails and domestic rabbits cannot be crossed. Dr. C. E. Adams of the University of Cambridge has studied this cross; sperm and eggs of the two genera will cross-fertilize, but the developing embryos die in a few hours after about four cell divisions, due to major dissimilarities in the chromosomes of the two species.

The story of the domestication of rabbits is shrouded in mystery. The first recorded rabbit husbandry was in early Roman times, when rabbits were kept in leporaria, or walled rabbit gardens. Rabbits reproduced in these enclosures and were captured and killed for food. In the Middle Ages, sailing vessels distributed rabbits on islands in various sea lanes, to be used as a source of food by sailors. Wherever these releases were made, the rabbits increased greatly in number at the expense of the indigenous animals. As exploration of the world increased, the European wild rabbit was further distributed by sailors. In 1859, a single pair was released in Victoria, Australia, and in 30 years gave rise to an estimated 20 million rabbits. Other releases of a few rabbits in Australia also gave rise to millions of rabbits in the areas of release. The wild rabbit became a serious pest in Australia and New Zealand, due to the favorable environment, abundant feed, and absence of predators.

The European wild rabbit, while released in North America, was never able to gain a foothold and does not exist on the continent.

In the Middle Ages, rabbits were kept in rock enclosures in England and western Europe. True domestication probably began in the sixteenth century, in monasteries. By 1700, seven distinct colors had been selected: non-agouti, brown, albino, dilute (blue), yellow, silver, and Dutch spotting. By 1850, two new colors and the Angora-type hair had been developed. Between 1850 and the present day, the remaining colors and fur types have been developed and selected.

POTENTIAL OF THE RABBIT FOR MEAT AND FUR PRODUCTION

The domestic rabbit has the potential to become one of the world's major livestock species. In the future, as the human population exerts increasing pressure on the world's food resources, it is likely that rabbits will assume an increasingly important role as a source of food. They possess various attributes that are advanta-

Fig. 1-2. The interior of a modern commercial rabbitry of simple but adequate construction. (Courtesy of OSU Rabbit Research Center)

geous in comparison to other livestock. Rabbits can be successfully raised on diets that are low in grain and high in roughage. Recent research has demonstrated that normal growth and reproductive performance can be achieved on diets containing no grain at all. As competition between humans and livestock for grains intensifies, rabbits will have a competitive advantage over swine and poultry, since these animals cannot be raised on high roughage diets or diets that don't contain grain. Rabbits convert forage into meat more efficiently than ruminant animals such as cattle and sheep. From a given amount of alfalfa, rabbits can produce about five times as much meat as beef cattle.

The ability of rabbits to convert forage into meat efficiently will be of special significance in developing countries, where population pressures and food shortages are greatest. In many cases, there is abundant local vegetation which cannot be consumed directly by people, but which could be fed to rabbits. A few does can be kept by villagers on a backyard scale, to produce enough meat to satisfy the needs of a family, using weeds, tropical forages, vegetable tops,

Fig. 1-3. A small backyard rabbitry in Haiti. Rabbit production has great potential in developing countries, because rabbits can be fed on forages and by-products that can't be used directly by humans. (Courtesy of *The Journal of Applied Rabbit Research*)

and table scraps as feed for the rabbits. Keeping cattle under such circumstances is not feasible because of their larger feed and space requirements, the long time taken to reach slaughter weight, and the problem of using a large amount of meat at once when refrigeration is lacking. Rabbits act as "biological refrigerators," since the meat from one animal can be consumed without the need for storage.

An exciting characteristic of rabbits is their high reproductive potential. This, of course, is well known, being the subject of numerous jokes regarding fertility. Because of their rapid growth rate, short gestation period, and ability to rebreed immediately after parturition (giving birth), the reproductive potential is staggering. Several animals released in Australia resulted in a few years in tens of millions of rabbits. In commercial production, this high reproduction potential is of great importance. Recent research has demonstrated the feasibility of post-partum breeding, so it is possible for a doe to have a litter, be rebred immediately, wean the litter at 28 days, and have another litter 3 days later. No other type of livestock has this amazing reproductive potential. Such intensive breeding requires a high level of management skill and is not recommended until further research is completed.

The future is bright for genetic improvement of rabbits raised commercially. Because of the short generation time, rapid selection progress can be made. The heritability of growth and carcass traits is high, so rapid improvement of these traits through selection can be made. There has been comparatively little genetic selection of rabbits for such important commercial characteristics as carcass traits, so there is scope for considerable progress in these areas. Compared to other types of livestock production, there has been little commercial development of high performing hybrids, use of well designed crossbreeding schemes, or other techniques that are routine in the other types of livestock enterprises.

Rabbits lend themselves to both small- and large-scale production. France is the world's largest producer and consumer of rabbits. The size of the average French doe herd is six animals. Thus the French industry is based upon a large number of small producers. In contrast, in Hungary there are rabbitries with 10,000 does, producing meat rabbits for export to Italy. The future looks bright for both types of production. In the US, there is increasing interest in large-scale commercial production, with units of 500 or 1000 or several thousand does. At the other end of the scale, many people

Fig. 1-4. A 10,000-doe rabbitry in Hungary, producing about 300,000 fryers annually. Rabbits are suited to both large- and small-scale production. (Courtesy of *The Journal of Applied Rabbit Research*)

keep a few does in the backyard to raise meat for the family. In times of economic stress, such as the depression of the 1930's, World War II, and the 1980's energy crisis, interest in self-sufficiency increases, and backyard rabbit production increases. Because they are noiseless, rabbits can be raised in a suburban situation without infringing on the peace of neighbors. Only a small space is needed for raising rabbits, and they adapt themselves to a variety of conditions, being raised successfully in many cities, in small towns, and on farms in every state of the US. They appeal to all classes of people with a diversity of backgrounds. Many of these people have had a lifelong yen for raising animals but have been so situated that they could not realize their dreams, and are now deriving a great deal of satisfaction and relaxation from working with them. The amount of capital needed for the equipment and for the animals is reasonable; caring for them does not involve strenuous physical exertion, so the work can be carried on with much satisfaction by the physically disabled and is especially useful for occupational therapy. The size of the animal makes it exceptionally valuable also in youth programs.

Rabbit meat is a wholesome, tasty product. Compared to most

Fig. 1-5. Rabbit is a high quality, nutritious, and attractive meat. (Courtesy of D. J. Harris, Corvallis, Oregon)

other meats, it is high in protein and low in fat, cholesterol, and sodium. The meat is white, fine-grained, delicately flavored, nutritious, and appetizing. It is low in caloric content also. The size of the carcass, the fine quality of the meat, and the wide range in methods for preparation make it an excellent and economical meat for use in any season of the year. In many areas it is available in the markets either in the cut-up and packaged, fresh or frozen form, or in the whole carcass. While there appears to be a preference shown by consumers for the cut-up and packaged product, chefs and those in charge of the meat purchasing for institutions such as hospitals, clubs, and hotels prefer it in the whole carcass form so they may cut it to suit their own requirements and methods of preparation.

While the main product of commercial rabbit production is meat, the skins are also important. The furs are used in various apparel items such as fur coats. There is a market for all sizes and colors of domestic rabbit skins, although the price paid for the skins by the larger fur buyers is not sufficient to justify many of the assertions that have been made that one could engage in breeding rabbits for their pelts alone and make a satisfactory profit, for the returns from both meat and pelts must be combined in order to derive the maximum profit on the labor and capital invested. The market values vary from time to time depending on season, fashion dictates, etc. The center of the fur industry in the United States is New York City.

Rabbit skins are used in many ways, the best quality being employed in making fur garments and fur trimmings, the poorer quality being used by the felting industry and for manufacturing toys, specialty articles, etc. The normal furs are used chiefly for making imitations of high priced furs, and the fur industry has become so proficient in this line that by plucking, shearing, dyeing, etc., it is able to imitate many of the wild and more expensive furs. These imitations are sold under a variety of trade names, and each imitation must be properly labeled. The better quality garments that are made from the heavily furred rabbit skins are warm and luxurious, and they wear well. Those skins that are not suitable for manufacturing the better quality products are used for lining men's and boys' clothing, making toys, trimming children's garments and coats, and manufacturing felt hats. At the time the fur is cut from the skins for use by the felting industry, the skins are shredded and a glue that is especially strong is extracted. This glue is used principally by furniture makers.

The Rex rabbit differs from other breeds in having a coat with no conspicuous guard hairs, giving a very attractive fur. There has recently been extensive interest in the United States in Rex rabbit production. Whether this will develop into an integral component of the American rabbit industry remains to be seen.

PRODUCTION OF PHARMACEUTICALS

Associated with the production of rabbits for meat and fur is the preparation of pharmaceutical products. The brains, blood, and various internal organs are used for producing "biologicals" for medical use and research. For example, rabbit brains are a source of thromboplastin, which is used to control the dosage of anticoagulant given to prevent thrombosis (heart attack), phlebitis, and other abnormal clotting conditions of the human body. The blood is used to prepare complement, used in biomedical programs. Various enzymes for research are derived from rabbit tissues. Large processing plants use all parts of the rabbit, even the feet for "lucky rabbit's foot" souvenirs.

YOUTH PROGRAMS

The raising of domestic rabbits lends itself nicely to 4-H Club, Boy and Girl Scout, and FFA projects. The fact that in many cases they can be raised where larger farm animals or even poultry cannot be handled makes them especially useful animals for these groups. In this connection, rabbit breeders can be of material aid to these younger people by providing desirable breeding stock at nominal prices and by counseling with their leaders and the members of the youth groups with respect to methods for raising or caring for their animals. In many sections where the youthful rabbit raisers may need capital for developing their projects, local bankers cooperate with them and arrange to make loans for that purpose. The boy or girl signs a note and is expected to repay the principal and interest out of the profits from the endeavor. This cooperation by business executives is helpful and gives the young rabbit raiser an insight into business procedure. Many youth projects have resulted in prizes and trophies being awarded at fairs and other exhibitions.

In order to teach the young person the fundamentals of animal

Fig. 1-6. 4-H members showing their rabbits. (Courtesy of D. J. Harris, Corvallis, Oregon)

husbandry, these youth groups may begin with young rabbits at weaning age. When the young people in a family group want to raise rabbits, it may be best to purchase an adult doe in order that their interest may be kept keen by the chronological events such as the doe making a nest and kindling, and the young people taking care of the litter, selling the products, etc. Many of these small beginnings on the part of young people have developed into sizeable undertakings.

HOBBIES AND PETS

Because the domestic rabbit is cage-raised, it lends itself more readily than other farm animals to handling by blind or otherwise disabled persons and opens up a new field of activity for them. They derive a great deal of satisfaction from producing meat rabbits, spinning Angora wool, and making garments.

Fig. 1-7. Rabbits make fine pets! (Courtesy of Charles and Vicki Hertel, Vanher Rabbitry, Forest Grove, Oregon)

People may desire to raise rabbits because they enjoy working with animals and thus can advantageously combine a hobby with prospects of a supplemental income. There are many ramifications to this type of activity. Some people may develop an interest in attempting to improve a strain of rabbits by studying its characteristics, in an effort to produce animals as nearly perfect as possible, and derive a great deal of pleasure from showing them.

Complete rabbit rations can be purchased in small quantitites at most feed stores, and these complete pellets are clean, easy to store, and convenient to feed. Caution should be taken, however, in purchasing very young rabbits for small children, such as Easter bunnies, etc., because in too many of these cases the rabbits are improperly handled or cared for, and may be abused and die. For a child's pet, a rabbit that is a quarter to half grown is a more desirable size, because it has passed its more delicate stage of development and is less likely to be injured while the child is being instructed by the parent as to the proper method for holding and playing with it.

LABORATORY USE

A large number of rabbits are used by laboratories. Because the animal is small and does not require a large amount of space in the laboratory, and the feeding and care of it is relatively inexpensive, this species is exceptionally well adapted to certain types of research. These include performing nutritional studies, testing new medical products, developing information relative to inheritance of malformations, and studying diseases. The rabbit is being used more and more in connection with preliminary research tests with the larger types of farm animals, and its blood is used quite extensively in making antisera.

FACTORS LIMITING RABBIT PRODUCTION

Despite the promising potential of the rabbit as a meat- and fur-producing animal, a number of factors presently limit the profitability of rabbit enterprises. These are related to problems of nutrition, disease, genetics, and the high labor requirement for intensive rabbit production. Much less research has been conducted on

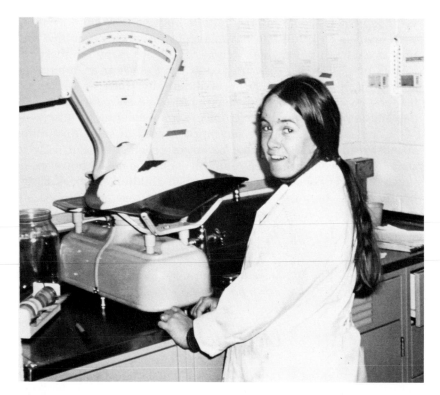

Fig. 1-8. Rabbits are widely used in biomedical research. In this picture, a rabbit used in nutrition research is being weighed. (Courtesy of OSU Rabbit Research Center)

commercial rabbit production than with other livestock species. Therefore, many more unsolved problems exist, and less information is available on optimal feeding, breeding, disease prevention, and management systems. In the area of nutrition, for instance, it is only since 1970 that data on specific nutrient requirements for energy, protein, amino acids, vitamins, and minerals have been obtained. In most cases, the existing data have been collected in experiments using small numbers of animals, with diets that are not representative of commercial feeds. Thus much refining of this information is needed, through continued research.

Diseases such as enteritis and snuffles are very important factors that prevent rabbit production from reaching its potential. Enteritis is a complex of several diseases which cause diarrhea, dehydration, and death of young rabbits. Until the late 1970's, very little progress had been made in understanding the causes of the disease. Significant advancements in the identification of types of bacteria and dietary factors involved in development of enteritis have been made, but much remains to be done.

In the genetics and breeding areas, there has been relatively little sustained effort to develop superior breeding animals. The commercial rabbit industry in the United States has been based on rabbit raisers who have not been in the business for very long. One large processor has characterized rabbit raisers as "one-third coming into the industry, one-third in, and one-third leaving." The lack of many long-term commercial producers means that there have not been many sustained breeding and selection programs carried out for a sufficient period to make real progress. Some selection in the past has been for traits with a low heritability, such as litter size, whereas highly heritable traits such as milk production and growth rate have not received much attention. Development of superior breeding stock, with the potential for high performance in all productive traits, would do much to ensure the growth of the rabbit industry.

Another factor which limits the profit potential of large-scale rabbit production is the high labor intensity of rabbit raising. Under present management situations, there is a great deal of hand labor involved in feeding, mating, cage cleaning, and virtually all other facets of rabbit production. This is in contrast to the extensive mechanization and low labor requirements for poultry production. Once a rabbitry reaches a size above 600 does where hired labor is required, the labor costs become a major factor. Additionally, rabbits require "tender loving care," and with large rabbitries employing hired labor, this is not always easy to provide. For successful development of large commercial rabbit enterprises to occur in North America and other areas with high labor costs, management systems employing greater automation will need to be developed.

In contrast, for backyard production in both developed and developing countries, the labor requirements are more or less irrelevant. A few does and their offspring for family meat production are easy to manage, with the care often provided by the children. Diseases such as enteritis seem to be much less prevalent under these conditions, probably because of a more varied diet and less stressful conditions than animals experience in a large rabbitry. Because of low labor costs, and often abundant forage resources, some developing countries may prove to be ideal sites for large-scale rabbitries.

The future is bright for rabbit production. Increasing interest in research on rabbit production at universities and experiment stations throughout the world will undoubtedly provide answers to many of the problems currently plaguing rabbit producers.

SOURCES OF HELPFUL INFORMATION

For many years, the United States Department of Agriculture maintained the U.S. Rabbit Experiment Station at Fontana, California. This station was the source of much useful information on rabbit production. The station was closed when it appeared that rabbit production was not going to become a major agricultural enterprise in the US. Rabbit research was at a very low ebb in the 1960's and early 1970's. Since that time, interest in the rabbit as a meat animal has been rekindled, due in part to the increasing awareness of the competition between livestock and humans for grain. A USDA-supported program of rabbit research has been established at Oregon State University's Rabbit Research Center. This program is also heavily supported financially by the rabbit industry. The Research Center publishes *The Journal of Applied Rabbit Research,* which contains reports of the latest research on commercial rabbit production. Most of the land-grant universities, through their extension departments, sponsor 4-H Rabbit Club activities in their respective states, and several have sponsored rabbit schools. These schools are similar to the forums or courses that for many years have been conducted for other types of farm animals and are usually held annually at the university, although occasionally they are held in the section of the state where the largest centers of rabbit population are located. These schools have been extremely valuable to the rabbit industry, with members of the university faculty and other well informed representatives of the rabbit industry participating. One of the most valuable features of these rabbit school programs is the time allotted to questions and answers.

Many of the state agricultural universities issue bulletins on rabbit production and assign a member of the extension department to the specific duty of assisting the industry in the state. Advice may also be obtained by contacting agricultural agents and farm advisors.

The American Rabbit Breeders Association (ARBA), with home offices in Bloomington, Illinois,[1] assists the rabbit industry in many ways by maintaining a registration and recording system, affording memberships to persons interested in breeding and marketing rabbits and allied products, promoting and conducting public and private exhibitions, providing judging systems, licensing official judges and registrars, and making and revising official standards. The association also organizes and assists local, county, and state associations and specialty clubs, maintains information bureaus, and furnishes at cost bulletins, guide books, and other printed matter. It assists in marketing, and in securing legislation and publicity. An annual convention and show are held.

Contact with members of local rabbit clubs is an excellent means for beginners to obtain information relative to rabbit problems, such as facts on cooperative buying and marketing of products, lists of reliable breeders, ordinances with relation to the industry, etc.

On the whole, feed manufacturers have spent a great deal of time and money in research work in order to develop efficient rations for rabbits. They also issue bulletins and sometimes furnish the breeder with hutch cards and other record cards. Many of them have field representatives who make visits to rabbitries and assist the breeders with their rabbit problems.

A list of useful general books and periodicals on rabbit production follows.

BOOKS AND PERIODICALS ON RABBIT PRODUCTION

Books

Arrington, L. R., and K. C. Kelley. *Domestic Rabbit Biology and Production.* Gainesville: The University Presses of Florida, 1976.

Mannell, P. *How to Start a Commercial Rabbitry.* Monett, Missouri: Bass Equipment Co., 1973.

---

[1]American Rabbit Breeders Association, Inc., P.O. Box 426, Bloomington, Illinois 61701.

Periodicals

The Journal of Applied Rabbit Research. OSU Rabbit Research Center, Oregon State University, Corvallis, Oregon 97331.

Rabbits. Countryside Publications, Ltd., 312 Portland Road, Highway 19 East, Waterloo, Wisconsin 53594.

Domestic Rabbits. American Rabbit Breeders Association, Inc., P.O. Box 426, Bloomington, Illinois 61701.

Rabbit and Cavy Gazette. Tri County, Inc., 4304 Powell, Kansas City, Kansas 66106.

2

Selecting a Breed and Purchasing Stock

SELECTING A BREED

The prospective rabbit raiser should decide on the purpose for which the rabbits will be raised, and then select a breed that will be best suited to this and one that will also satisfy his or her personal preferences. There is no one breed that is best for all purposes, but there are many with such different characteristics that there should be little difficulty in making a selection.

With respect to body conformation, there is considerable variation from the "racy type" of the Belgian Hare to the compact body shape of the medium weight and heavy meat breeds. Weights range from a mature weight of less than 2½ pounds for the Netherland Dwarf to over 20 pounds for some of the giant breeds.

The length of the coat for the different breeds ranges from the short-furred Rex to the Angora, which has an annual growth of 8 to 10 inches of wool. There are also many different coat colors, and the rabbits may be solid black, blue, chocolate, fawn, gray, white, etc., or with spots, or of mixed colors.

For commercial meat production, the New Zealand White is the principal breed. It has a number of desirable traits including a rapid growth rate, good carcass quality, good prolificacy, and good mothering ability, and in general possesses all the characteristics desirable for a meat-producing animal. The other major meat breed is the Californian. It tends to finish out at a lighter weight than the New Zealand White, but in most other respects is comparable. European producers have found that crossing the Californian buck with the New Zealand White doe produces a high quality market animal. In Hungary, the "White Pearl" is raised extensively for meat. The White Pearl is the product of a New Zealand White buck bred to a Californian–New Zealand White crossbred doe. Thus for commercial meat production, the New Zealand White and the Californian are currently the breeds of choice.

For backyard raising of rabbits as pets and for home meat production, the choice of a breed is not critical, as maximum production and profit are not being sought. Personal preference as to color and type are greater factors. If children are involved, they will probably be more interested in a variety of colors. For strictly pet raising or backyard meat production, there is nothing particularly wrong with indiscriminate crossing. Children in particular may want rabbits of various colors and crosses; this may stimulate their curiosity and result in a lifelong interest in rabbits.

Fig. 2-1. New Zealand White. (Courtesy of OSU Rabbit Research Center)

For show purposes, the selection of a breed will be based on personal preferences, availability of good breeding stock, etc. The dwarf breeds require much less feed than medium or giant breeds, which might be a consideration in breed selection.

Fig. 2-2. Californian. (Courtesy of *Rabbits* magazine)

Fig. 2-3. Sandy Flemish Giant. (Courtesy of *Small Stock Magazine*)

A large market exists for laboratory animals, which are used in biomedical research. Generally the New Zealand White is the main breed used in research, although large numbers of Dutch are also used. The Florida White was developed as a laboratory animal and

Fig. 2-4. White Flemish Giant. (Courtesy of OSU Rabbit Research Center)

might be more extensively used by scientists if they were made aware of its existence. Its feed requirements are considerably less than those of the New Zealand White, which is a significant factor when research animals are to be kept for long periods.

PURCHASING BREEDING STOCK

After it has been decided which breed of rabbit one wishes to raise, lists of breeders who have that particular stock for sale can be obtained from the officers of the local, state, and specialty rabbit clubs and from the Secretary of the American Rabbit Breeders Association. (Most countries have similar organizations.) County agents are another source of names of rabbit raisers. Advertisements in rabbit journals and other periodicals that carry classified ads are good sources of listings. One should, however, avoid the flashy type of advertisement that features the statement that a fortune can be made in raising rabbits, for this is not true, although an experienced, conscientious, industrious person with proper equipment and a well selected herd should be able to realize a reasonable return from raising them.

Fig. 2-5. Dutch. (Courtesy of *Rabbits* magazine)

Fig. 2-6. Havana. (Courtesy of *Rabbits* magazine)

Fig. 2-7. Siamese Satin. (Courtesy of *Rabbits* magazine)

Fig. 2-8. English Spot. (Courtesy of *Rabbits* magazine)

When an entire herd is being sold, it is well to inquire carefully into the reasons, as such sales may or may not be excellent opportunities for buying good, healthy breeding stock. It is always best to deal with reputable breeders, and the inexperienced will do well to depend on the advice of an established breeder in selecting animals. The source rabbitry should be clean and well managed, with no observable snuffles or other disease problems. It is never economical to purchase inferior breeding stock, for actually one good producing doe may make more net profit than several inferior ones.

The novice is advised to begin rabbit raising operations on a small scale, preferably with 1 buck and 2 to 10 does, then to expand as experience and the market outlet would indicate. He or she may start with a few junior animals when they are weaned, or with mature stock. The former method offers an opportunity to become acquainted with the animals and to gain experience in the business before handling too many rabbits; the latter method is quicker, but naturally the stock will cost more. However, when rabbits are to be purchased for raising by a younger member of the family, the additional cost of an adult doe is justified because youth demands action. By having to supply a nest box and nesting material, preparing for the kindling of the doe, and caring for the litter, followed by marketing the meat, skins, or animals, there is a new event happening at about the time the young person's interest in the undertaking might be lagging. Then, on receiving some income from the sale of the products he or she is ready to go on and plan for another litter. On the other hand, if the stock is purchased at eight weeks of age, or at time of weaning, it seems like a long wait for the young rabbit raiser before the animals are ready to go into production, and he or she may lose interest.

In purchasing stock, use great care to avoid diseases. If animals are purchased from various sources, quarantine them before mixing with other animals. From a genetics point of view, it is desirable to obtain stock from a number of different sources to get genetic diversity. Another way to accomplish this is to obtain bucks from different sources, and quarantine them before using them in the herd. When buying stock, ask to see the records. If you are buying commercial stock, find out what selection procedures have been used. Get information on litter sizes and 21- and 56-day litter weights. Generally the best stock for meat production comes from successful commercial rabbit raisers. Many people start with a trio of two does and a buck, which should not be littermates. They

Fig. 2-9. Belgian Hare. (Courtesy of W. J. Barnes)

Fig. 2-10. Champagne d'Argent.

Fig. 2-11. Blanc de Hotot. (Courtesy of OSU Rabbit Research Center)

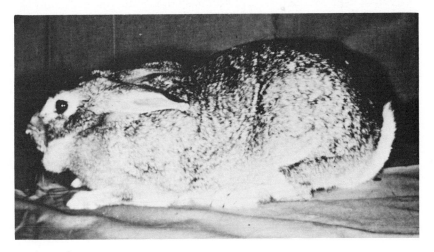

Fig. 2-12. Chinchilla.

should be carefully examined for soundness, good foot pads, normal teeth, good fur quality, and absence of ear mites and other pests and diseases. It is very important to start your rabbitry with the highest quality stock you can obtain. If you have had no rabbit experience, start with no more than 20 does. Find out if you really want to raise rabbits. If you find that you do enjoy it, then increase

Fig. 2-13. Netherland Dwarf.

by buying more breeding stock. Two hundred breeding does is a minimum economic unit. Rabbitries smaller than this do not make effective use of large quantity purchase discounts for feed, supplies, cages, and other equipment. The cost of selling fryers may also be greater for small producers, as they usually have to transport their fryers to pick-up points, while the truck usually comes directly to a large rabbitry. It is advisable to buy no more than 100 does, and then increase by saving your own replacements. A full-time rabbit operation for one person is about 500 does. If breeding stock is being purchased from a small herd, it is advisable to get the bucks from a different source than the does, for maximum genetic diversity.

If you are doing any custom breeding, keep one or more bucks in isolation for that purpose. Never use your buck on someone else's does, and then return the buck to your herd. Custom breeding is an easy way to introduce rabbit syphilis into your herd.

BREEDS OF RABBITS

Information on breeds of rabbits and The Standard of Perfection can be obtained from the American Rabbit Breeders Association (address: 1925 S. Main, P.O. Box 426, Dept. H7, Bloomington, Illinois 61701). The Standard of Perfection for 1981 through 1985 is listed in Table 2-1. Pictures of some of the more common breeds of rabbits are shown in this chapter. A full-color section features 32 photographs by David J. Harris.

BELGIAN HARE

Owned by

Eric Peterson
Hillsboro, Oreg.

BLANC DE HOTOT

Owned by

Julie Wichert
Chehalis, Wash.

BLUE VIENNA

Owned by

Melinda Bucy
Corvallis, Oreg.

BRITANNIA PETITE

Owned by

Debbie Meek
Centralia, Wash.

(Photos by David J. Harris)

Breeds of Rabbits

CALIFORNIAN

Owned by

Susie Smith
Corvallis, Oreg.

CHAMPAGNE D'ARGENT

Owned by

Linda Slinkard
Tacoma, Wash.

CHECKERED GIANT

Owned by

Jill Stahley
Beavercreek, Oreg.

DUTCH

Owned by

Andrew Crabtree
Corvallis, Oreg.

(Photos by David J. Harris)

Breeds of Rabbits

ENGLISH ANGORA

Owned by

Ruth Reed
Cornelius, Oreg.

ENGLISH LOP

Owned by

Almira and Charles Dickens
Beaverton, Oreg.

ENGLISH SPOT

Owned by

Freddie McCown
Lebanon, Oreg.

FLEMISH GIANT

Owned by

April Chunn
Woodland, Wash.

(Photos by David J. Harris)

Breeds of Rabbits

FLORIDA WHITE

Owned by

Nita Boatman
Colton, Oreg.

FRENCH ANGORA

Owned by

Dawn Yager
Newberg, Oreg.

FRENCH LOP

Owned by

Sharon Campbell
Shedd, Oreg.

GIANT CHINCHILLA

Owned by

Dick and Grace Barbee
Portland, Oreg.

(Photos by David J. Harris)

Breeds of Rabbits

HARLEQUIN

Owned by

Sharon Etenburn
Colton, Oreg.

HAVANA

Owned by

Cathy Cook
Boring, Oreg.

HIMALAYAN

Owned by

Brian Smith
Corvallis, Oreg.

HOLLAND LOP

Owned by

Hans Albrecht
Newport, Oreg.

(Photos by David J. Harris)

Breeds of Rabbits

LILAC

Owned by

    Eric Peterson
    Hillsboro, Oreg.

MINI LOP

Owned by

    Linda Johansen
    Corvallis, Oreg.

NETHERLAND DWARF

Owned by

    Linda Johansen
    Corvallis, Oreg.

NEW ZEALAND WHITE

Owned by

    Gene Knieling
    Aumsville, Oreg.

(Photos by David J. Harris)

Breeds of Rabbits

PALOMINO

Owned by

    David Phillips
    Corvallis, Oreg.

POLISH

Owned by

    Cathy Hunt
    Corvallis, Oreg.

REX

Owned by

    Melinda Bucy
    Corvallis, Oreg.

RHINELANDER

Owned by

    Betty Kelly
    Chehalis, Wash.

(Photos by David J. Harris)

Breeds of Rabbits

SATIN

Owned by

Darwin Oakes
Monroe, Oreg.

SILVER FOX

Owned by

Kari Staggs
Sumner, Wash.

SILVER MARTEN

Owned by

Sharon Etenburn
Colton, Oreg.

TAN

Owned by

Charles Etenburn
Colton, Oreg.

(Photos by David J. Harris)

Breeds of Rabbits

Fig. 2-14. Britannia Petite. (Courtesy of *Rabbits* magazine)

Table 2-1. Breeds of Rabbits Recognized by ARBA, 1981, with Ideal Weights

Breed	Ideal Weights (pounds)	
	Senior Does	Senior Bucks
American (Blue, White)[1]	11	10
Angora, English	6½	5½
Angora, French	over 8	over 8
Belgian Hare	8	8
Beveren (White, Blue, Black)	10	9
Blue Vienna	9½	9
Britannia Petite	2¼	2¼
Californian	9½	9
Champagne d'Argent	10½	10
Checkered Giant, American (Black, Blue)	over 12	over 11

(Continued)

Table 2-1 (Continued)

Breed	Ideal Weights (pounds)	
	Senior Does	Senior Bucks
Chinchilla, American	11	10
Chinchilla, Giant	14–15	13–14
Cinnamon	10	9½
Creme d'Argent	10	9
Dutch (Black, Blue, Chocolate, Tortoise, Steel Gray, Gray)	4½	4½
English Spot (Black, Blue, Chocolate, Gold, Gray, Lilac, Tortoise)	7	6
Flemish Giant (Black, Blue, Fawn, Light Gray, Sandy, Steel Gray, White)	13 or over	12 or over
Florida White	5	5
Harlequin (Japanese, Magpie)	8	7½
Havana (Black, Blue, Chocolate)	5¼–5½	5¼–5½
Himalayan (Black, Blue)	3½	3½
Blanc de Hotot	10	9
Lilac	6–7½	6–7
Lop, English (Solid, Broken)	11	10
Lop, French (Solid, Broken)	12	11
Lop, Holland (Solid, Broken)	3	3
Lop, Mini (Solid, Broken)	6	5½
Netherland Dwarf (Self, Shaded, Agouti, Tan Pattern)	2	2
New Zealand (Black, Red, White)	11	10
Palomino	10	9
Polish (Black, Chocolate, Blue-eyed White, Ruby-eyed White)	2½	2½
Rex (Black, Blue, Californian, Castor, Chinchilla, Chocolate, Lilac, Lynx, Opal, Red, Sable, Seal, White, Broken)	9	8
Rhinelander	8½	8
Sable	9	8
Satin (Black, Blue, Californian, Chinchilla, Chocolate, Copper, Red, Siamese, White)	10	9½
Silver (Brown, Fawn, Gray)	6	6
Silver Fox (Black, Blue)	10½	9½
Silver Marten (Black, Blue, Chocolate, Sable)	8½	7½
Tan (Black, Blue, Chocolate, Lilac)	4½–5½	4–5

[1]Varieties of breeds are shown in parentheses.

The Rabbitry and Its Equipment

The type of building and equipment needed will depend on the location of the rabbitry, the climate, the size of the enterprise, and the amount of money to be invested. Every rabbitry presents its individual problems, but whatever the size of the proposed undertaking, the construction and equipment should be planned to save labor in caring for the herd. Neatness in design and convenient arrangement of the equipment for the rabbitry will make for a pleasant environment in which to work and will also create a favorable impression on prospective buyers of breeding stock or rabbitry products.

Before deciding on a location for engaging in rabbit raising and investing too much capital, you should thoroughly consider your own local conditions and such items as available markets and labor. In a town or city, check to make sure that no local ordinance forbids such an enterprise. This chapter describes the equipment that will or may be required.

HUTCHES AND CAGES

A *hutch* is a small unit of solid construction used for housing a few animals on a backyard scale. An example is shown in Fig. 3-1. They generally are of wood and chicken wire construction, and may have a wire-mesh floor, or a solid floor bedded with straw. These inexpensive hutches are satisfactory for the backyard rabbit raiser who has a few does. They can be constructed easily, using inexpensive material which may be on hand. Hutches are also used in developing countries, and are constructed of local building materials

Fig. 3-1. An inexpensive, portable wood-wire hutch suitable for backyard rabbit raising. Note the hay feeder between the two cages. (Courtesy of U.S. Department of the Interior)

such as twigs or bamboo (Fig. 3-2). Rabbits are very adaptable and can be raised in a wide variety of types of hutches, provided that there is adequate ventilation and provision for manure removal, and as long as the rabbits can be kept dry.

Fig. 3-2. A rabbitry in Malawi (East Africa) constructed of inexpensive local materials. Rabbits are quite suitable for small-scale production in developing countries. (Courtesy of J. I. McNitt and *The Journal of Applied Rabbit Research*)

Fig. 3-3. A quonset-style hanging wire cage. This style of cage can be readily used for hay feeding. (Courtesy of D. J. Harris, Corvallis, Oregon)

Modern commercial rabbitries do not use hutches. They use hanging wire cages. These are usually suspended from supports on the ceiling of a rabbitry. They provide good ventilation and waste disposal, and place the rabbits at a convenient height for the rabbit raiser to work with them. A variety of different types of wire cages are used successfully. The quonset-style cage (Fig. 3-3) is one of the best, because it requires less wire than a rectangular cage, reaching into all corners of the cage is easy, and the cage door doesn't fall down when one is reaching inside the cage. Quonset cages suspended back to back provide a ready-made hay feeder (Fig. 3-3) that is useful when hay is fed for enteritis control or to prevent fur chewing. Generally either 14 or 16 gauge wire is used (Fig. 3-4); 12 gauge wire is ideal but is probably too expensive for routine use. Another style of cage, which has been referred to as the *European-style* cage, has two compartments. The young can be kept in one compartment and the doe in the other. Before weaning, the young have access to both compartments; at weaning, the door separating the compartments is closed. It is believed that this system produces less stress to the litter than when the doe is totally removed. This has not been experimentally proven, however.

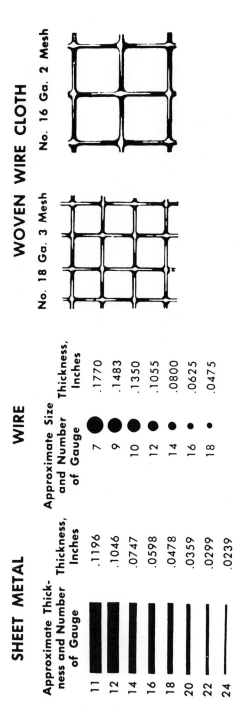

SHEET METAL

Approximate Thickness and Number of Gauge	Thickness, Inches
11	.1196
12	.1046
14	.0747
16	.0598
18	.0478
20	.0359
22	.0299
24	.0239

WIRE

Approximate Size and Number of Gauge	Thickness, Inches
7	.1770
9	.1483
10	.1350
12	.1055
14	.0800
16	.0625
18	.0475

WOVEN WIRE CLOTH

No. 18 Ga. 3 Mesh   No. 16 Ga. 2 Mesh

Fig. 3-4. The sizes and identification of wire grid, wire, and sheet metal. (Courtesy of Hoeltge, Inc., Cincinnati)

The dimensions of the rabbit cage will vary, depending upon the breed, the management system used, and the personal preferences of the rabbit raiser. For medium breeds and commercial production, a cage 30 inches deep × 30 inches wide is satisfactory if the young are weaned at four weeks. If they are weaned at eight weeks, a cage 30 inches deep × 36 inches wide should be used. The height should be about 20 inches. For the sides and top, 1 × 2–inch mesh is used, and for the floor, the mesh should be ½ × 1 inch. A type of wire called "baby-saver" is available; it decreases in mesh size from top to bottom, so that kits don't fall out the sides of the cage or crawl through to another doe's cage. The door should be of adequate size to allow easy access to all parts of the cage, and introduction of a nest box.

Wire for cage construction can be purchased from rabbit supply houses or wire manufacturing companies. Check with other rabbit raisers, or current issues of rabbit magazines, to find suppliers. It is best to buy locally to have minimal shipping charges. Commercial raisers should build their own cages, using J clips and J clip pliers to hold them together. If only a few cages are needed for a backyard rabbitry, they can be purchased from another producer, or kits of pre-cut cages can be purchased, requiring only to be clipped together.

Bucks should be kept in 30 × 30–inch cages. Some producers use a round buck cage, so that during breeding, the doe can't get into a corner and prevent the buck from mating. For junior does, prior to breeding, a 15 × 30–inch cage is adequate, or else two or three junior does can be housed together in a larger cage up to three weeks before intended breeding, when they should be separated. Hanging wire cages should be suspended at a height convenient to the rabbit raiser, so that he or she can readily reach into all parts of the cage. In general, cages should be single-tiered. If forced-air ventilation is used, then a double-tiered arrangment (Fig. 3-5) may be considered. However, snuffles and other respiratory ailments are almost always a problem with double- and triple-tiered cages. Adequate ventilation to prevent build-up of humidity and ammonia is extremely critical. Also, with double or triple tiers, it is difficult to readily observe animals or nest boxes on the top and bottom tiers for signs of illness or other problems. With double or triple tiers, various types of waste disposal systems have been used, including automatic scrapers (Fig. 3-6), and deflection boards to deflect feces and urine into a collection area.

Fig. 3-5. A two-tier arrangement of cages. (Courtesy of J. C. Lowit)

Feedlot cages are sometimes used, to save on labor and cage construction costs. Large cages, of any suitable dimensions, are constructed. Several hundred fryer rabbits per cage are fed in a feedlot system from weaning to marketing. Feed is given in large feed hoppers. This system reduces some of the high labor requirements which exist when litters are kept individually in cages. Studies using limited numbers at the OSU Rabbit Research Center have shown that this system can be successfully used. A fairly high stocking density is needed to keep the animals from running and playing, which increases energy expenditure and feed requirements. A density of two to three rabbits per square foot may be satisfactory. Fighting is not usually a problem. Junior does, from

Fig. 3-6. A two-tier caging arrangement with an automatic manure scraper powered by a small electric motor. (Courtesy of OSU Rabbit Research Center)

weaning to four months, can also be kept in group cages. An additional advantage of feedlot or group cages is that there is some evidence that increased exercise may aid in prevention of enteritis.

THE RABBIT BUILDING

Modern commercial rabbitries are generally of a pole frame construction, with metal sides and roof. They are of two basic types: those with natural ventilation, and those with a controlled environment. A building with natural ventilation in temperate climates may have an open side toward a direction that does not have prevailing winds. In some areas, such as in Arkansas, rabbitries commonly are open-sided, with a roll-up curtain of plastic, burlap, or canvas which can be dropped down in the winter and rolled up in the summer for better ventilation (Fig. 3-7). With natural ventilation, only one tier of cages should be used.

Fig. 3-7. An Arkansas rabbitry, with open sides and a roll-up curtain that is let down in the winter. (Photo by P. R. Cheeke)

For a controlled environment rabbitry, forced-air ventilation systems are employed. Generally about 20 air changes per hour are desirable. The capacity of entry and exhaust fans, and the air circulation system used, should be determined in consultation with an agricultural engineer. A temperature of about 60°F is optimal for rabbit production. Evaporative cooling systems may be used in hot climates. This type of cooling uses cold water running through mats or coils.

A solid concrete floor may not be the best type to use in a rabbitry. Concrete floors lead to excessive humidity and ammonia levels, as liquid wastes cannot be readily removed. If solid concrete floors are used, provision must be made for rapid removal of solid and liquid wastes. A better system is to use pits beneath the cages, with concrete alleyways. Concrete alleyways 3 feet in width between rows of hanging cages are desirable. Beneath the cages, a porous pit of layers of gravel and sand, with a drainage tile to remove liquids, is a good system. Manure is allowed to accumulate, and may be removed annually, semi-annually, or as required. As long as the sand and gravel layers remain porous, the urine doesn't accumulate, and the humidity of the building will not increase. The pits may be cleaned manually or with scraper devices.

Various devices to automatically remove manure have been developed. They include scrapers on a cable, tractor-driven scrapers, and flushing water systems. Most of them share a common characteristic: they generally don't work very well! Many automatic scraping systems can be seen stacked up outside rabbitries, because they weren't satisfactory. Rabbitries with these systems usually are characterized by high humidity, a strong odor of ammonia, and many sneezing rabbits with snuffles.

In many areas, insulation of the rabbitry is desirable to control environmental temperature. This is important in both hot and cold areas. In hot climates, an insulated building is necessary to complement the action of cooling systems, and to minimize radiation of heat from the roof into the rabbitry. Both the walls and the ceiling of an environmentally controlled building should be insulated. With an open building, insulation of the ceiling will aid in control of high temperatures by reducing radiation from the roof into the rabbitry.

A good policy in a commercial rabbitry is to restrict visitors. Other rabbit raisers may bring diseases with them when they visit your rabbitry. Strangers cause stress to rabbits. A compromise policy is to install a viewing window at one end of the building. Visitors can look inside, but disease organisms and noise are kept out.

A new, modern commercial rabbitry should have an office area for recordkeeping, etc. It should be equipped with office supplies, including a calculator. Large rabbitries will find a small computer a good investment, to enhance recordkeeping and economic analysis, and to produce daily chore sheets. Other components of the rabbitry include bulk feed tanks and a feed storage room. If the volume of feed used is very substantial, bulk tanks are advisable. Bagged feed is more expensive than bulk, and with increasing costs of labor and materials, the relative difference between the two is likely to continue to rise. A screen may be installed between the bulk bin and the feed cart, to remove fines from the feed, if necessary.

Under certain circumstances, radically different approaches to the housing of rabbits may have merit. For example, it is possible to construct a rabbitry underground in certain locations. The advantages are that control of temperature in a range desirable for rabbit production may be more feasible than with above-ground rabbitries in some climates. Another idea is to have an underground airduct for the incoming air in a controlled environment building. The incoming air is cooled as it is drawn in below ground. This may have application in hot climates. Other innovations include using a flushing manure removal system, with solid:liquid separation and fermentation of the solids in a methane generator. Some rabbit raisers have combined their waste disposal systems with aquaculture (fish ponds) or greenhouse irrigation. Rabbits have been kept in greenhouses, with their body heat contributing to the heating of the greenhouses. For the ingenious person there are many possibilities, particularly if only a few rabbits are to be raised, for using unique housing systems.

FEEDING EQUIPMENT

Feeders

Various types of feed hoppers are commercially available (Fig. 3-8). They should have sufficient capacity to hold at least a one-day feed supply, and should be designed so feed is not scratched out (scrabbled) and wasted. Guards placed 2–3 inches apart over the opening may be needed to prevent young rabbits from getting in the hopper. Some feeders have a mesh bottom, which allows fines to fall through. This assures the rabbits of good quality pellets. This is desirable because the presence of fines may reduce feed intake and growth performance. Crocks may be used in small rabbitries, but they require a lot of labor for cleaning, as they are often soiled with feces and urine. Wastage is often a problem.

Hay Mangers

Hay feeding may be considered desirable by some rabbit raisers. There is evidence that it may help reduce the incidence of enteritis. Use of home-grown hay may help to reduce feed costs. Various types of V-shaped hay feeders that attach to the outside of the cage may be built. If quonset-style cages are used, the hay can be fed directly on the tops of the cages (Fig. 3-3).

Fig. 3-8. An example of a J feeder, with a mesh bottom to allow fines to sift out of the feed. (Courtesy of OSU Rabbit Research Center)

WATERING EQUIPMENT

All rabbit raisers with more than about six does should consider installing an automatic watering system. A properly designed and installed automatic watering system will provide a dependable supply of water and remove the hazard of spreading infection by water siphoning from cage to cage. Experiments have shown that rabbits using automatic watering systems gain weight more rapidly than rabbits watered with crocks. Rabbits learn to use the automatic valves readily (Fig. 3-9). An automatic watering system is adequate for use throughout the year in rabbitries that are protected so the exposed water pipes will not freeze, but where there is more exposure, it may be necessary to drain the pipes during short cold spells. In some colder areas, such a system can be used all year if it is allowed to drip to prevent the supply pipes from freezing, or if heating cables are installed inside the pipes to prevent freezing. Even in regions where it would be necessary to discontinue using it during the winter months, the amount of labor saved for the remainder of the year might justify installation.

Fig. 3-9. A young rabbit drinking from an automatic waterer. (Courtesy of USDA)

You may locate necessary materials for installation by referring to advertisements in rabbit magazines, or you may purchase them from rabbit and poultry supply houses. A system generally will consist of a break pressure tank equipped with a float valve, ½-inch supply pipe, one dew-drop valve for each cage, and valves for eliminating air bubbles, draining the pipes, and cutting off the water supply. The break pressure tank may be the standard tank used for this purpose, or a half-barrel. A 1-gallon capacity tank is desirable for warm areas because the small volume of water will be consumed readily and the tank will fill at short intervals and assist in keeping the water in the supply pipes cool; the half-barrel will supply several hundred cages and is especially useful in case the water supply contains sediment. By installing the supply pipe outlet several inches from the bottom of the barrel there will be enough water volume so this sediment will gravitate to the bottom of the barrel and not clog the watering valves. A trap for catching sediment may be installed between the tank and the supply pipe which furnishes water to the cages.

The break pressure tank should be about 1 to 2 feet above the highest cage, or a foot above the highest point of the supply pipe, in case it is necessary to raise the supply pipe to clear feeding alleys, etc. If the pipe has to be raised, it is a good plan to install a vent pipe at the highest point, with the open end of the pipe at least a foot above the surface of the water in the tank to prevent air bubbles accumulating in the supply pipe. A convenient method for determining the proper height of the tank is to fasten a rubber hose to the outlet from the tank and to the supply pipe, then to raise and lower the tank until the proper tension is obtained on the water valves. About 2 pounds per square inch (psi) at the valves is suitable. If there is too much pressure, the rabbit cannot trip a valve with its tongue; if the pressure is too weak, the valves will drip. Several days are usually required for the valves to become seated and stop dripping. If they begin to drip after they have been in use for some time, it may be due to minerals contained in the water collecting on the metal and preventing them from seating properly; you can correct this by soaking the valves in a 5% solution of muriatic acid. Generally, you can fix a dripping valve by removing and cleaning it. If not, it should be replaced, as water dripping in the rabbitry contributes to excess humidity.

The supply pipe should be on the outside of the cage, so that any dripping will not wet the rabbits, and so that the water line is not chewed on. The valves should be about 9 inches from the cage floor for the medium weight and heavy breeds and 7 inches for the small breeds. One valve for each cage is adequate. After an automatic watering system is installed, it should be thoroughly flushed several times to remove any particulate matter which may cause the valves to leak.

NEST BOXES

Wooden boxes without lids are used quite extensively as nest boxes throughout the year in those areas where winter temperatures are above freezing. You can make one by using a box 12 inches long, 24 inches wide, and 12 inches high (Fig. 3-10). Cut one end of the box down to about 6 inches. Nail a 1 × 12 × 12–inch board across the top of the box at the opposite end. Cut off the two projecting corners of the sides, slanting from the edge of the 12-inch board across the top to the edge of the 6-inch board. Protect the edges of the boards against chewing with strips of tin. The doe is

Fig. 3-10. A box-type wooden nest box.

able to get away from her litter and is often seen on top of the nest box. Satisfactory results have been obtained with nest boxes of dimensions as small as 16 × 10 × 8 inches. Advantages of smaller nest boxes are that the doe makes a more compact nest, the materials cost less, and the box takes up less space in the cage.

Injury of young litters by the doe jumping into the box may be prevented by a slight change in the nest box. A door, size 6 × 6 inches, should be made in one end, approximately 6 inches from the floor. Before the young are old enough to get out of the box, the end with the opening is turned away from the cage wall so the doe can get into the box without jumping over the side. When the young are about large enough to get out of the box, in order to keep them in it a few more days, the box is turned so its opening is against the wall. By this time the doe is not likely to injure the young when she jumps over the side into the box.

A drop nest box (Figs. 3-11 and 3-12) has a number of advantages. The nest box is below the floor of the cage. This allows does to mimic the nesting behavior of wild rabbits in holes or depressions. A major advantage is that if the young rabbits do crawl out of

Fig. 3-11. A "drop" or "subterranean" nest box. (Courtesy of *The Journal of Applied Rabbit Research*)

the nest box or are carried out attached to a teat, they fall back into it as they are crawling around the cage. This eliminates deaths from exposure of kits, because rabbits, unlike many other species, will not return their young to the nest. The use of drop nest boxes may also reduce the problem of does kindling on the wire.

Another good style of nest box is suspended on the front of the cage. The litter is very accessible for inspection by the rabbit raiser, who can remove dead kits, etc., without opening the cage or disturbing the doe. The nest box can be equipped with a hinged door, so that the doe can be locked out of it. This prevents her from jumping into the box frequently and trampling the kits. Suitable inside dimensions of the nest box for most breeds are 16 × 10 × 16 inches. The front-loading nest box should have a lid (Fig. 3-13) to prevent the doe from jumping out.

A system which has been successfully employed at the OSU Rabbit Research Center in studies to measure milk production is to lock the doe out of the nest box for all but one 10-minute period per day. Since kits generally nurse once each day, this is an adequate exposure to the doe. When the door is opened, the doe usually

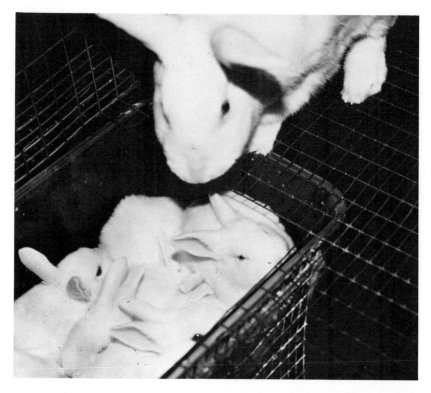

Fig. 3-12. A well filled drop nest box. (Courtesy of OSU Rabbit Research Center)

jumps in, nurses the litter, and then leaves. The use of this technique may reduce losses of kits due to trampling. It should be emphasized that if the does are stressed by visitors, unusual noises, etc., they may not jump into the nest boxes in the allotted time. This system requires a high level of management skill.

Various types of bedding can be used in nest boxes, including straw, wood chips, newspaper, sawdust, and shredded sugarcane products. The doe will supplement the bedding with pulled hair to make a nest (Fig. 3-14). Does may eat straw or hay used in the nest box; this is not necessarily a problem, as the ingested fiber may be helpful in preventing enteric diseases. Another innovation is the use of disposable nest box liners, constructed of cardboard. These are removed and burned after use by one litter. This may have value in sanitation and disease control. Regardless of the type of nest box used, it should have adequate drainage.

Fig. 3-13. A modern commercial rabbitry with front-loading nest boxes. (Courtesy of OSU Rabbit Research Center)

Fig. 3-14. An example of a typical young litter in the nest box. (Courtesy of D. J. Harris, Corvallis, Oregon)

WINTER NEST BOX

You can insulate the box type of nest box for winter use by lining it on the inside with one or two layers of corrugated cardboard or several thicknesses of paper and then completely filling it with straw so the doe will have to burrow into it to make a nest.

You can also make a nest box for use in low temperatures by placing the standard size nest box inside a larger box so there will be a space of 3 inches on all sides except for the entrance and the top, the 3-inch space to be filled with closely packed straw or other suitable insulating material. A boxwood lid covered on the underside with two thicknesses of cardboard or several thicknesses of paper will supply the necessary top insulation. Make three holes ¾ inch in diameter in the end of the lid opposite the opening into the nest box to prevent moisture or condensation within the box and to provide ventilation.

Put corrugated cardboard or newspapers on the bottom of the inner box to keep the newborn litters from coming in contact with the cold boards, and then pack the nest box with clean straw so the doe will have to burrow into it to make a hollow for her nest. If the doe nurses her newborn litter and promptly covers it up with fur, the young can survive temperatures as low as −15°F to −20°F in this type of nest box.

SPRINKLING SYSTEMS

Rabbits are very susceptible to heat stress. Air temperatures around 90°–100°F may cause discomfort and even loss of animals. A properly installed sprinkling system on the roof will help reduce the high temperatures and, when thermostatically controlled, will be a safeguard when sudden weather changes occur. The thermostat should be set so the sprinkler will be turned on when the temperature in the rabbitry reaches about 85°F.

IDENTIFICATION EQUIPMENT

An adjustable tattoo box enables one person to mark a rabbit for identification. The box should be 20 inches long, 8 inches high, and 8 inches wide, with a movable 1 × 6 × 18¼–inch floorboard that may be raised or lowered to accommodate the size of the rabbit. A small board that slides into slots spaced 1 inch apart is placed in back of the rabbit to keep it confined in the front end of the box. A top with an opening to allow the rabbit's ear to protrude is fastened to the box at the back end with a 3 × 2⅜-inch T hinge and at the front end with a door hook (Fig. 3-15). This type of restrainer can also be used to hold a rabbit for collection of a blood sample (Fig. 3-16).

Figures or letters or a combination of the two are tattooed in the inner surface of the rabbit's ear with either a tattoo needle or the plier-tong tattooing instrument that may be secured from rabbitry supply houses.

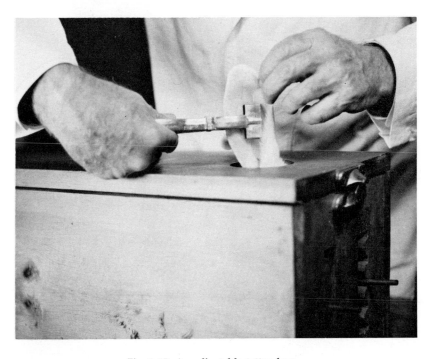

Fig. 3-15. An adjustable tattoo box.

Another way of identifying rabbits is with ear tags. These are wing tags for chickens and are available from poultry supply houses. They are easily inserted, using a simple tool (Fig. 3-17). For temporary identification, culling, or other purposes, marking the ears with felt-tipped pens is useful.

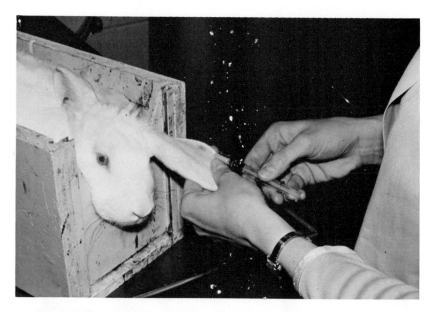

Fig. 3-16. Restraining a rabbit for collection of a blood sample from the ear. (Courtesy of OSU Rabbit Research Center)

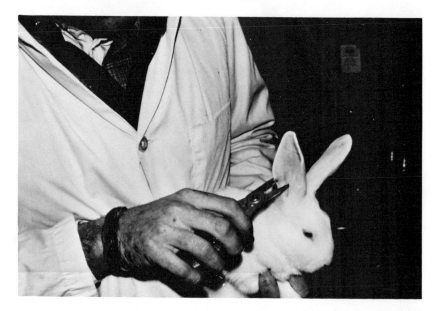

Fig. 3-17. Inserting an ear tag for easy identification. (Courtesy of OSU Rabbit Research Center)

UTILITY CART

A cart equipped for hauling feed, rabbits, nest boxes, and other equipment is a great convenience and a time and labor saver. A special bed on the cart for holding rabbits can be used for taking does to the buck's cage for breeding and for transporting rabbits out of the rabbitry. When a scale is attached to the cart, weights can be entered immediately on the cage cards. Those rabbits that are not to be marketed can be tattooed and retained in the rabbitry. The bed of the cart should be at a convenient height to eliminate bending over or stooping.

OTHER EQUIPMENT

Other equipment needed in the rabbitry includes nail clippers for nail trimming, wire brushes for cage cleaning, and a propane torch or a vacuum cleaner for removing hair from cages.

4

Rabbit Management

Rabbits vary considerably in temperament and respond readily to kind treatment. If they are handled properly they will be gentle and easy to manage, and these characteristics should be considered in selecting breeding stock. A doe that is fairly aggressive for a few days following kindling should not be condemned if she is gentle at other times. Aggressiveness indicates that she is alert and ready to protect her newborn litter. Some of the does that are the best mothers show this trait.

When entering the rabbitry, practice caution so as not to startle the animals. A familiar voice speaking to them will give warning and prevent them from becoming frightened.

It should be emphasized that good management is the key to successful rabbit raising. The quality of the stock, the quality of the feed, and the sophistication of the cages, equipment, and building will do nothing to overcome the detrimental effects of poor management. Rabbit production involves a high degree of management skill compared to other livestock endeavors. Of critical importance in good management practices are sanitation and ventilation, to control enteritis and respiratory infections. The beginning rabbit raiser should not underestimate the necessity for cleanliness, ventilation, and close observation of the animals. Close observation is extremely important, since early detection allows correction of any problems before they become serious or even uncorrectable.

HANDLING RABBITS

Rabbits should never be lifted only by their ears or legs, for

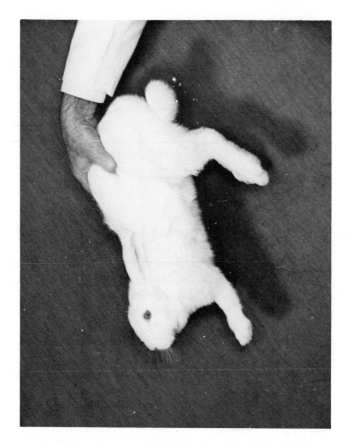

Fig. 4-1. The proper method of lifting and carrying fryers.

they may be permanently injured. You may lift and carry a small rabbit or fryer comfortably without damaging the pelt or bruising the carcass by grasping the loin gently but firmly, with the heel of the hand toward the tail of the animal (Fig. 4-1).

With medium and heavy weight rabbits, grasp a fold of skin over the shoulder with one hand and place the other hand under the rump to support the weight of the animal (Fig. 4-2).

For carrying, grasp a fold of skin over the shoulder and lift, holding the rabbit against your body with its head under one arm, the forearm being extended along the side of the animal and the hand under its rump for support. This prevents struggling, and the rabbit may be carried comfortably (Fig. 4-3). Gentle handling of rabbits should result in less scratching or biting attempts.

Fig. 4-2. The proper method of lifting medium or heavy weight rabbits.

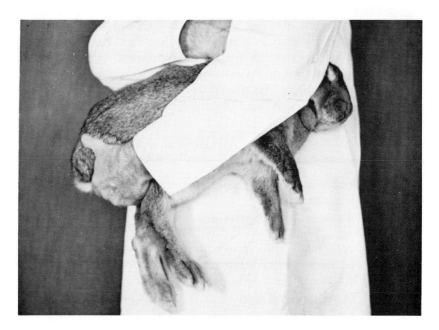

Fig. 4-3. The proper method of carrying medium or heavy weight rabbits.

NUMBER OF BUCKS

One buck should be maintained for each 10–15 does; this breeding schedule will not overwork him. A mature, vigorous buck may even be used every day for a few days in an emergency in order to have several litters kindle at about the same time and facilitate transferring young. However, in normal use he should not be used for more than three or four services a week, although recent research indicates that more frequent service may be acceptable. Frequency of use of bucks is an area that requires further research.

AGE TO BREED

Individual rabbits vary somewhat in the rapidity with which they develop, so both development and age must be taken into consideration in determining the proper time to start them in production. Sexually, the smaller breeds mature much earlier than the heavier breeds, the small Polish usually being ready to start production at four months of age, the medium weight New Zealand, Californian, etc., at five to six months, and the heavy Flemish, at six to seven months of age.

For best results, junior bucks and does should be fed in such a manner that they will make normal growth, develop strong, healthy bodies, and be firm in flesh by the time they are to be mated for the first time, without being excessively fat. Bucks should be put into service about a month later than does, as they are slower to mature sexually.

BREEDING SCHEDULE

For production of show rabbits, it may be advisable not to attempt to produce more than two or three litters a year, with the time of matings so arranged that the offspring will be of the proper age and development for the desired show classification.

For commercial rabbit production, the objective should be to produce and raise as many marketable fryers per doe per year as possible. It takes about 30–40 offspring per doe per year to meet expenses, or the equivalent of about five litters per year. In the past, fryers were kept with the doe until marketing at eight weeks. The trend now is for earlier weaning, and earlier breed-back, to attempt to increase productivity. Many producers now breed back at 14 or 21 days. In intensive production systems, does may even be bred within 24 hours of kindling. It is remarkable that does will rebreed immediately after giving birth; in fact, their receptivity is very good at that time. Under post-partum breeding systems, litters must be weaned at 28 days, so the doe can be given a nest box in preparation for kindling three days later. No other type of livestock has such a potential for high reproductivity as the rabbit. However, this system may increase the percentage of does that are culled annually. Intensive breeding increases nutritional requirements, so a high quality feed is needed. Intensive breeding is not recommended for new rabbit raisers. Probably a 35-day breed-back should be first selected, and if satisfactory results are obtained, it can be shortened to a period that suits the producer and his or her management skills. With early breed-back, more cages are needed than when does and litters are kept together until marketing of the fryers. This increase in caging costs may be more than compensated for by increased production.

THE MATING PROCESS

The doe gives evidence of being in heat by behaving restlessly; by rubbing the chin (chinning) on the cage, water crock, feed troughs, etc.; and by making an effort to join other rabbits in nearby cages. The appearance of the vulva, whether it is pale or pinkish in color, is not always indicative of the rabbit being in heat. However, a doe with a dry, pale vulva is less likely to be receptive than one with a pinkish red, moist vulva.

The doe is rather prone to object to another rabbit being placed in her own cage and quite often will attack and even injure the intruder, so she should always be taken to the buck's cage for mating. If she is ready for service and the buck is active, mating should occur almost immediately (Fig. 4-4). When it is completed the buck usually falls over on his side (Fig. 4-5) and the doe should be returned to her own cage immediately.

Sometimes a doe will squat in the corner of the cage and will not accept service; in this case, restraining her for mating will expedite and ensure service in difficult cases, making many matings possible that would not be made otherwise. Restraining her, how-

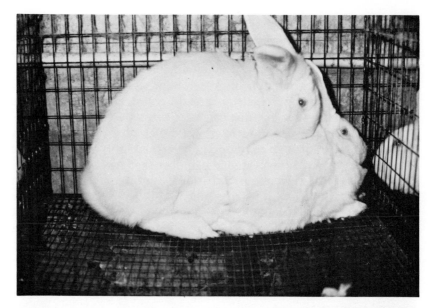

Fig. 4-4. An example of natural mating. (Courtesy of D. J. Harris, Corvallis, Oregon)

Fig. 4-5. When mating is completed, the buck usually falls over on his side. (Courtesy of OSU Rabbit Research Center)

ever, does not necessarily mean she will conceive, if there is any condition that would prevent it. The conception rate from forced mating is lower than with unrestrained mating.

Figure 4-6 shows the proper method for restraining the doe. Either the right or left hand is used to hold the ears and a fold of skin over the doe's shoulders; the other hand is placed under her body and between her hind legs. The thumb is placed on one side of the vulva, the index finger on the other, and the skin is pushed gently backward but avoiding any pinching of the vagina (Fig. 4-7). This procedure throws her tail up and over her back. The weight of the doe's body is supported by the hand, and the rear quarters are elevated, but only to the normal height for mating. Bucks accustomed to being handled will not object to this assistance by the attendant, and many does will respond and accept service naturally when the buck mounts. Forced mating of rabbits should only be used as a last resort.

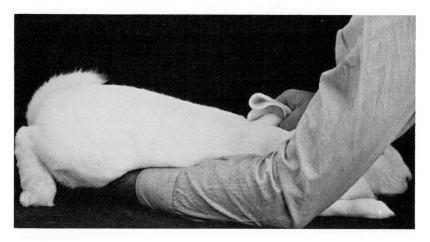

Fig. 4-6. Restraining a doe for mating—side view. (Courtesy of USDA)

The buck and doe should not be left together unattended for more than a few minutes, as the buck may be injured. If mating doesn't occur within five minutes, it is advisable to put the doe in with another buck. Sometimes she will refuse service with one buck but will readily accept another. If she still won't breed, she is probably non-receptive for that day, and should be rescheduled for the next day.

Fig. 4-7. Restraining a doe for mating—rear view. (Courtesy of USDA)

ARTIFICIAL INSEMINATION

In large rabbitries, artificial insemination (AI) may have useful application. The major advantages over natural matings are: (1) With AI, one buck can service 2000–5000 does annually. Therefore, far fewer bucks are needed, reducing feed and cage costs. (2) Does can be bred by AI regardless of their willingness to mate. This allows for synchronized breeding and kindling. This in turn would allow an all-in, all-out system of management, in which bred does are put into a building, they nearly all kindle the same day, the litters are all weaned the same day, and the entire group is marketed the same day. The house can then be sterilized and a new batch of bred does brought in. This system has been used at Bikal State Farm in Hungary, which has a herd of 10,000 does.

Semen is collected in an artificial vagina, with a doe used as a teaser, or bucks can be trained to mount an arm covered with a rabbit skin (Fig. 4-8) and ejaculate in the collection vessel. The

Fig. 4-8. Collecting semen for artificial insemination. The technician is holding a collection tube (artificial vagina) and is wearing a rabbit skin on her arm, which the buck mounts. (Courtesy of OSU Rabbit Research Center)

semen is diluted with semen extenders and used fresh, or it can be frozen. Rabbit semen can be frozen for years without losing its viability, if it has been properly prepared and stored. The technician inseminates the doe using a glass pipette (Fig. 4-9). It is necessary to induce ovulation artificially following AI; this can be done by injecting a hormone preparation within two to four hours after insemination. Further information on AI in rabbits, with complete

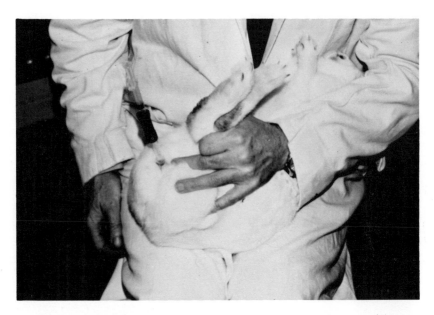

Fig. 4-9. The position of the insemination pipette for artificial insemination. (Courtesy of OSU Rabbit Research Center)

details on materials and methods, can be found in articles by Heidbrink et al. (1979)[1] and Adams (1981).[2]

GESTATION PERIOD

The gestation period, or time from mating of the doe to kindling of the litter, averages 31 days. About 98% of normal litters will be kindled between the thirtieth and thirty-third days, but a small percentage may be kindled as early as the twenty-ninth or as late as the thirty-fifth day. In cases of prolonged gestation, the litter may contain only a few individuals with one or more abnormally large kits. Often the young may be born dead.

---

[1]Heidbrink, G., et al., "The Practical Application of Artificial Insemination in Commercial Rabbit Production," *The Domestic Rabbit: Potentials, Problems, and Current Research* (Corvallis: Oregon State University Rabbit Research Center, 1979).

[2]Adams, C. E., "Artificial Insemination in the Rabbit: The Technique and Application to Practice," *The Journal of Applied Rabbit Research,* vol. 4 (1981), pp. 10–13.

FACTORS THAT PREVENT CONCEPTION

There are many factors that influence conception rate. Sterility, extreme age, poor physical condition, pseudopregnancy, poor genetic quality, sore hocks, injuries, retained fetuses, and disease are among the most important factors. Pay special attention to the physical condition of the doe. If she is too thin, you are probably underfeeding, or if she's too fat, you're overfeeding. Both conditions have negative effects on reproduction. Intensive breeding (on a 14-day or less remate schedule) can cause a doe to lose weight and condition, thus reducing her ability to conceive.

Sterility

In its natural environment the wild rabbit breeds during the spring and early summer and is barren during the fall and winter. During this barren period the ovaries become somewhat shriveled and inactive, and fail to produce normal egg cells; bucks may fail to produce sperm, or the sperm may lack motility or be abnormal in development. In developing the domestic rabbit, humans have shortened the barren period somewhat. Its duration and intensity vary considerably. Some does and bucks are fertile throughout the year and for successive years. Others will not conceive for extended periods. When does are out of production for an extended time, it is more difficult to get them to conceive; but if the herd has received proper care, a large percent of both does and bucks should be over the barren period in a short time. In extreme cases, however, the period may last four to five months. Usually these prolonged periods occur in areas where excessive temperatures have prevailed, especially when unseasonably or excessively high temperatures occur or continue for some time, or when the high temperatures are associated with drought conditions. Indications are that the sperm production of the bucks is more likely to be impaired by these high temperatures than ovulation in the does, but both sexes can be affected.

Another cause for the prolonged sterile periods may be that the ration has not been properly balanced, or the proper amount of feed wasn't used to keep the rabbits in desired breeding condition. While the animal is molting, the development of a new coat may tax its vitality, and conception may be delayed. Occasionally an animal is permanently infertile and should be disposed of.

A decrease in conception in the winter may be caused by inadequate feeding. In the cold of winter in unheated rabbitries, the rabbits use more of their daily ration to produce heat to keep warm. Therefore, less energy is available for reproduction processes. To offset this increased body heat demand, the daily feed allotment to does should be increased by about 25% in the winter.

Because there is so much variation among does and bucks in regard to the regularity of breeding, the rabbit breeder may well give considerable attention to overcoming this factor through proper selection of breeding stock. Breeding stock should be selected from parents that produce regularly. Attempts to increase production during the sterile period by the use of vitamins and other feed supplements have not been effective.

During the late autumn and early winter, when the percentage of does that conceive is below that of the spring and summer, the birth weight of the young may be below normal, litters may contain fewer individuals, and the does may neglect their young.

Another factor that may influence seasonal fertility is the lighting program. In the wild, the rabbit is a seasonal breeder; this pattern is possibly regulated both by temperature and by light. During the fall, as day length decreases, a light-sensitive gland, the pineal gland, detects the decrease in light and decreases the secretion of certain reproductive hormones by the pituitary gland at the base of the rabbit's brain. By maintaining a longer day length in the rabbitry by using artificial lights, you may be able to prevent the winter decline in reproduction. A lighting period of 16 hours per day seems adequate in most regions; the length of the lighting period should be as long as the longest day in your region. This is the principle used in the poultry industry to keep birds laying in the winter. A great deal more research is needed to elucidate the role of environmental factors such as temperature and light in controlling rabbit production.

Young does and bucks may be sexually immature, while other does and bucks may be too old, having passed their period of usefulness. The proper age for the animals to be put into production was discussed earlier, and they may be retained in the breeding herd as long as they maintain good physical condition and produce satisfactory litters. This may be until they are 2½ to 3 years old. There is wide variation, and some individuals may reproduce satisfactorily for four years or more. However, in some commercial herds, up to 100% of the does may be replaced in a year.

A high culling rate may be desirable to continually upgrade the herd. If proper selection procedures are used, each doe that is culled can be replaced by a doe of higher genetic quality.

Physical Condition

Rabbits that are abnormally fat or thin will have impaired fertility or they may become sterile, and the ration should be adjusted and breeding delayed until they are in the proper physical condition. For those that are too fat, a pelleted diet should be restricted and a limited quantity of a good quality hay fed. For those that are too thin, the complete pellets or a grain and hay ration should be fed in increased amounts.

Pseudopregnancy

Pseudopregnancy can result from a sterile mating or from stimulation caused by one doe riding another, or by a doe riding the young in her own litter. This condition lasts for about 17 days. During this time the doe may not conceive, so if the does have been kept in groups they should be separated and put into individual cages at least 18 days before being mated. Pseudopregnancy is discussed further in Chapter 9.

Sore Hocks or Injuries

Sore hocks or injuries may affect the vitality of does and bucks and should be corrected before the animals are mated. They should also be examined carefully before being mated, and if any symptoms of disease are found the affected animals should be isolated and held in quarantine until completely recovered, or culled from the herd. Because sore hocks may have a genetic disposition, the breeding of rabbits with this condition may not be advisable.

Retained Fetus

In rather rare instances, a doe may fail to deliver the entire litter, and the tissues of the retained fetus will be absorbed and the bones will remain in the uterus. These cases can be diagnosed accurately by palpation. Because these does will seldom conceive again, they should be culled from the herd.

DETERMINING PREGNANCY

Test-mating does by returning them to the buck's cage to determine whether they have conceived is not a dependable practice. Some does will accept service again after they have conceived, and others will not accept service even though they have not conceived. Noting the development of the abdominal region and the gain in flesh by the doe as the period of gestation advances is not always accurate and will delay definite diagnosis until late in the period.

Palpating or feeling the development of the young in the uterus with the thumb and forefinger is an accurate and quick method for determining pregnancy. To make this test, restrain the doe by holding the ears and a fold of skin over the shoulders in either the right or left hand, with your free hand placed under the body slightly in front of the pelvis (Fig. 4-10). To make the test accurate, you must relax the doe so the abdominal muscles will not be tense. Generally, you can place the doe on top of the cage for palpation. If it is necessary to use a table or cart, cover the top with a feed sack or carpeting to prevent her from slipping.

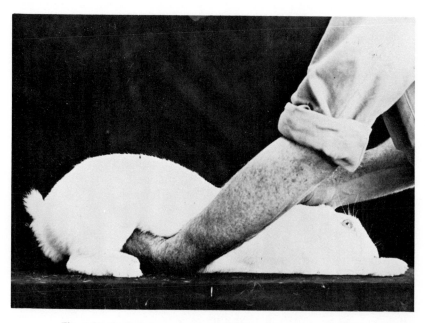

Fig. 4-10. Restraining a doe for palpating. (Courtesy of USDA)

You must be acquainted with the relative size and location of the uterus and the embryos as pregnancy advances. Fig. 4-11 (left) shows the position of the uterus (the digestive tract has been removed) and illustrates the size of the uterus of a non-pregnant doe (left) and that of a doe at the end of 10 days of pregnancy (right). It should be noted that the uterus has expanded to accommodate developing embryos; as the period of gestation advances, the embryos grow larger and the uterus is pushed forward as shown in Fig. 4-12.

There is little danger in palpating, provided it is done at the proper stage of fetus development and the proper technique is followed, but you must use caution and not put too much pressure on the tissues, in order to prevent injury to the developing embryos. The test will be more accurate and there will be less danger of injury if the examination is made about two weeks following mating. On the tenth and twelfth days of pregnancy the embryos are about the size of a marble and are distributed in the uterus as indicated in Fig. 4-12 (left). Just enough pressure must be used with the thumb placed on one side of the uterus and the forefinger placed on the other side to enable the one doing the palpating to note the marble-shaped bodies or embryos by allowing the thumb and finger to slide over them gently. If the technique has been perfected, and no developing embryos are found, the doe should be returned to the buck's cage for another service. She should be kept on the ration that is suitable in quantity and quality for dry does until she is known to have conceived or is culled.

It would be well for the inexperienced person to repalpate in a few days the does that were diagnosed as non-pregnant. If a mistake was made at the first handling and a doe is now found to be pregnant, she should be placed immediately on a management regime that is suitable for pregnant does.

Later than the fourteenth day it is more difficult to distinguish between the developing young and the digestive organs when palpating (Fig. 4-12, right). After the technique has been developed, however, it is possible to determine pregnancy by the tenth day. In palpating earlier than 10 days following mating, the embryos are very small and you must make sure that pellet-shaped fecal material in the large intestine is not confused with the small embryos in the uterus. You can avoid confusion by remembering that, with the animal in the proper position for palpating (Fig. 4-10), the uterus lies at the bottom of the abdominal cavity while the large intestine is above it, nearer the backbone of the animal.

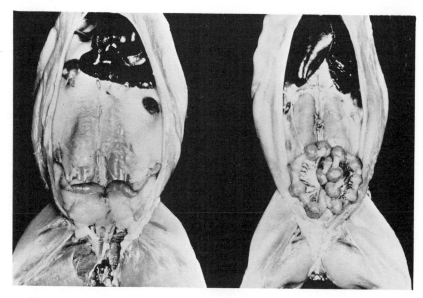

Fig. 4-11. Specimens showing the relative location and size of the uterus of a non-pregnant doe (left) and of a doe that is 10 days pregnant (right). (Courtesy of USDA)

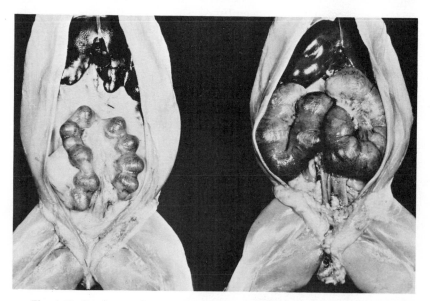

Fig. 4-12. Specimens showing the relative location and size of the uterus and developing embryos at the end of 14 (left) and 21 (right) days of pregnancy. (Courtesy of USDA)

As one gains proficiency in the practice and becomes better acquainted with the anatomy of the organs in the abdominal cavity, it is possible to identify retained fetuses and the presence of abscesses or cysts in the reproductive tract. When any of these conditions are detected, the does should be culled.

KINDLING

The nest box should be placed in the cage 28 days after the doe has been bred. It should contain bedding or straw, shavings, or similar material. The doe will make a nest of straw or other materials (Fig. 4-13), after which she pulls fur (Fig. 4-14) from the hip area, the dewlap, and around the mammary glands, to complete the nest (Fig. 3-14).

A doe will usually consume less feed than normal for two or three days before parturition, and a small amount of green feed each day may tempt her appetite and have a beneficial effect on the

Fig. 4-13. A doe carrying straw in her mouth during preparation of her nest.

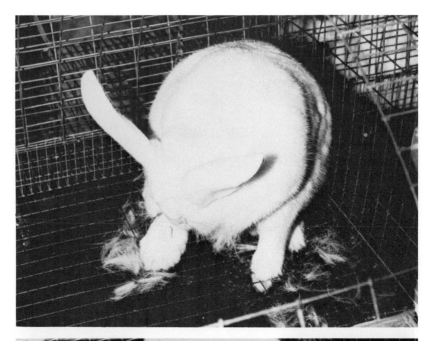

Fig. 4-14. Upper: a doe pulling fur to make a nest. Lower: the doe carrying fur for completion of the nest. (Courtesy of D. J. Harris, Corvallis, Oregon)

digestive system. She should be made as comfortable as possible and should be undisturbed at the time of kindling. A majority of the litters will be kindled during the night. Either the anterior or breach presentation is normal, and as a rule there are no complications at delivery if the fetuses are normal in size. Occasionally there may be only a few kits in the litter, and in these cases one or more may be abnormally large and kindling may be delayed a day or two.

As each kit is delivered the doe licks it and may nurse it immediately. When the entire litter is kindled, she pulls more fur from her body and covers the litter (Fig. 4-14). A normal litter that is clean and has full stomachs and a comfortable nest has made a good start in life.

CARE OF YOUNG LITTERS

Following kindling, you should inspect the litter and remove any dead or deformed young. If this inspection is done quietly after the doe has left the nest box, the doe will not be disturbed and there is no danger of causing her to disown the young. Examine the kits to make sure they have nursed, as will be shown by full stomachs. If a doe does not feed her litter or has not produced enough milk, the litter should be fostered to other lactating does. Does that repeat this abnormal behavior with the next litter should be culled.

Occasionally a doe will make two nests in the nest box and divide the litter when kindling. When this happens, rearrange the bedding in one nest with the depth of the nest and the fur covering regulated to meet the essential requirement for keeping the young comfortable. Make sure that there is bedding under the young and that there is good drainage from the nest box. If there are too many in the litter, transfer some to other litters, or if there are too few, bring in young from other litters. These transfers should be made a day or two following kindling and between litters that do not vary more than one to three days in age. Some does will accept kits of varying ages.

Sometimes does fail to pull enough fur to cover their litter during cold weather. When you discover this, pluck fur from the doe's body to cover the young before they are chilled. The fur is easily plucked at kindling time. If the temperatures are high and the doe pulls an excessive amount of fur, adjust the covering to the quantity needed to keep the newborn litter comfortable and save the surplus fur for an emergency when more may be needed for other litters.

Inspect the litter periodically to make sure that all is going well.

NEST BOX MANAGEMENT

To be satisfactory, a nest box should provide seclusion for the doe during kindling and protection and comfort for the litter afterwards. There are many types, and no one nest box is suitable for use in all rabbitries and in all seasons. Different kinds are discussed in Chapter 3, "The Rabbitry and Its Equipment."

The bedding material should be pliable, absorbent, and of the type the doe can mix with the fur she pulls from her body, with the choice depending upon availability and upon type of nest desired. Straw, hay, leaves, cottonseed hulls, etc., can be used. If the does are being fed a ration consisting only of pellets, they may eat any palatable material used for bedding, and in this case, soft wood shavings or unpalatable bagasse may be used. These may also be used during the warm season when only enough bedding to make a shallow nest is needed, but when low temperatures prevail the nest box should be filled so completely with new, clean straw that the doe will have to burrow into it in order to form her nest.

Shredded paper is a poor absorbent, excelsior is harsh and does not mix readily with the fur, and both of these materials may cause suffering or death of the kits by becoming wrapped around their legs or necks. Shredded redwood bark and peat moss stain the coats, and the dust from them irritates the respiratory tracts of the young rabbits.

It has often been said that "the litter is made in the nest box," and during the time the young rabbits spend there, their weight should increase seven to eight fold. A very important aspect of this is the milking ability of the does, which can be assessed by the 21-day weight of the litter.

The nest box may be removed from the cage when the litter is 12–21 days old, but the time for taking it out should be determined by the weather conditions. If it is necessary to keep it in the cage longer, it should be thoroughly inspected periodically and any soiled bedding replaced with clean. The longer the nest box is left in, the more likely that eye infections and other disease problems will develop, so the nest box should be removed as early as possible. Recent work suggests that in most cases the nest box can be removed when the litter is 12–14 days of age.

Does only nurse their litters once per day. One management practice used quite extensively in Europe is to remove the nest box, and only put the litter in with the doe for about five minutes per day. She usually jumps in and feeds them. Removal of the nest box reduces nest box mortality caused by the doe jumping in several times a day and trampling some of the kits. With the use of a front-loading nest box (Fig. 3-13), the opening can be closed to keep the doe out except for a once-per-day nursing.

After the nest boxes are removed, they should be thoroughly washed and disinfected. They should be stored where wild rodents cannot get to them, as the smell of rodent urine may cause does to refuse to use the nest box.

FOSTERING YOUNG

Frequently does give birth to a larger number of young than they can nurse. It is good herd management to foster a doe's excess kits to another doe with a smaller litter. In raising Angoras or rabbits for the meat market, there is a distinct advantage in reducing the size of the large litter to the number that the doe can develop uniformly; in the case of show rabbits it is especially important to reduce the litter even to four or five so that the young can have an opportunity to develop to the maximum of their inherited possibilities.

In order to distribute the transferred young for fostering, it is advisable when planning the breeding program to mate the does so that several will kindle as near as possible to the same date. The newborn litter should be inspected as soon as possible after the doe has quieted down following kindling, and a memorandum made of the number to be removed from or added to each litter. When all the does due at that time have kindled, the surplus young should be removed and permanently marked with a tattoo, ear punch, etc., so that the transferred young in each litter can be identified at weaning.

When transferring the young it is not necessary to use any method for destroying the scent of the human hand or the scent of the dam of the young being transferred. Does do not make any distinction of young, even if they are of different colors or sizes (Fig. 4-15).

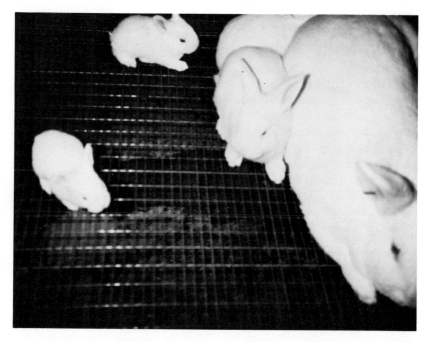

Fig. 4-15. An example of fostering, where small kits have been added to a litter of larger kits. Does accept these fostered kits readily, even when they are different ages, as in this picture. (Photo by J. I. McNitt)

When selecting litters for fostering, it is advisable to watch carefully for any evidence of infection among the litters or does, as the transfer procedure could be the means for spreading disease.

CAUSES OF LOSSES IN YOUNG LITTERS

Disease accounts for only a small percentage of the mortality that occurs that first week following kindling, and most losses during this time are due to improper equipment or feeding and management methods. Some cases may be due to the doe failing to produce milk, and you can diagnose these by feeling the doe's udder to determine whether or not she is producing any milk. If she is not nursing the litter, the milk glands will be undeveloped and the young will be shriveled and wrinkled; if she is nursing them, the udder will be well developed and when the teats are stripped there will be evidence of milk. The well nourished young will be plump; milk may be detected through the abdominal wall depending on how recently they have nursed. If the doe has not produced any milk, it may be because the ration she received during the gestation period was inadequate in quantity or quality.

Does having a first litter often do not use the nest box, for a variety of reasons, and have their litter on the wire. Does should not be culled at this point, but if a doe drops the second litter on the wire, she should be culled. Typically, there is a 20–30% incidence of this problem with the first litter does. The use of drop nest boxes helps to reduce the problem.

At parturition you will obtain better results by making it possible for the doe to be secluded and undisturbed. Many losses of new litters are caused by the presence of strangers in the rabbitry when the doe is due to kindle, by the presence of strange cats, dogs, or the natural enemies of the rabbit such as opossums, rats, snakes, etc. These predators sometimes cause trouble in the city as well as in the country, and even if they cannot gain access to the cage they may be so close that the doe can detect their presence and instead of going into the nest box to kindle she may kindle on the cage floor. If she has already kindled when she discovers the presence of predators, in an attempt to protect her litter she may jump into the nest box and because she is frightened will stamp with her hind feet and crush her young. The predators seek more food when nursing their own young and consequently cause more trouble in the rabbitry in the spring. Evidently they can locate the cage where a doe is kindling or where a litter has just been delivered by the scent of blood. The losses are more likely to occur at night, and the presence of the intruders may not be detected by the caretaker. The rabbits, however, generally give warning by stamping their back feet, and if this warning is heard an immediate inspection of the rabbitry should be made.

FEEDING THE DOE AFTER KINDLING

Does reduce their feed intake prior to kindling. This may in part be due to a reduced gut capacity, caused by the presence of the fetuses in the body cavity. Following kindling, as lactation begins, their feed intake increases markedly. Sometimes a young first or second litter doe will suddenly die when the litter is one to two weeks of age (young doe syndrome). This may be due to enterotoxemia or mastitis. It is desirable to gradually increase the amount of feed offered to the doe for the first week or so following kindling until full feed intake is reached. Sometimes apparently healthy litters will suddenly die at five or six days of age. This may be due to milk enterotoxemia, again caused by overfeeding the doe following kindling. Be sure not to overreact and underfeed the doe, as this may reduce milk production excessively.

WEANING

Litters may be weaned at 28 days of age. Milk production is declining by then, and the young are consuming solid feed well. Feed is used more efficiently if it is eaten directly by the fryers, rather than eaten by the doe and converted to milk. There is less weaning stress if they are weaned at a young age. There is a stress at weaning, which may cause the fryers to go off feed and lose weight for a few days. This occurs particularly if the fryers are moved to a new cage. Rabbits are territorial animals, and establish a home territory. When the fryers are removed from the doe and put in a new cage, the stress is not from being taken from the doe, but from being taken from their territory. If the doe is removed, and the kits left in the cage in which they were born, the stress of weaning is less severe. The doe is more tolerant of the stress of being moved to a new cage.

Be sure that the weaned rabbits know how to drink. If after the first day of weaning, they have not eaten much, it may be a water problem. Put in a water crock; if they rush to it to drink, then you know they haven't learned to drink from the automatic waterers. Put a toothpick in the valve or loosen the valve, to make it drip slightly. This should quickly teach them to drink.

DETERMINATION OF SEX

The sex of the young rabbits may be determined accurately a day or two following kindling, and sexing at this time is necessary when one sex may be needed to supply a market for either does or bucks for breeding purposes, when rabbits are being produced for laboratory work, or when Angora bucks are to be kept as "wool-

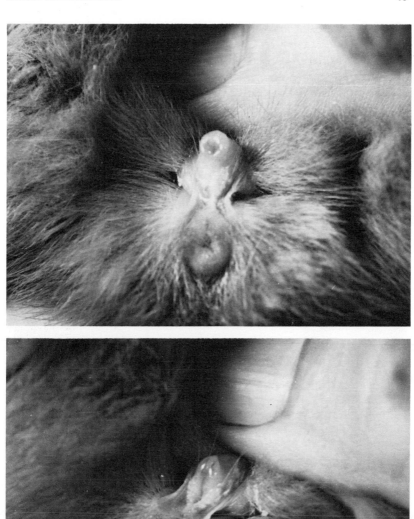

Fig. 4-16. Sex differences in the external genitalia of young rabbits. Upper, male. Lower, female. (Courtesy of L. R. Arrington, Clemson, South Carolina)

lers," in order that any surplus to be disposed of will be the undesired sex.

The external organs of both sexes of the newborn rabbits have very much the same appearance, and a special technique is required for identification of sex at an early age. To prevent the continual wiggling of the little rabbit, restrain it firmly but gently. Place it on its back in the palm of your hand, with its head extended toward the heel of the hand. Use the index finger to press the tail back and down. Press down on the sexual organs gently but with enough pressure to expose the reddish mucous membrane which in the case of the buck can be made to protrude sufficiently to form a circle; in the case of the doe it will protrude and form a slit that will have a slight depression at the end next to the rectum.

Until the technique of sexing rabbits has been perfected (Fig. 4-16), it may be a good plan to sex young at weaning time and then practice with several at about three weeks of age. This will make it easier to determine the sex of the three-day-old rabbit. Constant irritation of the tender parts may be detrimental, so sexing should not be practiced on the same rabbit at too short intervals.

TATTOOING AND EAR TAGS

An efficient, permanent system for identification is a necessity. Tattooing figures or letters, or a combination of the two, in the rabbit's ear does not disfigure it, is permanent, and is easily accomplished. When young are being fostered, a hand tattoo needle is satisfactory for making one or more dots in each kit's ear so the transferred young can be identified. It is also used by many breeders for the regular tattooing work in the rabbitry; others prefer the plier or tongs with removable figures and letters. After the inside of the ear is thoroughly cleaned with alcohol, either instrument may be used to perforate the inner surface of the ear. Tattoo ink or India ink should be rubbed into the perforations immediately (Fig. 4-17). The registration number for purebred stock is usually tattooed in the right ear and the rabbit's individual mark or number in the left ear. A tattoo box that has movable parts so it can be adjusted to different sized rabbits (Fig. 3-15) holds the animal steady so one person can do the tattooing.

Rabbits can also be identified by the use of ear tags (Fig. 3-17). They are quickly and easily inserted with a set of ear tag pliers.

Fig. 4-17. A permanent identification mark tattooed in a rabbit's ear.

CARE OF THE HERD DURING PERIODS
OF HIGH TEMPERATURES

Rabbits must be protected from rain and sun. Good circulation of air throughout the rabbitry is a must, but strong drafts and winds should be avoided. It is essential that they have a supply of water available at all times. Temperature, humidity, and air currents all have a direct bearing, and each rabbitry is an individual problem. Adequate shade should be provided.

Rabbits suffer more from heat than cold; it is necessary to give the herd special attention during periods of high temperatures. They are more uncomfortable in high temperatures the first few hot days in the season. Does that are well advanced in pregnancy and newborn litters are the most susceptible to injury. The does give evidence of suffering by excessive moisture around the mouth and occasionally slight hemorrhage around the nostrils, rapid respiration, and restlessness; newborn litters by extreme restlessness. Rabbits that show symptoms of suffering should be removed to a quiet, well ventilated place. Considerable relief can be given by placement of wet feed sacks in the cage for the animal to lie on. In the case of the doe that has advanced to the stage where hemorrhage is occurring and quick action is necessary, placing cracked ice between the folds of a wet feed sack and placing it in the cage so she can lie on it is quite effective and may save many does about to kindle. Immersing the entire rabbit in cold water for three seconds is another emergency measure to save heat-stressed rabbits.

Sprinkling the roof and floor of the rabbitry will give considerable relief. If a roof sprinkler is thermostatically controlled, it will take care of quick weather changes and is especially useful if the caretaker is not available for regulating the sprinkler. The rabbits must be kept dry, for wet coats are predisposing causes for pneumonia and respiratory troubles.

FUR EATING

When there are several rabbits in a cage and the habit of fur eating develops, the eyelashes and whiskers are eaten first, then the fur on the head and on the body. Rabbits that are alone in a cage eat the fur on their sides or back of their rumps and are capable of reaching fur on the sides of their body where it would seem impossible. If rabbits can reach the coat of another rabbit in an adjoining cage, they may chew its fur. Sometimes does chew the fur on their own young.

In cases in which rabbits are eating their own fur or the fur of other rabbits, the coats have an uneven appearance (Fig. 4-18). This habit is most likely due to a faulty ration or to the rabbits not receiving the proper amount of feed, and is usually associated with a ration that does not contain enough protein or fiber. Check the analysis of the ration to make sure that it contains sufficient protein and fiber. Keeping a good quality hay or straw available at all times and feeding small quantities of green feed daily will assist materially in preventing the fur chewing habit from developing. If the feeding of hay does not solve the problem, increasing the protein

Fig. 4-18. Examples of fur chewing. The dark patches are areas of exposed skin. These rabbits were fed a diet containing sunflower leaves, which contain tannins that react with protein to cause a protein deficiency. (Courtesy of OSU Rabbit Research Center)

content of the ration might help. The addition of 5 pounds of magnesium oxide per ton of feed sometimes aids in control of fur chewing.

SANITATION

Sanitation is very important in controlling disease. Ideally, cages should be cleaned daily. Any manure hanging on the bottom of the cage should be removed with a wire brush. This helps control enteritis and coccidiosis. A wire brush mounted on a long handle is a handy tool. A battery-driven electric drill with a wire brush head can be mounted on a handle and used for cleaning the bottoms of cages. Cages should be brushed or sprayed with a bleach solution (1 ounce of bleach per quart of water). Rabbits excrete large amounts of calcium carbonate in their urine; calcium deposits may build up (Fig. 4-19). Calcium carbonate is soluble in acid, so a weakly acidic solution (e.g., vinegar) will aid in removing these deposits.

Hair should not be allowed to build up on cages and elsewhere in the rabbitry (Fig. 4-20). Hair can be removed from cages by burning with a propane torch. A vacuum cleaner also does an excellent job.

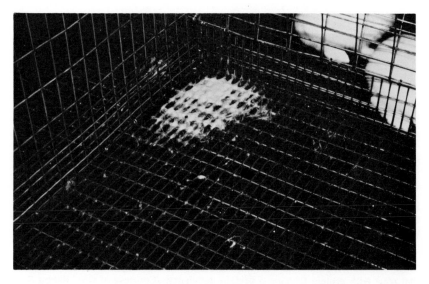

Fig. 4-19. An example of a deposit of calcium carbonate in a rabbit cage. Rabbits excrete large amounts of calcium in their urine. (Courtesy of OSU Rabbit Research Center)

Fig. 4-20. Accumulation of hair in a rabbitry. (Courtesy of D. J. Harris, Corvallis, Oregon)

BREEDING HERD REPLACEMENTS

An extremely important part of herd management is providing adequate replacements for the breeding herd. In commercial rabbitries it is common to replace 50% of the breeding does each year. In fact, if you are not replacing a sizeable portion of the breeding herd annually you are probably not improving the quality and health of the herd as rapidly as you should. Snuffles, sore hocks, malocclusion, mastitis, poor reproductive performance, and many other reasons will result in breeding animals being removed from the herd. As a general rule, save 1 replacement doe per month for every 12 does in production. Also, 1 replacement buck for every 5 bucks in service should be adequate. The continual replacement of old bucks with young bucks is extremely important. Since each buck is bred to many does, his influence on the genetic quality of the herd is much greater than that of an individual doe. Young bucks tend to have greater libido and will work harder than old bucks.

The criteria used in selection of young stock are covered in Chapter 10, "Rabbit Breeding and Genetics." Proper selection of breeding stock has a great impact on the success of a rabbitry and on the potential for profit.

HERD RECORDS

Herd records pay big dividends when the time comes for selecting breeding stock and culling. A useful and uncomplicated system of records for the commercial breeder and also the breeder of purebred animals involves the use of cage cards for the does, a card for keeping each buck's breeding record, and an extended pedigree record or other permanent record. It is not necessary that an elaborate system of bookkeeping be maintained, but a simple record of income and expense enables the rabbit raiser to determine profit or loss.

The cage cards (Fig. 4-21) for making notation of the date of breeding, buck and doe numbers, date of kindling, number of young born and retained, litter number, date and number weaned, and weaned weight of the litter are readily available from feed companies and other commercial sources. Some rabbit raisers may wish to include a record of the weight of the litter at three weeks of age to indicate the doe's milk production. The records that show whether

RABBIT CAGE RECORD CARD

NAME OR
EAR NO. _____

SIRE _____

BORN _____

DAM _____

CAGE NO. _____

SERVED BY	DATE	TESTED	KINDLED	NUMBER OF YOUNG					JRS. SAVED		WEIGHT	REMARKS
				BORN	LEFT	ADDED	RAISED	DIED	BUCKS	DOES		

Fig. 4-21. An example of a cage record card.

BUCK RECORD CARD

EAR NO. _____ SIRE _____ DAM _____ CAGE NO. _____

BORN _____ WEIGHT 2 MOS. _____

DOE SERVED	DATE	LITTER SIZE	WEIGHT	JRS. SAVED		DOE SERVED	DATE	LITTER SIZE	WEIGHT	JRS. SAVED	
				Bucks	Does					Bucks	Does

Fig. 4-22. An example of a buck cage record card.

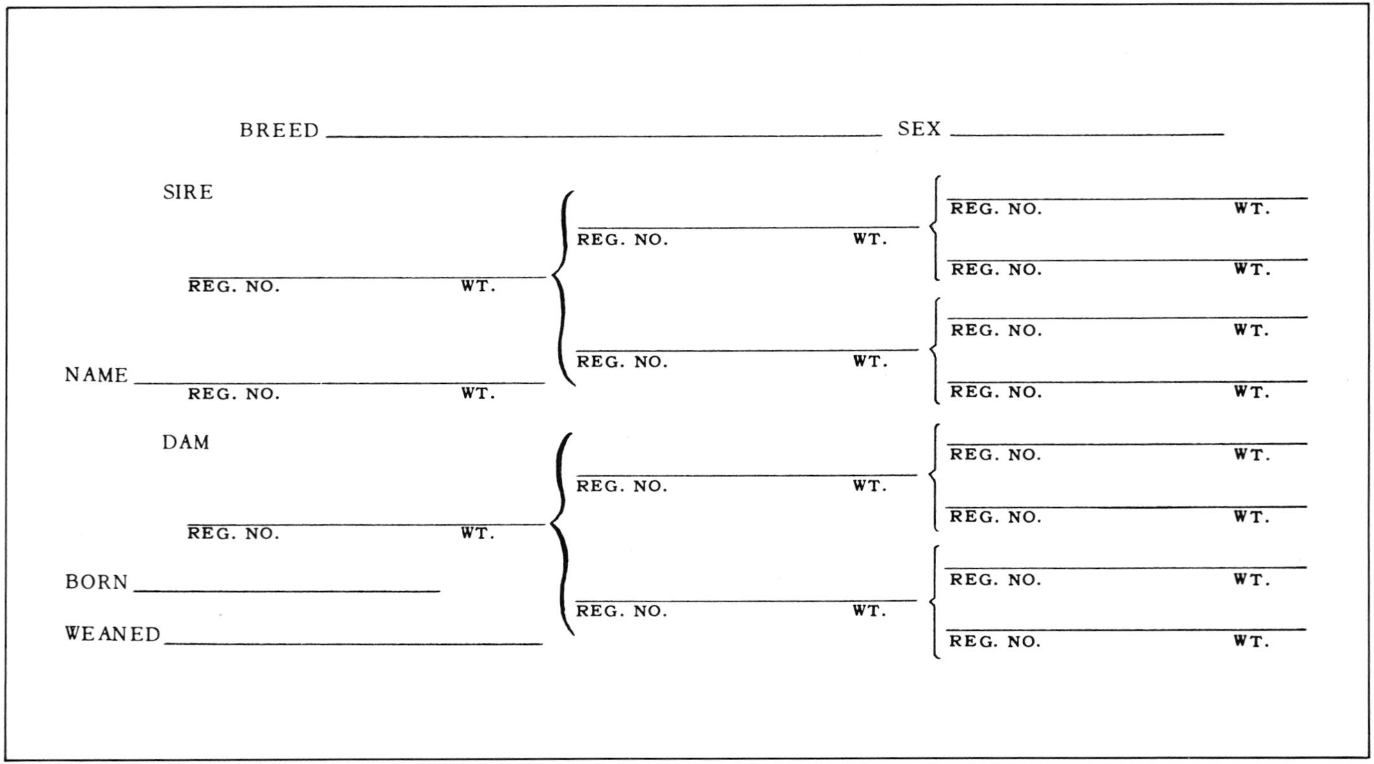

Fig. 4-23. An example of a pedigree card.

the doe conceives regularly throughout the year, whether she is prolific, and whether she has the ability to properly nurse and care for the litter are especially useful in determining which ones are profitable.

Some breeders object to the cage card because during periods of high humidity the cards become limp and fall out of the holders, and the records become illegible. Often the cards become torn, dirty, or lost, making it necessary to keep duplicate records. A cellophane cover will protect them, or information can be transferred to permanent records more frequently.

The buck record card (Fig. 4-22) is extremely important, for it will furnish information as to whether or not a buck has settled his does throughout the year, and information on the relative growth performance of his offspring.

Permanent records which contain both pedigree and production information should be maintained for each breeding animal. Information should be transferred to the permanent records when the cage cards are full, or at regular shorter intervals. Some rabbit raisers may wish to store herd records on computer tapes. Commercial computer programs are available for this purpose.

An extended pedigree (Fig. 4-23) includes at least three generations for each buck and doe in the breeding herd, and can be supplemented with notes and comments entered on the pedigree blank as to record of performance, show winnings, and desirable and undesirable characteristics for each of the ancestors in the pedigree. It is valuable when planning matings for herd improvement. In fact, having these records available is the only way to obtain a complete picture of all the factors involved, for it is impossible to remember all essential details. The extended pedigrees are also necessary for use in making out applications for registration of rabbits.

REGISTERING RABBITS

The American Rabbit Breeders Association maintains a registration and recording system, and purebred rabbits can be registered only by a licensed registrar of that association. A list of registrars may be obtained from ARBA.

The registrar examines the rabbit to be registered, to make sure it is healthy and has no serious defects. If, after checking, the registrar finds the animal qualified, he or she will fill in the registration application blank, giving information as to quality of fur, body type, head, balance, eyes, weight, bone, and color. The registrar will then add personal remarks, make copies of three generations of the pedigree of the rabbit, and give the names of the breeders and the owner of the sire, date of birth, etc. This registration blank will have a number at the right top and bottom corners, which will be tattooed in the rabbit's right ear; the left ear is reserved for the breeder's marks.

The registration application blanks are in triplicate; the original is mailed to the National Office by the registrar, the duplicate acts as a receipt and is given to the owner of the rabbit being registered, and the triplicate is kept for reference by the registrar to be used in case the original becomes lost.

If the National Office finds the application to be correct, it makes up a Certificate of Registration, checks the registration number that appears on the pedigree, and affixes the proper merit seal. If the sire and dam are registered, a red seal is affixed; if the sire and dam and the grand-sires and grand-dams are registered, a red and white seal is affixed; if all 14 ancestors shown on the pedigree are registered, a red, white, and blue seal is affixed. This is the merit system and shows how many generations are purebred and free of defects.

On the back of each application for registration and certificate are three spaces for use of the owner who wishes to transfer the ownership of an animal. After the owner fills in the information called for, the certificate is then mailed to the National Office with a small fee. The office then records the transfer of ownership on the back of the original registration certificate and stamps it, transferring the original application officially.

SHEDDING OR MOLTING

The rabbit's coat is prime when the hairs have a good sheen, are tight, and have attained their maximum length. The skin is white and the hair flows back into place evenly when the coat is rubbed from the rump to the shoulders.

Unprimeness is indicated by a dull, uneven coat, and loose hair. The hair does not flow back evenly when the coat is rubbed from the rump to the shoulders. Patches of new fibers can be seen, and these new fibers will appear in a growth pattern that varies from animal to animal. The skin of these new hair growth areas is dark and easily detected on rabbits with colored coats.

The pattern of shedding in rabbits has not been definitely established. There is a juvenile molt that begins when the rabbit is about two months old and lasts until it is four to six months of age. Heavy feeding of the young tends to cause the molt at an earlier age. In addition, there is the annual molt with mature rabbits. This molt varies in time of appearance in different geographical areas.

Rabbits may be thrown into molt by disease, going "off feed," the sudden occurrence of unseasonably high temperatures, or other stresses. Evidence of molting in the herd is the accumulation of loose hair on the wire sides and in the corners of the cage, and the droppings being bound together by embedded fibers.

Shedding first appears on the sides of the rump and the thighs, followed by appearance on the back, then increasing in areas down over the sides. There is a pronounced degree of similarity in the size and location of the ingrowing new coat areas on both the right and left sides of the rabbit.

ENVIRONMENTAL EFFECTS ON
RABBIT PERFORMANCE

Temperature

Rabbits are very susceptible to heat stress, as they have few functional sweat glands and have difficulty in eliminating body heat when the environmental temperature is high. Heat-stressed animals stretch out to maximize body surface area for heat elimination, and pant. Panting eliminates body heat, because heat is required to evaporate water in the lungs. Animals respond differently to a sudden acute exposure to high temperature than to chronic exposure when reared under high environmental temperatures. In the tropics, New Zealand White rabbits can be successfully raised under conditions in which the temperature is consistently 90°–95°F, while rabbits of the same breed adapted to the cool conditions of the Pacific Northwest of the United States may die of heat stress when the temperature on rare occasions exceeds 90°F. Animals routinely kept under high temperatures develop metabolic mechanisms to adapt to heat stress. In areas of high temperature, such as the tropics, rabbits consume large quantities of water, and consume less feed than in temperate climates. Their productivity is reduced because of the lower feed intake. Provision of adequate water is critical under these conditions.

An ideal environmental temperature is 60°–65°F. This is known as the "comfort zone." At either higher or lower temperatures than this, the animal has to expend energy to maintain its body temperature. Rabbits are much more tolerant of low temperatures than high temperatures. A major consideration under low temperatures is that feed consumption is increased, so the animal can maintain its body temperature. Thus the lower the environmental temperature, the poorer the feed conversion, as a greater quantity of feed energy is being used to maintain body temperature. When limit feeding is practiced, provision must be made to provide extra feed in cold weather. It is also significant that water consumption also increases as the temperature drops, because of the increased feed intake. Restricted availability of water under cold conditions (e.g., from frozen water lines) will reduce performance more than restriction at the comfort zone.

Fig. 4-24. The Californian rabbit on the left had a patch of hair shaved on its rump, and was then kept in a cold environment for a few days. The hair grew back in as pigmented fur. The animal on the right was raised in a warmer environment. (Courtesy of OSU Rabbit Research Center)

An interesting response to cold temperature occurs in some breeds such as the Californian, Siamese Satin, and Sable. If the newborn kits are exposed to cold temperature, or if fur on an adult is shaved and then the rabbit exposed to cold, the fur will temporarily grow in black in areas where it is normally white (Fig. 4-24).

There is some evidence that fluctuations in temperature may trigger outbreaks of enteritis. Enteritis outbreaks are sometimes noted following the start of a cold snap. One possibility to account for this is that a sudden drop in temperature triggers an increase in feed intake. This could cause carbohydrate overload, leading to proliferation of pathogens in the gut, with the production of lethal toxins.

Light

Optimal lighting conditions for rabbit production have not been established. It is believed that the winter decline in fertility that is often observed in some parts of the world may be due at least in part to decreasing day length. Use of lights to maintain a total day length equal to the longest day at a particular latitude is rec-

Fig. 4-25. A rabbit that has been hypnotized. (Photo by N. M. Patton)

ommended. Commercial rabbitries should have lights on a time clock, and use supplementary winter lighting to help maintain normal breeding during the fall and winter. It is possible that the spectrum of the light source may also have an influence on animal performance.

HYPNOSIS

You can readily hypnotize a rabbit by laying it on its back and gently stroking the chest, abdomen, and sides of the head. When hypnotized, a rabbit is in a trance-like state (Fig. 4-25). Hypnosis may have some value as a means of restraining animals for minor surgery; probably it is mainly used to get the attention of 4-H Club members touring the rabbitry!

5

Principles of Rabbit Nutrition

The rabbit is classified as an herbivorous non-ruminant. It has a simple, non-compartmentalized stomach, like the human and pig, and an enlarged cecum and colon (hindgut), like the horse and guinea pig. The hindgut is an area of bacterial growth, somewhat analogous to the rumen of cattle and sheep, which has an influence on digestive processes, nutrient requirements, and the types of feedstuffs rabbits can utilize.

NUTRIENT CATEGORIES

The nutrients that rabbits require in their feed can be grouped in the following categories:

Protein
Carbohydrates
Fats
Minerals
Vitamins

Each of the known nutrients can be placed in one of these categories. While more than 50 nutrients have been identified, it is fortunate that in feed formulation only a few require critical attention.

PROTEIN

Protein is a fundamental component of animal tissue. It is a major component of muscle tissue, cell membranes, certain hormones, and all enzymes. Proteins are made up of basic units called *amino acids* (a-mee-no acids). While over 300 different amino acids are known in the plant world, only about 20 are important in animal tissues. Each animal, and each tissue of an animal, has proteins of a characteristic structure. This structure is determined by the amino acids that the protein contains, and by the order in which they are joined together. Typically, an individual protein molecule will be made up of hundreds or thousands of amino acids joined together in a particular sequence. Some proteins are particularly rich in certain amino acids; for example, hair is very high in cystine (sis-teen), a sulfur-containing amino acid.

Certain animals require particular amino acids in their diets. Monogastric animals, such as pigs and chickens, and non-ruminant herbivores, such as rabbits, require these amino acids in their feed. Ruminants, such as cattle and sheep, do not need amino acids in their diet because the bacteria in the rumen manufacture them, and the animal eventually "eats" or digests the bacteria. The amino acids that are needed in the diet are called *essential amino acids,* meaning that they cannot be manufactured by an animal. The names of the essential amino acids, and their pronunciations, are shown in the following table.

Essential Amino Acids

Arginine	Are-ji-neen
Histidine	Hiss-ti-deen
Isoleucine	I-so-lew-seen
Leucine	Lew-seen
Tryptophan	Trip-toe-fane
Lysine	Lie-seen
Methionine	Meth-I-oh-neen
Phenylalanine	Fen-ill-al-a-neen
Threonine	Three-oh-neen
Valine	Vay-leen

Of these, lysine and methionine are the ones most likely to be deficient in rabbit feeds. This is because grains tend to be low in these amino acids. In the formulation of rabbit rations, it is not sufficient to just consider the amount of protein in the feed. The content of the essential amino acids also needs to be adequate.

Cereal grains are poor sources of protein and are used in human and animal nutrition primarily as sources of energy. Protein supplements are required because of the low protein content and quality of the grains. The major protein supplement used in rabbit feeds is soybean meal, although cottonseed meal, meat meal, linseed meal, and sunflower meal are also used. Alfalfa meal and other forages are also good sources of protein.

CARBOHYDRATES

Carbohydrates are made of carbon, hydrogen, and oxygen. They are synthesized by plants, from carbon dioxide and water, using solar energy. This process is called *photosynthesis*. The solar energy trapped by plants is used by animals, when the carbohydrates are metabolized, producing carbon dioxide and water as waste products.

The simplest carbohydrate is *glucose*. Most other carbohydrates are made up solely or partially of glucose. The most important carbohydrates in rabbit feed are *starch* and *cellulose*. Both are made up entirely of glucose. Starch is found in cereal grains and tubers (potatoes, cassava, etc.). Starch is readily digested by animals and is the major dietary energy source for most non-ruminants (pigs, chickens, humans). Cellulose is the structural component of plants, being a major component of plant fiber. No animals produce the enzyme, cellulase, that digests cellulose. Therefore, the only animals that can use cellulose as an energy source are those which have bacteria in their gut that accomplish the digestion. Cattle and sheep have a rich bacterial population in the stomach (rumen) that digests cellulose. These animals can eat hay, straw, and other roughages, and use them as an energy source because the bacteria digest them. Rabbits, having a bacterial population in the hindgut (cecum and colon), are able to digest cellulose to a minor extent.

The primary function of carbohydrates in rabbit diets is to provide energy, which is expressed in calories. High levels of grain may cause carbohydrate overload of the hindgut, leading to enteritis. Additionally, the indigestible carbohydrate (fiber) may have beneficial effects in preventing enteritis. These aspects will be discussed in the section on carbohydrate digestion.

FATS

Like carbohydrates, fats function primarily as sources of energy. They contain, on an equal weight basis, about 2¼ times as much energy as carbohydrates. Thus they are used in the formulation of high energy diets.

Fat is often added to rabbit rations at levels of 2–5% of the diets. Added fat increases the palatability of feeds, reduces fines, and acts as a lubricant in the pelleting process. It also facilitates absorption of fat-soluble vitamins in the gut. A level of 2–5% dietary fat seems to help in promoting a shiny, lustrous hair coat, which is useful in show rabbits. A supplement of corn oil once or twice a week will do the same thing.

Technically, fats are called *triglycerides*. They are a combination of glycerol and three fatty acids. Fatty acids that are fully saturated with hydrogen are called *saturated fatty acids*. Those which are capable of holding more hydrogen are called *unsaturated fatty acids*. Unsaturated fatty acids can be converted to the saturated form by the addition of hydrogen (hydrogenation). This happens in the rumen, so beef and lamb fat tend to be high in saturated fatty acids. Hydrogenation does not occur in the rabbit gut, so rabbit meat fat is not of the saturated type.

Cholesterol is a complex substance that is often considered with fats. It has been implicated in human health, as it is a constituent of the deposits that form in atherosclerosis (fat deposition in the arteries). Rabbits develop atherosclerosis very readily, so they have been widely used as laboratory animals in the study of this disease. Because alfalfa contains substances (saponins) which reduce tissue cholesterol, and because most rabbit diets contain alfalfa, rabbit meat is low in cholesterol.

MINERALS

Mineral elements are components of the ash content of feeds. The mineral needs of rabbits are easily satisfied, by use of a calcium-phosphorus supplement, and trace mineralized salt, which provides the trace elements. Trace elements are those which are needed in traces, or very small quantities. Copper, manganese, and iodine are examples.

Minerals function in several ways. They may be part of the structure of the body. Calcium and phosphorus function in this way as the major components of bone. They may regulate the properties of biological fluids such as blood and cell protoplasm. Sodium and potassium function in this way. Many trace elements are "cofactors" for enzyme systems; that is, the presence of the mineral is necessary for the enzyme to have activity. Copper, selenium, and zinc are examples of this group. Iodine is a part of the thyroid hormone. Sulfur functions as a component of amino acids (methionine and cystine) and of some vitamins (thiamine and biotin). Iron is a component of a protein that carries oxygen in the blood (hemoglobin). Cobalt is a part of vitamin B_{12}. Phosphorus is a component of a molecule (ATP) that transfers energy in cellular metabolism. Thus minerals have many diverse roles in animal nutrition.

The functions and the deficiency and/or toxicity symptoms of minerals in rabbits will be briefly described.

Calcium and Phosphorus

These elements are important in the structure of bone and teeth. Rabbits are quite unusual in their metabolism of calcium. They absorb it very efficiently, and excrete the excess in the urine. This accounts for the chalky white deposits seen in many rabbitries (Fig. 4-19). Legumes, such as alfalfa, are rich sources of calcium. Grains are very low in calcium but quite high in phosphorus. A combination of grain and alfalfa is thus complementary, and generally meets calcium and phosphorus requirements.

Vitamin D functions in most animals in regulating calcium absorption and bone mineralization. The significance of vitamin D in regulating calcium absorption in rabbits is unclear. They seem to be highly efficient in calcium uptake, and continue to absorb it in large quantities after the metabolic requirement is satisfied. In other species, the amount of calcium absorbed is controlled by a metabolite of vitamin D, and calcium is absorbed only as needed.

Deficiencies of calcium, phosphorus, or vitamin D produce rickets in young animals, and osteomalacia in adults. Young rabbits with rickets exhibit enlarged joints, crooked legs, arched backs, and beaded ribs. Adults may experience demineralization of the bones, until their skeletons become paper thin and fragile, and broken backs occur readily.

Toxicities due to calcium and phosphorus in rabbits are virtually unknown.

Magnesium

Magnesium functions as a component of bone, as a cofactor in enzyme systems, and in transmission of nerve impulses. A magnesium deficiency causes convulsions, hyperirritability, and death. Magnesium deficiency is common in cattle in certain areas (grass tetany). However, it is probably unlikely to occur in rabbits, since legumes (alfalfa, clover) are excellent sources of the element. High dietary levels of calcium increase the magnesium requirement, so it is conceivable that high alfalfa diets could benefit from magnesium supplementation. There have been reports that rabbits chewing fur may respond to supplementation with 5 pounds of magnesium oxide added per ton of feed.

Excess magnesium, added as magnesium sulfate (Epsom salts), can cause severe diarrhea.

Sodium, Potassium, and Chlorine

These elements function in maintaining proper ionic relationships (acid-base balance) in the blood and other body fluids. Potassium occurs abundantly in legumes such as alfalfa, and grains are good sources also, so a deficiency in rabbits is unlikely. Provision of salt at a level of 0.5% of the diet satisfies the sodium and chloride needs. European researchers have suggested that these elements in diets should be provided such that the sum of sodium and potassium, minus chloride, should be about 25 milliequivalents per 100 grams of feed. When enteritis occurs in rabbits, these elements are drawn into the gut, causing a disturbance of fluid balance in the body. The result is dehydration, which may be lethal. Sodium, potassium, and chloride are electrolytes (charged molecules in solution); administration of electrolyte solutions in the drinking water or by injection to animals with enteritis is sometimes beneficial.

Sulfur

Sulfur is a component of the sulfur amino acids and the vitamins thiamine and biotin. Thus it is only required as a component of these nutrients. Inorganic sulfate is used in formation of connective tissue. In poultry, responses to feeding inorganic sulfate (e.g., sodium sulfate) have been noted. It is not known if such responses occur in rabbits.

Iron

Iron is a component of several organic molecules that function in energy metabolism. Hemoglobin, a blood pigment in the red blood cells, contains iron. Hemoglobin functions in oxygen transport in the blood. A deficiency of iron results in decreased hemoglobin formation and anemia. Iron deficiency in rabbits is unlikely, because most commercial rabbit diets contain adequate iron.

Copper

This element is closely involved with iron metabolism. A copper deficiency impairs iron utilization, causing anemia. Copper is also a cofactor for several enzymes. A peculiarity of copper deficiency is that a graying of black fur occurs (Fig. 5-1). This is due to the role of copper in the synthesis of melanin, a pigment in hair and fur.

Fig. 5-1. A copper-deficient rabbit. Note the graying of the normally black fur. (Courtesy of S. E. Smith, Cornell University)

Cobalt

No specific metabolic requirement for cobalt is known. Its only nutritional role is as a part of the structure of vitamin B_{12}. This vitamin is synthesized in the hindgut of the rabbit by bacteria. When rabbits eat their night feces (coprophagy), they satisfy their vitamin B_{12} requirement. In fact, a large excess of the vitamin is obtained in this way.

Manganese

Manganese deficiency in rabbits causes a malformation of the

Fig. 5-2. A manganese deficiency, showing crooked front legs due to impaired bone formation. (Courtesy of S. E. Smith, Cornell University)

skeletal system (Fig. 5-2), including crooked legs; brittle bones; and decreased weight, density, length, and ash content of the bones. This is due to the metabolic role of manganese in the formation of the organic matrix of bone. A deficiency in rabbits fed practical diets is unlikely.

Zinc

Does fed zinc-deficient diets have been shown to have im-

Fig. 5-3. A zinc deficiency, showing loss of hair and crusting of the skin (dermatitis) on the ears. (Courtesy of C. E. Joseph, Los Angeles, and *The Journal of Nutrition*, American Institute of Nutrition)

paired fertility. Loss of hair and dermatitis are also observed (Figs. 5-3 and 5-4). Zinc functions as a cofactor of numerous enzymes, and is involved in DNA metabolism. Zinc is bound by phytic acid in soybean meal and grains, thus reducing its availability to some animals, such as swine and poultry. It is likely that in rabbits the zinc-phytate complex is destroyed by bacterial activity. Zinc deficiencies in commercial rabbit production have not been reported.

Fig. 5-4. A zinc deficiency, showing a zinc-deficient rabbit (right) contrasted with a zinc-adequate control (left). Stunted growth, altered posture, and abnormal fur are characteristics of zinc deficiency. (Courtesy of C. E. Joseph, Los Angeles, and *The Journal of Nutrition,* American Institute of Nutrition)

Iodine

Iodine is a constituent of the thyroid hormone thyroxin. In an iodine deficiency, the thyroid gland in the neck enlarges in an attempt to synthesize more thyroxin. This enlargement is called a *goiter.* Reproducing animals produce weak or dead offspring, which have readily observed goiters. Rabbit rations should always be supplemented with iodized salt.

Selenium

For many years, selenium was known only for its toxic properties. Feeds grown in areas which have soils with a high selenium content (the Great Plains states) may sometimes contain sufficient selenium to be toxic to livestock. Toxicity symptoms include loss of hair and blindness. In 1958, Oregon State University researchers discovered that white muscle disease (stiff lamb disease, nutritional muscular dystrophy) in sheep could be prevented by selenium. Subsequent work has demonstrated that selenium functions as a part of an enzyme, glutathione peroxidase, that is involved in the removal or detoxification of peroxides, such as hydrogen peroxide, that are formed in tissues during normal metabolic processes. Vitamin E functions by preventing peroxide formation; thus vitamin E and selenium are very closely related in nutrition. The rabbit is interesting in that it apparently depends completely on vitamin E for protection against peroxide damage. No selenium deficiency symptom has ever been demonstrated in rabbits, so it appears that selenium is not a required nutrient for rabbits.

Trace mineral deficiencies should not be a problem in rabbit production. The use of trace mineralized salt at a level of 0.5% of the diet will ensure that requirements are met. In addition, alfalfa meal is generally a good source of mineral elements.

VITAMINS

The discovery and identification of vitamins has occurred almost entirely in the twentieth century. While there were hints of the existence of factors which could prevent disorders such as beriberi and scurvy in humans, it was not until the period following 1900 that chemical techniques became sufficiently sophisticated to allow the identification of these substances. The term "vitamin" came from the fact that one of the first vitamins to be studied was a chemical type called an "amine." The compound was called "a vital amine"; this was later shortened to "vitamine," and then to "vitamin." A substance that was found in butter was called "fat-soluble A," and the substance found to protect against beriberi was called "water-soluble B." Later these were called "vitamin A" and "vitamin B." It was soon discovered that "vitamin B" was actually made up of several vitamins, so it was called "the vitamin B complex."

These designations continue to this day; the fat-soluble vitamins are vitamins A, D, E, and K, while there are numerous members of the water-soluble vitamin B complex group, and vitamin C. The last vitamin to be discovered was vitamin B_{12}, in 1948. Thus the Golden Age of the discovery of vitamins was 1900 to 1948.

In spite of the fact that vitamins are newcomers to our knowledge of nutrition, they have become legends in their own time. People ascribe tremendous results to gulping large quantities of vitamins. A great commercial industry has developed, with an unlikely alliance between the large drug companies and the "health food" movement. The drug companies manufacture vitamins, and the "health food" industry promotes and sells them, at "megavitamin" dose levels. Most reputable nutritionists are somewhat appalled at this development, since the extensive scientific studies of the effects of vitamins do not support this massive overdosing.

This background is highly relevant to a discussion of rabbit nutrition. Since, in popular opinion, the thing to do at the first sign of illness is to take some vitamins, you should be aware that the dietary vitamin needs of rabbits are in most cases quite low. Large amounts of money have been spent unnecessarily to feed rabbits vitamins for which they have no need. They are simply excreted in the urine.

Definition of a Vitamin

Vitamins are defined as having the following properties.

1) They are organic compounds. The term "organic" is used in the original chemical terminology, rather than in the current popular jargon. An organic compound is one composed primarily of carbon and hydrogen. This is in contrast to inorganic substances, such as the minerals.

2) They are components of natural food, but are distinct from the other organic compounds, the carbohydrates, fats, and protein.

3) They are essential for normal growth and maintenance of tissue, and have a specific, essential role in metabolism.

4) When they are absent from the diet, or not properly absorbed, specific deficiency symptoms result.

5) They cannot be synthesized by animals, so they must be obtained from the diet.

6) They are required in very small quantities.

There are some exceptions to the fifth generalization listed. Vitamin D can be synthesized if there is exposure to sunlight. Most species, including rabbits, can manufacture their own vitamin C. Niacin can be made in tissues from the amino acid tryptophan.

FAT-SOLUBLE VITAMINS

There are four members of this group: vitamins A, D, E, and K. It should be noted that vitamin K exists in water-soluble form also, so it has some properties of the water-soluble vitamin group as well. The fat-soluble vitamins are not excreted readily, so they are stored in the body for extensive periods of time. Thus they do not need to be fed continuously, and it takes a prolonged feeding period on a deficient diet for deficiencies to develop. With the exception of vitamin K, fat-soluble vitamins are not synthesized by bacteria in the gut.

Vitamin A

Technically speaking, vitamin A is not found in plants; rather it occurs in plants as carotene, a substance which animals can convert to vitamin A. Vitamin A is required for the growth and maintenance of all body tissues, particularly the epithelial tissues, such as the skin, the digestive tract, and the reproductive tract. It is an essential component of compounds that function in vision. Symptoms of vitamin A deficiency in rabbits are retarded growth, nervous system effects such as incoordination and paralysis, blindness, and hydrocephalus (enlarged head) of fetuses born to vitamin A–deficient does. An interesting deficiency symptom in rabbits is that the ears droop. Vitamin A is required for cartilage formation, so in a deficiency, the ear cartilage is defective and cannot support the weight of the ear. Rabbit rations low in alfalfa meal should be supplemented with vitamin A (alfalfa is the richest plant source of vitamin A activity). Vitamin A activity of feeds can be reduced by feed processing (e.g., pelleting) and feed storage.

Vitamin D

The principal function of vitamin D is to regulate calcium absorption. In most species, the amount of calcium absorbed in the intestine is controlled by a "calcium binding protein" that transports calcium through the intestinal wall to the blood. The activity of this calcium binding protein, and thus the amount of calcium absorbed, is regulated by vitamin D. This does not seem to be the case in rabbits, as they absorb calcium efficiently regardless of their need for it. Thus the role of vitamin D in metabolism in the rabbit is obscure.

Vitamin D can be synthesized by the skin of animals exposed to sunlight. For animals kept under confinement conditions, it should be added to the diet. Vitamin D toxicity is probably of more significance than deficiencies in rabbit production. Several cases of vitamin D toxicity have occurred when excessive levels of the vitamin were inadvertently added to rabbit feeds. Toxicity symptoms are loss of appetite, impaired movement, and calcification of soft tissues such as kidneys and arteries.

Vitamin E

This vitamin is also called α-tocopherol (alpha toe-coff-er-all). Vitamin E is very closely linked to the mineral element selenium in its metabolism and function. Both nutrients function by preventing tissue destruction by toxic peroxides formed during metabolism. Vitamin E acts as an antioxidant to prevent peroxides from being formed. Selenium is a part of the enzyme glutathione peroxidase, which converts toxic peroxides into harmless substances such as water. In a deficiency of either vitamin E or selenium, tissue breakdown due to peroxide damage occurs. This results in destruction of muscle tissue (nutritional muscular dystrophy), infertility, absorption of fetuses, and a variety of other effects, which vary according to the species of animal involved. Rabbits seem to depend entirely on vitamin E for protection against peroxides. As mentioned earlier, attempts to demonstrate a selenium deficiency in rabbits have not been successful. Alfalfa and grains are quite good sources of vitamin E, but it is recommended that rabbit diets be routinely supplemented with vitamin E, as there are losses in feed processing.

Vitamin K

Vitamin K has a very specific metabolic function; it is essential for blood clotting. In a vitamin K deficiency, a blood protein, prothrombin, is not activated to allow it to participate in the clotting process. While vitamin K deficiency is not often encountered in animals, there are some classic examples of induced deficiencies. Sweet clover poisoning of cattle is caused by feeding molding sweet clover hay; it causes profuse bleeding and hemorrhage. Sweet clover contains coumarin, which is converted by molds to a potent antagonist of vitamin K, called *dicumarol*. Dicumarol is very similar in structure to vitamin K, but cannot substitute for it in prothrombin synthesis. The result is an induced vitamin K deficiency. Another example is the rat poison warfarin. This induces a vitamin K deficiency, causing death by internal bleeding. The sulfa drugs, such as sulfaquinoxaline, are vitamin K antagonists which increase the vitamin K requirements. Finally, some of the mold toxins (mycotoxins) in moldy hay and grain can act as vitamin K antagonists. Symptoms of vitamin K deficiency are prolonged bleeding following a minor injury, and abortion and placental hemorrhage in does. A vitamin K deficiency in rabbits is unlikely, because the vitamin is synthesized in the gut by bacteria, and obtained by the rabbit when it eats its feces (coprophagy).

WATER-SOLUBLE VITAMINS

The members of the vitamin B complex are all synthesized by bacteria in the cecum and colon of the rabbit. When the rabbit eats its night feces, these bacterially synthesized vitamins are consumed, and absorbed. Numerous studies have shown that rabbits do not respond to supplementation with B vitamins, because the bacteria supply more than adequate quantities via coprophagy. In addition, the grains and forages used in rabbit diets are good sources of these vitamins. Therefore, only a very brief description of each of these vitamins will be given, as there is little likelihood of deficiencies being encountered in rabbit production.

Thiamine (Vitamin B₁)

Thiamine is a cofactor for certain enzymes involved in carbohydrate and fat metabolism. A deficiency causes loss of appetite, accumulation of pyruvic acid in the blood, and muscle paralysis.

Riboflavin (Vitamin B_2)

Riboflavin is a component of several compounds that function in the complete oxidation of glucose within cells. These compounds are involved in the chemical transfer of the solar energy of glucose to specific biochemical reactions in metabolism. Riboflavin deficiency causes reduced growth and a lowered feed efficiency.

Niacin

The classic condition of niacin deficiency is pellagra, a disease that until the 1940's was responsible for thousands of human deaths each year in the southern part of the United States. Niacin can be synthesized from the amino acid tryptophan. Since corn is very low in both these nutrients, niacin deficiency has been a problem in humans and animals for which corn is a major dietary ingredient. Again, niacin is synthesized by gut bacteria, so a deficiency in rabbits is unlikely. Niacin functions metabolically in a manner similar to riboflavin. It is a component of cofactors that are involved in oxidation of carbohydrate within cells.

Pyridoxine (Vitamin B_6)

This vitamin functions in protein metabolism. It is a cofactor for several reactions involved in amino acid metabolism. A classic deficiency symptom is convulsions. A deficiency in rabbits is extremely improbable, due to this vitamin's abundance in forage and grains, and the intestinal synthesis by bacteria.

Pantothenic Acid

This vitamin also is essential for energy metabolism. It has a role in the oxidative breakdown of sugars and fatty acids to carbon dioxide and water. No deficiency of pantothenic acid in rabbits has ever been produced.

Biotin

Biotin deficiency causes loss of normal hair pigmentation. This has occurred in mink due to the feeding of raw eggs, which contain a biotin antagonist called *avidin*. Biotin has a metabolic function in fatty acid metabolism. Again, because of the intestinal synthesis of B vitamins in rabbits, no dietary supplementation is needed.

Choline

This compound can be synthesized by animals, so it is questionable that it should even be called a vitamin. Experimentally, choline deficiency has been produced in rabbits, causing poor growth, anemia, muscular dystrophy, and death. Its abundant distribution in feeds, and body and intestinal synthesis provide adeequately for the choline needs of rabbits.

Folic Acid

Folic acid (folacin) functions in the interconversion of amino acids and in nucleic acid synthesis. Its function is closely related to that of vitamin B_{12}. Folic acid deficiency causes anemia. Deficiencies in rabbits are unknown.

Vitamin B_{12}

Like folic acid, vitamin B_{12} functions in the synthesis of nucleic acids. Anemia is the primary deficiency symptom. Vitamin B_{12} contains cobalt, and is synthesized by the gut bacteria as long as cobalt is present. Even when very low levels of cobalt have been experimentally fed to rabbits, it has been impossible to produce a vitamin B_{12} deficiency. The bacteria in the hindgut of horses and rabbits are extremely efficient at using cobalt for vitamin B_{12} synthesis. Horses thrive on pastures so low in cobalt that cattle and sheep dependent on such pastures will die of vitamin B_{12} deficiency. Thus a cobalt deficiency is actually a metabolic deficiency of vitamin B_{12}.

Vitamin C

Only a few species require dietary vitamin C; these include humans, monkeys, guinea pigs, and certain fish. Rabbits synthesize vitamin C from glucose in their tissues, so they have no dietary requirement for this nutrient.

DIGESTIVE PROCESSES IN THE RABBIT

Rabbits are monogastric herbivores (Fig. 5-5). They have a simple stomach, and an enlarged hindgut (cecum and colon). It has commonly been assumed that the enlarged hindgut is an area functionally similar to the rumen of cattle. This is not correct, but there are some similarities. In ruminants, there is no requirement for dietary essential amino acids, because bacteria make them in the rumen. In rabbits, the bacterial protein synthesized in the hindgut makes very little contribution to their protein needs, so they are dependent on dietary essential amino acids. Cattle can digest fibrous feeds, because the rumen bacteria produce cellulase, which breaks down cellulose. Rabbits do not digest fiber efficiently. In fact, fiber digestibility in the rabbit is lower than for most other species, even the simple monogastrics such as rats and swine. The reasons for this will be discussed in the fiber portion of the section on carbohydrate digestion. Ruminants and rabbits do share one

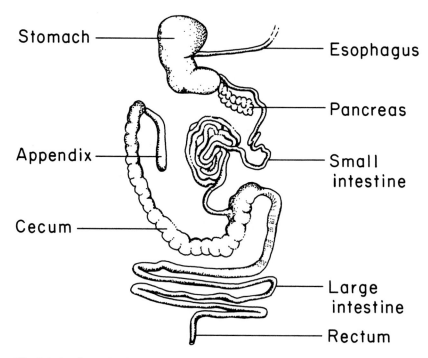

Fig. 5-5. A schematic of the major sections of the gastrointestinal tract of the rabbit.

characteristic related to their gut bacteria: the bacteria in both the rumen and the hindgut synthesize adequate quantities of the B vitamins. Both rabbits and ruminant animals only have dietary requirements for vitamins A, D, and E; the others are synthesized in adequate amounts by bacteria in the gut.

Digestion and Digestibility

Digestion is the preparation of feed nutrients for absorption. Absorption is the transport of the products of digestion from the digestive tract into the blood. During digestion, large molecules such as proteins and starch are split apart by digestive enzymes into the basic units of which they are made (amino acids and glucose, for proteins and starch respectively). In rabbits, most of the digestion occurs in the small intestine, and is accomplished by digestive enzymes that are secreted into the digestive tract. Most of these enzymes are produced in the pancreas, and secreted through the pancreatic duct into the small intestine. There is also some fermentation (digestion by bacteria) in the cecum and colon. This is much less important to digestion in the rabbit than once believed.

Determination of digestibility is a technique used to measure how much of a particular feed an animal can digest. To do this, it is necessary to measure the feed intake, and the feces excreted. The difference between these is the amount of nutrient absorbed. This is shown diagrammatically in Fig. 5-6. Animals are kept in metabolism cages, which are designed so that the feces and urine can be separated and collected (Fig. 5-7). Determination of the digestibility of feeds is very important, because it provides an estimate of their nutritional value. If a certain feed contains 80% protein, but only 30% of it is digestible, then that feed has the equivalent of only 24% protein, because 70% of the protein it contains is simply excreted in the feces.

While the digestibility of many feeds has been determined for cattle, sheep, and swine, there has been comparatively little research on this subject with rabbits.

Protein Digestion

Protein is digested primarily in the small intestine, by several enzymes secreted from the pancreas. Trypsin and chymotrypsin are two of the principal protein-digesting enzymes. The digestion proc-

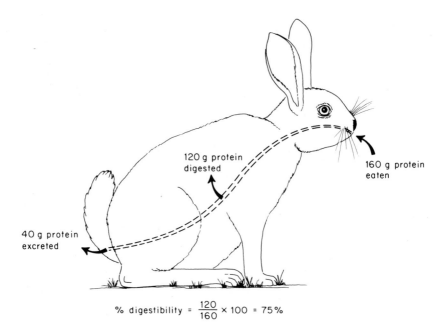

$$\% \text{ digestibility} = \frac{120}{160} \times 100 = 75\%$$

Procedure:

The rabbit is kept in a metabolism cage. Feed is consumed, and the feces excreted are weighed. Samples of the feed and feces are analyzed for their protein content.

Data collected:

Feed contains 16% protein
Feces contain 10% protein
Feed consumed = 1000 grams (g)
Feces excreted = 400 g

Calculations:

Protein consumed = 1000 g feed × 16% protein
$\qquad\qquad\quad$ = 1000 g × .16 = 160 g

Protein excreted $\quad$ = 400 g feces × 10% protein
$\qquad\qquad\qquad$ = 400 g × .10 = 40 g

Protein digested $\quad$ = protein consumed − protein excreted
$\qquad\qquad\qquad$ = 160 g − 40 g = 120 g

$$\% \text{ Protein digestibility} = \frac{\text{protein digested}}{\text{protein consumed}} \times 100$$

$$= \frac{120 \text{ g}}{160 \text{ g}} \times 100 = 75\%$$

Fig. 5-6. An example of the calculation of protein digestibility.

Fig. 5-7. Metabolism cages, which allow separate collection of feces and urine. These are used for such purposes as the measurement of nutrient digestibility. (Courtesy of D. J. Harris, Corvallis, Oregon)

ess consists of breaking the bonds which join amino acids together in the protein. Thus the dietary protein is broken into the individual amino acids of which it is composed. These are then absorbed into the blood. Protein not digested in this manner passes through the small intestine to the hindgut, where it is subjected to the action of bacterial enzymes. Bacteria in the hindgut synthesize amino acids, which they incorporate into their own proteins. This bacterial protein could be available to the rabbit when it eats its feces (coprophagy). However, research on nitrogen and protein metabolism in rabbits has demonstrated that the bacterial protein, consumed via coprophagy, makes a very small contribution to the animal's protein and amino acid needs. The rabbit is dependent on good quality dietary protein to meet its essential amino acid needs.

In cattle and other ruminants, the bacteria in the rumen synthesize protein from sources of nitrogen such as urea. This type of feed source is called *non-protein nitrogen* (NPN). In addition, the rumen bacteria convert low quality proteins, deficient in essential amino acids, to higher quality bacterial protein. This is economically advantageous, because low quality proteins and NPN sources are cheaper than high quality proteins. Because rabbits have a similar bacterial population in the hindgut, it is of interest to know if they can also efficiently use low quality proteins and NPN sources such as urea. Numerous studies have demonstrated that they cannot. Urea is of almost no value to rabbits as a nitrogen source for protein synthesis.

In comparison to other monogastric animals, rabbits digest the protein in forages very efficiently. A pig fed alfalfa meal will digest less than 50% of the protein in the alfalfa. Rabbits, on the other hand, will digest 75–80% of the alfalfa protein, in spite of the fact that they don't digest the fiber fraction any more efficiently than swine do. This is probably due to coprophagy. As a result of more than one passage through the digestive tract, more efficient extraction and digestion of the forage protein occurs. This is one of the main reasons why large quantities of alfalfa and other forages are fed to rabbits, and serve as a major source of protein. In the future, as grain becomes less available for animal feeding, and we rely more on forages for livestock feed, the ability of the rabbit to use forage protein efficiently will become very important.

Carbohydrate Digestion

Dietary carbohydrates are of two types: the readily digestible sources, such as starch and sucrose, and the relatively indigestible types, such as cellulose and hemicellulose. Starch is the major carbohydrate in grain, while cellulose and hemicellulose are major components of the fiber fraction of forages.

Starch is digested in the small intestine of the rabbit, by an enzyme called *amylase*, which is secreted by the pancreas. Amylase splits starch into the glucose molecules of which it is composed. Glucose is then absorbed into the blood and used by the rabbit as an energy source. Because of the rapid time of passage of feed through the small intestine, significant amounts of undigested starch may reach the hindgut. Here it is fermented by bacteria. High levels of grain fed to rabbits may cause carbohydrate overload of the hindgut. The abundant starch allows bacterial populations to "explode." If certain toxin-producing organisms are present, the result can be enterotoxemia and death. Thus type and amount of dietary carbohydrate can influence the development of a major disease problem in rabbits.

The fiber fraction of feeds is poorly digested by rabbits. This is illustrated in Table 5-1.

Table 5-1. Digestibility of the Fiber of Alfalfa Hay
by Various Animals

Animal	Percent Fiber Digestibility
Cattle	44
Sheep	45
Goats	41
Horses	41
Pigs	22
Rabbits	14

Adapted from Maynard, L. A., et al., *Animal Nutrition*, 7th ed. (New York: McGraw-Hill Book Co., 1979), p. 31.

If rabbits digest fiber so poorly, how do they make efficient use of fibrous feeds? This apparent contradiction can be explained by recognizing that fiber only makes up 20–25% of forages. Thus a forage like alfalfa meal is 75–80% non-fiber. The rabbit efficiently digests the non-fiber fraction, such as the protein and soluble carbohydrates, and excretes the fiber fraction. European studies have suggested that there is a separation of large and small particles in the cecum. The small particles are retained for further digestion, while the large particles (i.e., fiber) are rapidly excreted. The ability of the rabbit to utilize high dietary levels of alfalfa and other forages is due to a high intake of these low energy feeds, with rapid excretion of the fiber and efficient digestion of the non-fiber components.

In many countries, there is interest in producing leaf protein concentrates (LPC) as human and animal foods. In this process, forages are green-chopped, macerated, and pressed to squeeze out the juice. Much of the protein comes out in the juice. The protein in the juice is then coagulated, skimmed off, and dried. The product, LPC, is a protein source equal in value to soybean meal. Rabbits are a biological method of producing LPC. They efficiently separate the forage protein from the fiber, excrete the fiber, and convert the protein into high quality meat. In many countries, rabbit production may be an economically and technologically more effective means of utilizing forages than mechanical LPC production.

While fiber is not useful as an energy source for rabbits, it is a very important component of rabbit feeds. Numerous studies have shown that low fiber diets promote increased enteritis. Fiber may have a specific protective effect, by having a scabrous action on the intestinal lining, and maintaining it in a healthy condition. Higher fiber levels also reduce the soluble carbohydrate level, which may aid in reducing carbohydrate overload of the hindgut.

Fat Digestion

Fats are digested in the small intestine, by the pancreatic enzyme lipase. Bile is also required, to emulsify fat (break it into small droplets) in the aqueous medium of the gut contents. Popular opinion seems to be that high dietary fat might be indigestible; this is not correct. Fat is readily digestible, and fat levels as high as 25% of the diet have been fed to rabbits with no ill effect. In practical feeds, levels of 3–5% are used; higher levels may reduce pellet quality, causing crumbling of the pellets.

Digestion of Minerals and Vitamins

These nutrients do not require digestion, as they are already in a form that can be directly absorbed. Thus digestion is a process that only applies to the major nutrient categories of proteins, carbohydrates, and fats.

Coprophagy

Coprophagy is defined as the act of consuming feces. Unsavory as this may sound, it is a normal behavioral pattern for many types of animals, including rabbits. The principal nutritional consequence of coprophagy in rabbits is that this is a means of providing the B vitamin requirements. All the members of the B complex group are synthesized by bacteria in the rabbit hindgut, and are made available to the animal after it consumes its feces. As a result, rabbits do not require B vitamins in their diet. Another consequence of coprophagy is that it provides a small amount of bacterial protein. However, it is doubtful that this is of practical significance.

Rabbits excrete two types of feces. The hard feces or day feces, which are produced in the large intestine, are the fecal pellets commonly seen. The feces that are consumed via coprophagy are the night or soft feces, produced in the cecum. These are consumed directly from the anus. They are excreted in grape-like clusters, surrounded by a gelatinous membrane. They may often be found intact in the anterior portion of the stomach in necropsied animals. Since the feces are consumed directly from the anus, raising rabbits on wire does not inhibit coprophagy. In fact, prevention of coprophagy for experimental purposes is quite difficult, and involves equipping rabbits with a collar to prevent them from reaching the anus. The term "night feces" is a misnomer, because these soft pellets are often seen during the day as well.

FEED ANALYSIS

A complete analysis of a feed for all known nutrients would be extremely expensive. Nutritionists have devised a system for analysis of feeds that gives a general idea of their overall feeding value. This is called the *proximate analysis*. For particular feedstuffs or when certain nutritional problems are encountered, more sophisticated analyses may be conducted for amino acids, minerals, vitamins, or other specific nutrients. In ration formulation, "book values" are generally used. Such values are tabulated in the National Research Council (NRC) publications on nutrient requirements of animals. It is generally not feasible to get complete analyses on specific feedstuffs that are being used by feed manufacturers in preparing feeds.

The components measured in the proximate analysis scheme are:

Crude protein
Fat (ether extract)
Crude fiber
Ash
Nitrogen-free extract (NFE)
Water

Crude protein is actually based on a measurement of nitrogen content. It is assumed that all the nitrogen in a feed is associated with protein. Crude protein is defined as nitrogen content times the factor 6.25. This is somewhat imprecise, since not all the nitrogen is from protein, and this measurement gives no indication of amino acid content of protein sources. The fat or ether extract is that portion of the feed that is soluble in ether. Crude fiber is a measurement of the plant cell wall components. The crude fiber determination has been largely replaced by measurement of acid detergent fiber (ADF). The ADF is a more specific measure of the cellulose and lignin content of a forage. Ash is obtained by burning a feed sample in a laboratory furnace, and weighing the incombustible residue. This corresponds to the total mineral content. The nitrogen-free extract (NFE) is the difference between 100% and the sum of all the other proximate components. It is composed primarily of soluble carbohydrates, such as starch.

The energy content of feeds is obtained by burning a feed sample in an instrument called a *bomb calorimeter* (Fig. 5-8). Energy is measured in units called *calories,* a measurement of heat. A calorie is the amount of heat required to raise the temperature of 1 gram of water by 1°C. In the bomb calorimeter, a known amount of feed is burned in a "bomb" which is surrounded by a known weight of water. The water takes up the heat, and the temperature rises. From the weight of sample, weight of water, and rise in temperature of the water, the total heat energy (calories) can be determined. Popular usage of the term "calorie" is incorrect. A calorie is too small a unit to be useful in nutrition. We use kilocalories (kcal). One

Fig. 5-8. A bomb calorimeter, used in the determination of the calorie content of feeds. The bomb (the container in which the feed sample is burned) is in the technician's left hand. The feed sample is put in a cup in her right hand, and then inserted in the bomb. (Courtesy of OSU Rabbit Research Center)

kilocalorie is equal to 1000 calories. When people talk about how many calories they have eaten today, they are actually talking about the number of kilocalories rather than calories.

The total energy content of a feed is called the *gross energy*. Gross energy is not useful for expressing energy content of feeds, since anything that burns will have a high gross energy content. It does not mean that an animal can "burn" it. Therefore, feed energy is expressed as *digestible energy* (DE). This is determined by feeding an animal a test feed and collecting the feces excreted. The gross energy content of both the feed and feces are measured in a bomb calorimeter. The feed gross energy then is corrected for the amount of indigestible energy excreted in the feces to estimate digestible energy. As a rule of thumb, the DE content is 4 kilocalories per gram for protein and carbohydrate, and 9 kilocalories per gram for fat.

Total Digestible Nutrients (TDN)

This is an indirect method of estimating DE. It is calculated by adding up the digestible components of a feed that can yield energy. The caloric content of a feed is due to its protein, fat, and carbohydrate content. Minerals and vitamins do not provide energy. TDN is calculated by the following formula:

% TDN = % digestible crude protein + % digestible crude fiber + % digestible NFE + 2.25 (% digestible fat).

The fat content is multiplied by 2.25, because fats have about 2¼ times the energy content of protein and carbohydrate.

Information on a Feed Tag

By law, a feed tag must provide certain information, varying somewhat by state or province. Crude protein is usually listed as "not less than." In other words, the feed manufacturer can provide more protein than listed on the tag. The manufacturer is not likely to consciously do so, as protein is expensive. Similarly, the crude fiber is listed as "not more than." Again, this is to protect the buyer. Fiber sources are generally cheaper than grains. By stating a maximum fiber level, the manufacturer assures the buyer that cheap, low quality fibrous feedstuffs haven't been added to dilute the feed. If the feed has less than the maximum fiber content listed, it means that higher cost ingredients have been used.

It is impossible to look at a feed tag and say conclusively that the feed is good or bad. The information provided is insufficient to allow a judgement to be made. Crude protein is not a measurement of protein at all, but a measure of nitrogen. There is no indication on the tag of the quality of the protein (its content of essential amino acids). There is no indication of the digestibility of the protein. A crude protein analysis does not distinguish between soybean meal and shoe leather. There is no information on a feed tag on the energy content of the feed, or on the specific level of minerals and vitamins.

RELATIONSHIPS BETWEEN FEED MANUFACTURERS AND RABBIT RAISERS

Misunderstandings sometimes occur between rabbit raisers and feed manufacturers. There are probably several reasons for this. One is that compared to other domestic livestock, rabbits are picky, finicky animals. A pig or feedlot steer will eat almost anything a feed mill can concoct. Rabbits, on the other hand, are quite discriminating. A subtle change in the feed, from a new batch of a particular feedstuff, may cause them to go off feed or to scratch large amounts of feed out of the feeder. Enteritis outbreaks seem to be associated with the feed. All the factors involved in enteritis haven't been identified, but certainly the feed seems to be one of them. When an outbreak occurs, the rabbit raiser blames the feed, while the feed mill may be unable to identify any problem with it. Greater understanding by both sides is needed. Feed manufacturers should appreciate that rabbits are unique animals, and that they develop conditions such as enteritis on certain feeds, for reasons that have yet to be identified. Rabbit raisers should recognize that a feed mill is not a "fly-by-night" operation, and that feed manufacturers want to produce a high quality product. The basic underlying problem is that we still don't know exactly how to feed rabbits. Much more research is needed to identify all the subtle factors that seem to influence how rabbits respond to commercial feeds. It is very frustrating on both sides for a rabbit raiser to lose large numbers of animals when a certain feed is used, while the feed manufacturer cannot find anything wrong with the feed. Hopefully this situation will change in the future, as more is learned about the nutritional needs and peculiarities of rabbits.

Feeds and Feeding

NUTRIENT REQUIREMENTS OF RABBITS

Since rabbits are kept under confinement conditions, they are totally dependent on the feed provided. Generally, they are fed nothing but a pelleted feed. That feed must contain all the nutrients they need, in adequate amounts and proper balance, in a pelleted package that must be palatable and well accepted by the rabbits. This diet must not only be satisfactory for the short term, but must be adequate for reproduction and longevity. Breeding does should be able to produce 12 or more litters. In order that a feed may give satisfactory results, it is necessary that nutrient requirements be met. This information is obtained from the National Research Council publication *Nutrient Requirements of Rabbits*.

The National Research Council (NRC) is a branch of the National Academy of Sciences. The NRC establishes committees charged with the responsibility of reviewing the world's scientific literature to find, examine, and evaluate information on the nutritional needs of each of the major types of livestock. These committees are made up of scientists with recognized expertise in the nutrition of the particular animal under consideration. After each committee has agreed upon its recommendations, a report is issued in which the nutritional requirements are published. These reports are used extensively in the feed industry by animal nutritionists, as the standards for the nutrient requirements for animals. Among the animals for which requirements have been established are rabbits, dairy cattle, beef cattle, poultry, warm water fishes, trout, salmon and catfish, horses, cats, swine, laboratory animals, sheep, mink, and foxes and dogs. A publication on each of these species is available from the NRC,[1] for a small fee.

Compared to those for many other species, the nutrient requirements of rabbits have not been well established. Only a limited amount of research has been conducted. In many cases, the work has used small numbers of animals, and diets that do not resemble practical commercial diets. Thus the data available are imprecise and will require considerable "fine tuning" with more research. Nevertheless, the present requirement figures are a much better guideline than nothing at all, which is the alternative.

The nutrient requirements as established by the NRC are shown in Table 6-1. Notice that there are many blanks in the table, showing that information on these nutrients was simply not available. It should be emphasized that these figures are guidelines and often are modified by nutritionists as their best judgement dictates. There is no specific energy requirement, in kilocalories per kilogram or pound of diet. The recommended figure of 2500 kilocalories of DE (digestible energy) per kilogram of diet is a fairly typical figure for commercial diets. This does not mean that a feed should contain exactly 2500 kilocalories of DE per kilogram. The rabbit, like other animals, adjusts its feed intake to meet its caloric needs. If fed a low energy diet, it eats more feed. If fed a high energy diet, feed intake is less, but calorie intake in both cases will be about the same.

An updated version of the NRC requirements has been published by F. Lebas, a prominent French rabbit nutritionist. His nutrient requirement figures are shown in Table 6-2. Lebas has introduced the term "indigestible fiber." His and other work suggests that indigestible fiber aids in preventing enteritis.

COMPOSITION OF FEEDS

Besides knowing the nutrient requirements of rabbits, you must have knowledge of the nutrient content of feedstuffs, in order to be able to combine them to provide a nutritionally adequate diet. Also important is information on any other characteristics of the feed ingredients that might affect their use: presence of toxins, palatability, pelleting ability, nutrient imbalance, etc.

Feeds can be classified into several groups.

---

[1]National Academy of Sciences, Office of Publications, 2101 Constitution Avenue, Washington, D.C. 20418.

Table 6-1. Nutrient Requirements of Rabbits Fed *Ad Libitum* (Percentage or Amount per Kg of Diet)

Nutrients[1]	Growth	Maintenance	Gestation	Lactation
Energy and protein				
Digestible energy (kcal)	2500	2100	2500	2500
TDN (%)	65	55	58	70
Crude fiber (%)	10–12[2]	14[2]	10–12[2]	10–12[2]
Fat (%)	2[2]	2[2]	2[2]	2[2]
Crude protein (%)	16	12	15	17
Inorganic nutrients				
Calcium (%)	0.4	—[3]	0.45[2]	0.75[2]
Phosphorus (%)	0.22	—[3]	0.37[2]	0.5
Magnesium (mg)	300–400	300–400	300–400	300–400
Potassium (%)	0.6	0.6	0.6	0.6
Sodium (%)	0.2[2,4]	0.2[2,4]	0.2[2,4]	0.2[2,4]
Chlorine (%)	0.3[2,4]	0.3[2,4]	0.3[2,4]	0.3[2,4]
Copper (mg)	3	3	3	3
Iodine (mg)	0.2[2]	0.2[2]	0.2[2]	0.2[2]
Iron	—[3]	—[3]	—[3]	—[3]
Manganese (mg)	8.5[5]	2.5[5]	2.5[5]	2.5[5]
Zinc	—[3]	—[3]	—[3]	—[3]
Vitamins				
Vitamin A (IU)	580	—[3]	>1160	—[3]
Vitamin A as carotene (mg)	0.83[2,5]	—[6]	0.83[2,5]	—[6]
Vitamin D	—[7]	—[7]	—[7]	—[7]
Vitamin E (mg)	40[8]	—[3]	40[8]	40[8]
Vitamin K (mg)	—[9]	—[9]	0.2[2]	—[9]
Niacin (mg)	180	—[10]	—[10]	—[10]
Pyridoxine (mg)	39	—[10]	—[10]	—[10]
Choline (g)	1.2[2]	—[10]	—[10]	—[10]
Amino acids (%)				
Lysine	0.65	—[7]	—[7]	—[7]
Methionine + cystine	0.6	—[7]	—[7]	—[7]
Arginine	0.6	—[7]	—[7]	—[7]
Histidine	0.3[2]	—[7]	—[7]	—[7]
Leucine	1.1[2]	—[7]	—[7]	—[7]
Isoleucine	0.6[2]	—[7]	—[7]	—[7]
Phenylalanine + tyrosine	1.1[2]	—[7]	—[7]	—[7]
Threonine	0.6[2]	—[7]	—[7]	—[7]
Tryptophan	0.2[2]	—[7]	—[7]	—[7]
Valine	0.7[2]	—[7]	—[7]	—[7]
Glycine	—[3]	—[7]	—[7]	—[7]

[1] Nutrients not listed indicate dietary need unknown or not demonstrated.
[2] May not be minimum but known to be adequate.
[3] Quantitative requirement not determined, but dietary need demonstrated.
[4] May be met with 0.5% NaCl.
[5] Converted from amount per rabbit per day using an air-dry feed intake of 60 g per day for a 1-kg rabbit.
[6] Quantitative requirement not determined.
[7] Probably required, amount unknown.
[8] Estimated.
[9] Intestinal synthesis probably adequate.
[10] Dietary need unknown.

Table 6-2. Nutrient Requirements of Rabbits

Nutrient	Unit	Growing 4–12 Weeks	Lac-tation	Ges-tation	Mainte-nance	Does and Litters Fed One Diet
Crude protein	%	15	18	18	13	17
Amino acids						
Sulfur amino acids	%	0.5	0.6	—	—	0.55
Lysine	%	0.6	0.75	—	—	0.7
Arginine	%	0.9	0.8	—	—	0.9
Threonine	%	0.55	0.7	—	—	0.6
Tryptophan	%	0.18	0.22	—	—	0.2
Histidine	%	0.35	0.43	—	—	0.4
Isoleucine	%	0.60	0.70	—	—	1.25
Valine	%	0.70	0.85	—	—	0.8
Leucine	%	1.05	1.25	—	—	1.2
Crude fiber	%	14	12	14	15–16	14
Indigestible fiber	%	12	10	12	13	12
Digestible energy	kcal/kg	2500	2700	2500	2200	2500
Metabolizable energy	kcal/kg	2400	2600	2400	2120	2410
Fat	%	3	5	3	3	3
Minerals						
Calcium	%	0.5	1.1	0.8	0.6	1.1
Phosphorus	%	0.3	0.8	0.5	0.4	0.8
Potassium	%	0.8	0.9	0.9	—	0.9
Sodium	%	0.4	0.4	0.4	—	0.4
Chlorine	%	0.4	0.4	0.4	—	0.4
Magnesium	%	0.03	0.04	0.04	—	0.04
Sulfur	%	0.04	—	—	—	0.04
Cobalt	ppm	1	1	—	—	1
Copper	ppm	5	5	—	—	5
Zinc	ppm	50	70	70	—	70
Iron	ppm	50	50	50	50	50
Manganese	ppm	8.5	2.5	2.5	2.5	8.5
Iodine	ppm	0.2	0.2	0.2	0.2	0.2
Vitamins						
Vitamin A	IU/kg	6000	12,000	12,000	—	10,000
Carotene	ppm	.83	.83	.83	—	.83
Vitamin D	IU/kg	900	900	900	—	900
Vitamin E	ppm	50	50	50	50	50
Vitamin K	ppm	0	2	2	0	2
Vitamin C	ppm	0	0	0	0	0
Thiamine	ppm	2	—	0	0	2
Riboflavin	ppm	6	—	0	0	4
Pyridoxine	ppm	40	—	0	0	2
Vitamin B_{12}	ppm	.01	0	0	0	—
Folic acid	ppm	1	—	0	0	—
Pantothenic acid	ppm	20	—	0	0	—

Source: Lebas, F., *The Journal of Applied Rabbit Research*, vol. 3, no. 2 (1980), p. 15.

Classification of Feedstuffs

Roughages: bulky feeds that are high in fiber and low in digestible energy, e.g., alfalfa meal, hay, pasture, silage, green chop, straw and chaff, corn cobs, cottonseed hulls, bagasse, wood.

Concentrates:

Energy sources: cereal grains (corn, wheat, barley, milo, oats, rye, buckwheat, triticale), milling by-products (wheat bran, mill run, wheat shorts, etc.), beet and citrus pulp, molasses, fats and oils, brewers and distillers grains, roots and tubers (potatoes, cassava).

Protein sources: concentrates that have over 20% crude protein, e.g., soybean meal, rapeseed (canola) meal, cottonseed meal, meat meal, fish meal, milk by-products, dehydrated alfalfa meal.

Mineral supplements: limestone, dicalcium phosphate, salt, trace mineral mixtures.

Vitamin supplements.

Non-nutritive additives: antibiotics, antioxidants, bacterial preparations, colors and flavors, emulsifying agents, enzymes, hormones, chemotherapeutics (drugs), pellet binders.

Some of the major feedstuffs in these categories will be discussed, with emphasis on any peculiarities related to their use by rabbits. Data on their composition will be given, listing only nutrients that are significant in rabbit feed formulation.

ROUGHAGES

The roughages discussed here are those that are usually fed in the dry state, either as hay or incorporated into a pelleted diet.

Alfalfa

Alfalfa meal is a very desirable feed for rabbits and, in much of the United States, is the largest single component of commercial rabbit feeds. Besides its value as a feed, it has other desirable attributes in the entire agricultural scene. It produces more protein per acre than any other crop; for example, two to four times as much as soybeans. It is a legume, so it doesn't require nitrogen fertilization. It is a perennial, so the energy costs associated with its production are less than for many annual crops. It improves the soil, adding organic matter and reducing erosion. Alfalfa meal is not consumed directly by humans, so its use by livestock is complementary, rather than competitive, in relation to human food needs.

The protein in alfalfa meal is well digested by rabbits, so a major part of the total protein requirement can be met with alfalfa. It is a good source of phosphorus, and is an excellent source of calcium and potassium. It provides indigestible fiber, which helps prevent enteritis. It is the richest common plant source of vitamin A activity; dehydrated alfalfa meal may have over 60 times as much carotene as yellow corn, and over 4 times as much as carrots. Alfalfa is palatable to rabbits at moderate dietary levels. Thus it has many qualities that will ensure its continuing use as a rabbit feed. As competition between humans and animals for grains continues, alfalfa will become an increasingly important rabbit feed. Recent studies at the OSU Rabbit Research Center have demonstrated good results with diets in which alfalfa replaced all of the grain.

Table 6-3. Composition of Alfalfa

	Content of Nutrient, on an "As Fed" Basis			
Nutrient	Fresh Alfalfa	Dehydrated Alfalfa Meal	Sun-cured Alfalfa Meal	Alfalfa Hay
Dry matter (%)	24	92	91	89
DE (kcal/kg)	620	2350	2200	2200
TDN (%)	14	53	50	50
Crude protein (%)	4.9	17.4	17.6	17.7
Lysine (%)	0.26	1.01	1.0	1.0
Methionine + cystine (%)	0.14	0.55	0.54	0.54
Crude fiber (%)	6.5	23.9	27.3	24.9
Fat (%)	0.8	2.7	2.1	2.4
NFE (%)	10.1	38.1	34.1	37.3
Ash (%)	2.2	9.8	9.6	8.1
Calcium (%)	0.45	1.32	1.3	1.33
Phosphorus (%)	0.08	0.28	0.28	0.28
Vitamin A equivalent (IU/g)	56.4	146.6	63.6	64.0

Clovers

Most clovers are somewhat similar to alfalfa in feeding value for rabbits. As they are legumes, they are good sources of protein. Clover is highly palatable, in both the green and dried forms. Good quality clover hay can be used as a substitute for alfalfa meal in rabbit rations, so long as contents of protein, TDN (total digestible nutrients), and calcium are checked. Analyses for some typical clovers are shown in Table 6-4.

Table 6-4. Composition of Clovers

	Dry Matter (%)	DE (kcal/kg)	TDN (%)	Crude Protein (%)	Crude Fiber (%)	Calcium (%)	Phos- phorus (%)
Fresh red clover	22.7	600	14	4.2	5.0	0.41	0.06
Red clover hay	87.0	2170	49	14.1	25.5	1.30	0.22
Fresh white clover	17.6	500	10	5.0	2.8	0.25	0.09
White clover hay	90.7	2200	51	17.0	22.0	1.72	0.29
Fresh crimson clover	17.6	500	10	3.0	4.9	0.24	0.05
Crimson clover hay	88.8	2190	50	14.8	24.6	1.22	0.24

Grasses

Grasses are generally somewhat lower in nutritional value than legumes like alfalfa and clover. They tend to be lower in protein, calcium, and vitamin activity. Tropical grasses are of lower feeding value than temperate zone grasses, because of a lower protein and higher fiber content. Most grasses, when incorporated into complete rabbit diets as a source of roughage, are quite palatable. They generally contain 0.2–0.4% calcium, and 0.2–0.3% phosphorus. Composition of some common temperate and tropical grasses is shown in Table 6-5.

Green Feeds and Succulents

For backyard rabbit raising, feeding of green feeds can be advantageous. If palatable greens are fed free choice, the amount of

Table 6-5. Composition of Common Temperate Zone and Tropical Grasses

	Percent Dry Matter	Percent Crude Protein	Percent Crude Fiber	Percent TDN
Bahiagrass, fresh	30.3	2.5	9.5	15
Bahiagrass, hay	90.8	4.3	30.5	50
Bermuda grass, fresh	35.0	3.6	9.8	20
Bermuda grass, hay	91.2	7.2	26.8	44
Brome grass, fresh	30.0	4.2	8.8	18
Brome grass, hay	91.4	8.9	29.1	45
Coastal Bermuda, fresh	28.8	4.3	8.2	18
Coastal Bermuda, hay	88.4	17.1	26.9	50
Dallis grass, fresh	25.0	3.0	7.2	15
Dallis grass, hay	90.9	6.5	29.1	50
Guinea grass, fresh	24.2	1.4	10.1	10
Guinea grass, hay	89.3	6.3	28.1	40
Johnson grass, fresh	24.8	3.6	7.4	14
Johnson grass, hay	89.0	7.1	30.1	45
Kentucky bluegrass, fresh	29.0	4.5	7.5	17
Kentucky bluegrass, hay	88.9	9.1	26.7	54
Napier grass, fresh	14.9	1.6	4.7	7
Napier grass, hay	89.1	8.2	34.0	45
Orchard grass, fresh	24.2	2.8	7.9	14
Orchard grass, hay	88.6	9.8	30.3	45
Pangola grass, fresh	20.0	2.2	6.0	12
Pangola grass, hay	87.5	8.4	24.0	40
Ryegrass, fresh	26.1	2.9	6.6	15
Ryegrass, hay	86.1	8.3	24.9	55
Sudan grass, fresh	14.3	3.0	3.5	8
Sudan grass, hay	90.7	10.6	28.3	45
Tall Fescue, fresh	25.0	4.4	5.9	15
Tall Fescue, hay	84.7	5.2	30.7	40

pelleted feed used can be reduced by about 50%, with no adverse effects on performance. Most greens are very high in water content, so large amounts have to be consumed to make a useful contribution to rabbits' nutritional needs. Because of the large quantity of fresh material required, and the problems associated with collecting and feeding bulky materials, it is generally not feasible to use greens except on a backyard scale. Greens can sometimes be useful in stimulating appetite in animals that have gone off feed. Green feeds should not be left in piles which become heated before being fed, as digestive disturbances may result. If fed on the cage floor they quickly become fouled with feces and urine, so greens should be fed either on top of the cage or in a feeder designed for this purpose. Rabbits are highly selective when fed green feeds. They tend to choose succulent leaves, flowers, etc., and reject coarser plant parts.

Feeding greens to rabbits is important in tropical areas, where concentrates are expensive, while tropical forages are abundant and can be readily harvested by hand. Labor costs for such work are generally much less than in Europe and North America. Under these conditions, it is possible to base a rabbit enterprise on the feeding of forage and by-product feeds (Fig. 6-1).

Examples of some common succulent feeds are clover, grasses, comfrey, vegetables and vegetable tops (carrots, lettuce, celery, etc.), amaranthus, kale, rape, various roots and tubers such as car-

Fig. 6-1. Feeding green forage (Coastal Bermuda grass) in a rabbitry in Haiti. This large commercial rabbitry uses green feed and wheat milling by-products as the basis of the feeding program. Low labor costs make harvesting and feeding of grass economical in this situation. (Courtesy of OSU Rabbit Research Center)

Table 6-6. Composition of Greens and Succulents

	Percent Water	Percent Protein	Percent Fiber
Apples	82.1	0.5	1.3
Bananas	75.7	1.1	0.5
Bean leaves	71.2	5.2	3.3
Cabbage	90.4	2.0	1.0
Carrot roots	87.1	1.3	1.2
Cauliflower leaves	90.0	2.7	1.0
Celery	94.1	0.9	0.6
Comfrey	86.8	2.6	1.8
Dandelions	86.3	3.2	1.5
Kale	88.4	2.4	1.6
Kudzu	73.6	4.6	8.1
Lettuce	94.6	1.2	0.6
Pea vines	87.8	2.7	3.2
Potatoes	80.0	2.1	0.5
Rape	83.1	3.0	2.5

rots, potatoes, and turnips, and various weeds such as dandelions. Composition of some of these feeds is shown in Table 6-6. Note that most of them are 80–90% water, so they are of rather limited nutritional value.

CONCENTRATES

Grains

Grains are plant seeds. Cereal grains are seeds of selected members of the grass family, including corn, wheat, barley, and oats. Other grains, such as buckwheat and amaranthus, are not cereals.

Grains are a major source of energy for both humans and livestock. Some grains, such as wheat and rice, are grown primarily for human consumption, while some like sorghum (milo) are grown in the United States mainly for livestock feed. The main factor that determines (or should determine) which grain is used in a feed is its cost, and in particular, the cost per unit of energy.

Fig. 6-2. Comfrey, a large-leaved succulent plant often used as a source of greens for rabbits. (Courtesy of Lawrence D. Hills, Henry Doubleday Research Association, England)

Fig. 6-3. Amaranthus is a potential forage and grain crop for rabbit feeding. (Photo by P. R. Cheeke)

Fig. 6-4. Amaranthus has a large seed head, containing a "grain" that may have potential as an animal feed. (Courtesy of D. J. Harris, Corvallis, Oregon)

Table 6-7. US Bushel Weights of Common Feeds

Feed	Lb/Bu	Feed	Lb/Bu
Wheat	60	Buckwheat	50
Shelled corn	56	Barley	48
Grain sorghum	56	Wheat screenings	32
Rye	56	Whole oats	32
Corn meal	50	Ground oats	22

In many areas, grains are sold on the basis of bushel weight, which is the weight of a particular volume of grain. Grains like corn and wheat are quite dense, while oats are fluffy. This is reflected in the bushel weights, shown in Table 6-7.

Comparing the composition of cereal grains, corn, wheat, and milo are high energy grains, while barley and oats tend to be lower in energy because of their fibrous hull. The protein content is variable, depending upon the species, variety, cultural and environmental conditions, etc. Adverse growing conditions, such as drought, usually result in an increase in percent protein. This is because the grain is shriveled, having less than normal starch content, so the protein makes up a higher percentage of the total weight. Corn and milo usually have about 9% protein, while wheat and barley tend to have somewhat higher levels. Where large amounts of grain are to be used, a protein analysis is certainly advisable as an aid in ration formulation.

Oats and corn tend to be highest in fat content of the common grains, while oats and barley are highest in fiber content. All grains are essentially devoid of calcium, but they are moderately good sources of phosphorus. For non-ruminant animals, the phosphorus is of low availability, being bound as phytic acid phosphate. The availability of grain phosphorus for rabbits is unknown. All grains except yellow corn are lacking in vitamin A activity.

Corn is generally used as a standard of comparison for grains. Since grains are used primarily as sources of energy, and corn is generally the highest energy grain, other cereals will usually be ranked somewhat lower. Using the NRC values for grain TDN for rabbits, and the value of 100 assigned to corn, the other grains rank as follows:

Relative Value as TDN Source

Corn	100
Barley	90
Oats	78
Rye	93
Sorghum (milo)	88
Red winter wheat	101
White winter wheat	95
Red spring wheat	95

One potential problem with the use of grain in rabbit diets is the possibility of carbohydrate overload of the hindgut, resulting in enteritis. Work at the OSU Rabbit Research Center has indicated that high levels of grain may result in the stimulation of bacterial growth in the intestine, leading to the production of bacterial toxins, causing enteritis. While not definitely proven, high energy grains like corn may be more likely to cause this effect than low energy grains like oats. Corn has a waxy endosperm, which may reduce its digestibility in the small intestine, increasing the likelihood of carbohydrate overload of the hindgut.

Composition of some of the important grains used in rabbit feeding is shown in Table 6-8.

Table 6-8. Nutrient Composition of Grains

Grain	DE (kcal/kg)	TDN (percent)	Crude Protein (percent)	Crude Fiber (percent)	Lysine (percent)	Sulfur Amino Acids (percent)
Yellow corn	3790	83	9.3	2.0	0.20	0.26
Barley	3330	75	9.5	6.2	0.27	0.34
Red wheat	3680	84	12.8	2.4	0.38	0.48
White wheat	3680	79	9.8	2.7	0.32	0.44
Oats	2950	65	12.1	10.6	0.34	0.33
Milo	3330	75	10.7	2.2	0.27	0.27

Other Energy Sources

Other concentrates which function as energy sources include wheat milling by-products (wheat bran, shorts, mill run), beet and citrus pulp, bakery waste, molasses, brewers and distillers grains, etc. Wheat bran and other wheat by-products are quite palatable to rabbits at moderate levels, and are comparatively good sources of both energy and protein, and also are rich in phosphorus. They can be used at levels of 20–30% of the complete diet with good success. Molasses has a total sugar content of about 50–60%. It has a fairly high mineral content (8–10%), composed of sodium and potassium salts. Molasses is highly palatable, and is used to increase the acceptability of feed by rabbits, through its taste, reduction in fines, and improved pellet quality. Levels of 3–10% of the diet are generally used. At higher levels, it may cause diarrhea due to the high mineral content. Dried beet pulp is the residue remaining after extraction of sugar from sugar beets. It is quite palatable to rabbits. Although it is fairly high in fiber, the fiber is of a quite digestible type because it is low in lignin. Citrus by-products, such as dried citrus pulp, are somewhat unpalatable and probably shouldn't be fed at levels higher than 10% of the diet. The composition of some of these products is shown in Table 6-9.

Table 6-9. Composition of Miscellaneous Energy Sources

	DE (kcal/kg)	TDN (percent)	Crude Protein (percent)	Crude Fiber (percent)	Lysine (percent)	Sulfur Amino Acids (percent)
Wheat bran	2610	57	15.1	10.3	0.58	0.52
Wheat mill run	2700	62	15.6	8.1	0.60	0.48
Beet pulp	3080	70	8.6	18.3	0.59	0.21
Dried citrus pulp	2050	47	6.4	11.6	—	—
Molasses	2460	55	3.9	—	—	—
Brewers dried grains	1900	43	25.3	15.3	0.9	1.0
Distillers dried grains	3500	81	27.2	9.1	0.6	0.9

Fats and oils also can serve as energy sources. Fats are palatable to rabbits, and levels as high as 25% fat in the diet have been successfully fed. Under practical conditions, added fat levels of 3–5% are used. Fats help reduce fines in feed, increase palatability, and act as a lubricant during pelleting. Vegetable oils provide essential fatty acids, which may aid in promoting good fur quality.

Protein Supplements

Protein supplements commonly used in rabbit feeds include soybean meal, cottonseed meal, sunflower meal, rapeseed meal, safflower meal, linseed meal, and peanut meal. In addition, alfalfa meal might be regarded as a protein supplement, since at the levels at which it is commonly used, it supplies a significant part of the total dietary protein. Protein supplements are normally considered to contain at least 20% crude protein.

Soybean meal is the protein supplement of choice for rabbit rations. It is highly palatable, and has a high digestibility and a good amino acid balance. Two types are commonly available: regular soybean meal, with 46% crude protein, and dehulled meal, with 49% crude protein. Either one can be used, depending on which is cheaper per unit of protein. Soybean meal is the residue remaining after the oil has been extracted by solvents. The meal is heated, to destroy a number of inhibitors. It should be noted that raw soybeans to be used in animal feeding should be heat-treated. Soybeans contain trypsin inhibitors, hemagglutinins, and several other toxic factors that are destroyed by heat.

Cottonseed meal can be used in limited quantities in rabbit diets. Cottonseed meal is lower in essential amino acids such as lysine and methionine than is soybean meal, so it is a poorer quality protein than soybean meal. It usually contains about 41% crude protein. Cottonseed meal should be used with caution in rabbit feeding. It has been successfully fed for prolonged periods at 5% of the diet; the upper safe limit has not been determined. It contains a toxic substance called *gossypol*. Gossypol causes tissue damage, especially to the heart. It also has been shown to cause infertility in males of some species, even at low levels in the diet. Therefore, it may not be advisable to include cottonseed meal at high levels in the diet of bucks. Gossypol can be detoxified by the addition of iron salts, such as ferrous sulfate. The effectiveness of this treatment for rabbits has not been determined. Cottonseed oil contains a toxic fatty acid called *sterculic acid*. This is present at low levels in expeller-produced cottonseed meal. Expeller-produced meal is the residue from mechanical removal of the oil, as opposed to extraction of the oil with solvents.

Sunflower meal is the residue remaining after oil has been extracted from sunflower seeds. Sunflowers are a major crop in the Soviet Union and northern Europe. Since about 1975, sunflower production has expanded rapidly in the United States, especially in North and South Dakota, and other northern states. Sunflower meal contains about 32% crude protein, and about 24% crude fiber. The dehulled meal contains about 47% crude protein and 11% fiber. The protein tends to be low in lysine and sulfur-containing amino acids. For this reason, it shouldn't be used as the sole protein supplement. It can be used at levels up to 10% of the total diet.

Rapeseed meal is of particular interest to rabbit producers in Canada and the northern US. Rapeseed is now the second most important crop, after wheat, in western Canada. It is grown primarily for its oil, which has applications in both food and industry. The meal remaining after oil extraction is used in animal feeding.

Rapeseed contains glucosinolates, which are compounds which inhibit the function of the thyroid gland. Glucosinolates interfere with the synthesis of the thyroid hormone. As a result, the gland enlarges, in an effort to produce more hormone. This enlarged gland is called a *goiter*. Plant breeders have very effectively selected for low glucosinolate varieties of rapeseed. As a result, the rapeseed meal now available is of a low glucosinolate type, and does not cause problems with livestock. To avoid the negative implications of the word "rape," Canadian producers are now referring to the low glucosinolate meal as *canola meal*. This can be used as a complete replacement for soybean meal in rabbit diets. Canola meal contains about 40–44% crude protein.

Safflower meal contains about 22% protein and 32% fiber; dehulled meal has about 40% protein and about 10% fiber. Safflowers are grown as an oil seed crop in the eastern and southwestern United States. The meal is high in fiber and low in protein. Safflower meal is similar in composition to alfalfa; research at Brigham Young University has shown that it can be used as a complete replacement for alfalfa meal in diets for does and fryers. Palatability tests have demonstrated that safflower meal may be even more palatable to rabbits than alfalfa meal.

Linseed meal is produced from flaxseed, which is grown primarily for its drying oils, used in paint manufacture. Linseed meal is now quite a minor protein supplement. It contains about 36% crude protein; the protein is low in lysine. Linseed meal contains mucilaginous gums which may have a laxative effect, and which may also have a favorable effect on the hair coat. It is possible that feeding a supplement of linseed meal to show rabbits could enhance the sheen and general appearance of the fur.

Peanut meal contains 45–55% crude protein. It is a common protein supplement in Europe, being imported from Africa and South America. It can be used satisfactorily as a replacement for soybean meal. Peanut meal is somewhat notorious in the feed trade for being the source of the original reported outbreak of aflatoxin poisoning. Aflatoxin is a mold toxin, produced by molds such as *Aspergillus flavus*. This toxin is very poisonous and is a carcinogen. *Aspergillus flavus* grows under warm, humid conditions, and has been a problem not only with peanut meal, but also with cottonseed meal, soybeans, and corn.

Several other plant proteins are sometimes available for animal feeding. They include crambe meal, mustard meal, sesame meal, palm kernel meal, and coconut oil meal. They are not commonly used in the United States.

Proteins of animal origin include meat meal, meat and bone meal, blood meal, feather meal, and fish meal. For reasons of cost, protein quality, and palatability, these protein supplements are not used to a significant extent in rabbit feeding.

NON-NUTRITIVE FEED ADDITIVES

Examples of non-nutritive feed additives are antibiotics, flavoring agents, enzymes, bacterial preparations, antioxidants, worming agents, coccidiostats, hormones, and other drugs. Very few antibiotics and drugs are approved by the Food and Drug Administration (FDA) for feeding to rabbits. Each new feed additive has to be cleared for each species of livestock to which it will be fed. This FDA clearance involves extensive testing for safety and efficacy. "Efficacy" means that the additive must give the response claimed by the manufacturer. If an additive is to be sold as a growth promotant, then the FDA must be provided data confirming that it does stimulate growth. Because of the great expense necessary to generate the data needed for FDA clearance, it is unlikely under present regulations that new drugs will be cleared for rabbits, unless the industry expands greatly. The cost of getting clearance would exceed the profit that the manufacturer could expect from the sale of the product. In the United States, the only drugs approved in 1982 for addition to rabbit feed were 10 grams of oxytetracycline per ton of feed, and 0.025% sulfaquinoxaline in the diet.

Antibiotics

Antibiotics have been in animal feed for many centuries. Contrary to what may be popular opinion, antibiotics are natural substances, present naturally in the environment. Antibiotics are substances produced by living organisms, usually molds, which inhibit the growth of bacteria. Thus antibiotics occur in moldy feed, in soil, and in other natural environments. Commercial production of antibiotics involves growing the appropriate mold in a fermentation vat and collecting the antibiotic that is produced. The first antibiotic to be discovered was penicillin, which is produced by a bread mold.

Antibiotics used as feed additives may function as growth

promotants. The mechanisms by which they cause this effect are not completely known. They may alter the balance of microorganisms in the gut to favor those bacteria that improve nutrient utilization. They may favorably influence the absorption of nutrients. They may reduce the population of toxin-producing organisms. Finally, they may prevent or cure low level disease conditions, with a consequent favorable effect on animal performance.

Concern has been expressed that the feeding of antibiotics to livestock may result in the development of pathogens that are resistant to them. This may decrease the effectiveness of antibiotics when they are required to control disease outbreaks. Of further concern is that the resistance factor may be transferred to human pathogens, making human diseases difficult to treat with antibiotics. One method of avoiding these potential problems has been the development of antibiotics which are to be used only for livestock. An example is virginiamycin. This antibiotic has been tested in Europe, and shows some effectiveness as a growth promotant in rabbits.

In view of increasingly rigid restrictions on the use of antibiotics, it is probably more useful for the rabbit industry, and rabbit scientists, to attempt to develop management and nutritional practices which give satisfactory performance, rather than using antibiotics routinely in the feed.

Pellet Binders

Substances such as bentonite (a clay) and lignin sulfonate (a derivative of wood) are used in feeds as pellet binders. These are quite important in rabbit feeds. Pellet quality is important in a rabbit diet, and the use of a binder is an effective means of making a good, firm pellet.

Flavoring Agents

Feed flavors have been developed for the purpose of stimulating the intake of feeds which may be unpalatable. There is little scientific evidence that they accomplish this goal. In general, feed flavors have a pleasant aroma that appeals to the buyer of the feed, but doesn't seem to alter animal performance. If a feedstuff or feed is unpalatable, it is apparently difficult to mask this with a flavor additive.

OTHER FEED ADDITIVES

Preprations containing live cultures of bacteria, enzymes, and mineral supplements have appeared at various times in the feed trade. These substances are promoted as growth or feed conversion stimulants. Unfortunately, scientific testing by unbiased researchers has generally shown little useful effect of these substances.

Producers should beware of publicity associated with some of these products. Extravagant claims of greatly improved growth or feed efficiency should be looked at critically. Frequently the promoters imply that universities and experiment stations (the "agricultural establishment") are against their product because they didn't discover it, or for some other reason. This is a good tip-off that the product is ineffective. Unfortunately, there is no magic substance which, when added to a well balanced feed, will have much effect on animal performance.

Salt

Rabbit diets should contain 0.5% trace mineralized salt. This will take care of their sodium chloride requirements, as well as providing the trace minerals such as iron, copper, zinc, and iodine. Salt spools are unnecessary, since a properly balanced commercial diet will contain sufficient salt. Salt spools or blocks corrode cages and feeders. The only situation in which a salt spool should be considered is in backyard rabbit production, if the rabbits are fed primarily greens with very little pelleted feed. If salt spools are used, they should be hung so they do not contact metal parts of the cage or feeder.

Water

Rabbits should have free access to fresh, pure water. With herds larger than a few does, an automatic watering system should be installed. It saves labor and eliminates contamination of the water. If crocks are used, they should be regularly cleaned to maintain sanitary conditions. The amount of water consumed varies with age of rabbits, type of ration, season, and stage of production. During warm weather, a doe and litter will drink about a gallon in 24 hours. In both cold and hot weather, water intake is increased. In cold weather, rabbits eat more feed, and as a consequence, increase their water intake also.

Use of heating cables in water lines in cold weather areas is advisable to prevent freezing, so as to maintain a continuous supply of water to the animals.

FEED PREPARATION AND PROCESSING

Feed processing consists of subjecting feeds to various treatments which may improve their nutritional value, destroy toxins, increase palatability, improve ease of handling, etc.

Pelleting is the most important feed processing procedure used in preparation of rabbit rations. Rabbits show a strong preference for pelleted feed over the same diet in a mash form. Pellets should be solid and firm, with a minimum of fines. Pellets should be ¼ inch or less in length, and ³/₁₆ inch or less in diameter. Weanling rabbits will waste large quantities of feed if the pellets are too large; they will take one bite of a pellet and let the rest drop through the cage. The pelleting process allows a variety of feedstuffs to be mixed together and then cohesively bound in a compact, homogeneous package. The animals are not able to sort out the ingredients, so they eat the entire balanced ration. Feedstuffs are processed in various ways prior to pelleting. Grains should be rolled or ground, to break down their cellular structure to facilitate digestion. Corn has a waxy endosperm which resists digestion; for example, whole corn will pass undigested through the entire digestive tract of a cow. Corn should be rolled or ground. Alfalfa and other roughages should be ground prior to pelleting. There is some indication that the fineness of grind of grains and roughages can influence the rate of food passage through the gut, which in turn may influence the digestibility of the feed, and the development of enteritis. French researchers have shown that small feed particles are retained in the rabbit cecum, while large particles are excreted more rapidly. Retention of small particles for a longer period may allow pathogenic bacteria to grow in the hindgut, causing enteritis. Therefore, it is probably advisable that feed ingredients for rabbits be coarsely, rather than finely, ground.

Heat treatment is necessary for certain types of feeds. For example, soybeans must be heated before being fed to livestock, to destroy a number of inhibitors that they contain.

If for some reason it is necessary to feed a mash diet, coarsely ground or rolled grains should be used. If finely ground products are used, the feed should be dampened to prepare a wet mash. The addition of molasses will aid in providing a palatable mix, and will retard spoilage. After a period of adaptation, rabbits will consume these diets in adequate amounts. In most cases, however, it is advisable to use a pelleted commercial diet.

Feed Storage

If stored in a dry, rodent-proof location, rabbit feed can be kept for a considerable period. With prolonged feed storage, there is a loss of vitamin activity, and the possible development of rancidity. However, buying feed in large quantities does result in a lower cost per ton of feed. Producers with large herds should consider the use of bulk tanks. These reduce labor costs of feed handling, and generally supply better storage conditions than storage of sacked feed. Bulk feed is less expensive than sacked feed because of lower labor and sacking costs involved. Since metal tanks may "sweat," causing moldy feed, wood or plastic tanks should be used if feed is to be stored for a prolonged period.

Feed Requirements and Feed Conversion

The total feed requirements needed to produce market fryers is dependent to a considerable extent on the composition of the diet. The higher the energy (TDN) content of the feed, the less feed that is required per unit of weight gain. Conversely, the lower the energy content, the more feed that is required. Thus it is possible to observe considerably different levels of feed intake, depending on the type of diet used. In the final analysis, it is the cost of production (cost of gain) that is of prime importance, not the price per ton of feed.

As a rule of thumb, a New Zealand doe and litter will consume about 100 pounds of feed from breeding to weaning. Weanling rabbits will consume about 4 to 6 ounces of feed per day, depending on their size.

Feed conversion or feed efficiency is the pounds of feed consumed divided by the pounds of body weight gain. It is commonly referred to as the *feed/gain ratio*. Weanling rabbits will consume about 3 pounds of feed per pound of gain. As a general rule, it will take 3.5–4.0 pounds of feed for a doe and litter per pound of gain of the litter.

Considering the fact that rabbit rations are typically quite high in roughage and low in energy, the feed/gain ratios commonly observed are remarkably good. Rabbits are as efficient as broiler chickens in their conversion of protein and energy into meat.

Rabbit producers should be aware that it is the cost per pound of fryer produced that is the "bottom line" figure, rather than the cost per ton of feed. If Feed A costs $200 per ton, and Feed B costs $225 per ton, which is the better buy? If feed conversion is 3.7 on Feed A and 3.1 on Feed B, then the cost per pound of gain is 37.0¢ on Feed A and 34.9¢ on Feed B. Thus Feed B is actually a better buy.

Feeding Systems

The two basic feeding systems are *ad libitum* or free choice feeding, and limit feeding, in which a controlled or limited amount of feed is offered daily. Each feeding system has its advocates. Free choice feeding, in which the hoppers are kept full of feed, is less labor intensive than limit feeding. It is widely used for does with litters, and for weaned litters. Maximum growth performance can only be achieved with full feeding. Another advantage is that there is less crowding at the feed hopper. Advocates of limit feeding assert that this system forces rabbit raisers to visually observe each cage every day, so that they are more likely to notice animals off feed, or other signs of illness. Limit feeding may also reduce enterotoxemia. You should be careful not to restrict feed intake to the extent that weight gains are severely affected.

A good manager will watch the feed hopper and the droppings closely. If the droppings become soft, it may be necessary to supplement with some hay or other fibrous feed. If no feces are being excreted, palpate the abdomen to examine the cecum. If it has become impacted, the rabbit will likely develop mucoid enteritis. European researchers believe that cecal impaction may be caused by insufficient roughage in the diet, or feed that is too finely ground. Finely ground particles in the gut seem to decrease intestinal motility, which causes constipation and impaction.

Creep Feeding

Creep feeding involves feeding the nursing kits a special feed to which the doe does not have access. The creep feed is a high energy, high protein feed. While creep feeding may give a slight improvement in growth rate, most producers find that the extra cost of the creep feed and the extra labor involved do not justify the use of this system.

Examples of Diet Formulas

A wide variety of diet formulas can be used. Typical rabbit diets will include a roughage source (e.g., alfalfa), a grain (e.g., barley, corn, oats), a protein supplement (e.g., soybean meal), salt, and mineral and vitamin supplements. The selection of particular ingredients will depend largely on their relative cost and availability.

Doe Lactation/Fryer Grower Diet

Ingredient	Percentage of Diet
Alfalfa meal	50
Corn	23.5
Barley	11
Wheat bran	5
Soybean meal	10
Trace mineralized salt	0.5

Low Enteritis Lactation/Grower Diet

Ingredient	Percentage of Diet
Alfalfa meal	54
Soybean meal	21
Trace mineralized salt	0.5
Dicalcium phosphate	0.25
Molasses	3
Tallow	1.25
Wheat mill run	20

Buck and Gestating Doe Diet

Ingredient	Percentage of Diet
Alfalfa meal	50
Oats	45.5
Soybean meal	4
Salt	0.5

Lactating Doe Diet

Ingredient	Percentage of Diet
Alfalfa meal	40
Wheat	25
Sorghum	22.5
Soybean meal	12
Salt	0.5

These are just examples; many other diets of similar composition would be satisfactory.

Enteritis occurs on a wide variety of commercial diets. Unfortunately, the present state of knowledge on rabbit nutrition does not offer a complete explanation for this problem. Currently, there is no magic diet formula that will prevent enteritis. This is a major problem on a worldwide basis. The low enteritis diet shown here has given a marked reduction in enteritis at the OSU Rabbit Research Center as compared to other diets containing cereal grains.

GRAZING RABBITS

Attempts have been made to raise rabbits in large pens or warrens to utilize grazing crops and save labor, but there are so many unfavorable factors involved that this system has not met with much success. Considerable investment is required because fences must be constructed that will keep the rabbits in and predators out. Raising grazing crops in small enclosures is also expensive, and sooner or later internal parasites (as in coccidiosis) become a problem with the rabbits.

Fig. 6-5. Grazing rabbits outside a research laboratory in Germany. (Photo by J. I. McNitt)

When a number of does are maintained in an enclosure, it is impossible to keep any accurate individual breeding or kindling records. The practice of allowing does to kindle in burrows rather than in nest boxes could be followed only in areas where the climatic conditions were such that the ground would not freeze or become wet and soggy. When the does do kindle in the burrows, they usually take care of their litters satisfactorily. If they are forced to use nest boxes in these pens, they are not discriminating in nursing, so some litters may get proper nourishment while others will not. Unless the pens are unusually large, there will be considerable fighting and injuries among the does and bucks. Harvesting the fryers requires considerable labor.

ORPHAN LITTERS

Occasionally a doe will die at kindling time or before the litter is old enough to eat the feeds that are given to more mature rabbits. If it is desirable to hand-raise the litter because of exceptional production or show records, in order to maintain some particular bloodline, or for sentimental reasons, it can be raised by hand, although commercially this practice is not a sound one.

As the eyes of the kits are closed until they are about 10 days of age, it will be necessary to feed the orphans with an eyedropper or doll's nursing bottle, using cow or goat milk, or evaporated milk diluted to whole milk consistency. Synthetic dog milk, available at pet stores, is a substitute. Another recipe is evaporated milk diluted 50:50 with water, with an egg yolk and 1 tablespoon of corn syrup added to each cup of mixture. The milk should be heated to the point at which it feels comfortable when dropped on the back of your hand. When the young are 12 to 14 days of age they should be offered oatmeal and a few blades of fresh growing grass, or a small quantity of tender leaves from garden vegetables. They can be taught to drink out of a saucer and to begin to eat small quantities of the rations fed to the rest of the herd by the time they are 15 to 18 days of age. The quantity may be increased gradually as the young mature, but overfeeding should be avoided. It is essential that all feeding equipment be kept in a sanitary condition; this is especially important where milk is fed.

It is also possible to foster orphan kits to other does. This is an advantage of breeding several does at once; if a doe dies, her litter can be fostered to other does with litters of the same age. The fostered kits will usually be readily accepted.

CONDITIONING SHOW RABBITS

Properly balanced rations that are fed to the general herd will be satisfactory for feeding rabbits that are being conditioned for shows, but the quantity fed must be regulated to meet each individual's requirements so as to have the desired development and finish when show time arrives. Small quantities of fresh green feed or root crops, especially carrots, are used by some breeders as a stimulating and regulating food. Others feed bread and milk because of their food value, and to add variety to the ration.

7

Toxins in Feeds

Many feedstuffs contain toxic factors. While many people are concerned about synthetic chemicals in our food chain, it is desirable to maintain perspective by being aware that there are a great many natural toxins in food and feeds, including a number of extremely dangerous compounds. Most of the serious food-related episodes of damage to human or animal health have involved natural toxins. These include "food poisoning" caused by bacterial toxins; the death of thousands of people in Europe from ergot in rye and other grains; milk sickness in frontier America that depopulated entire villages due to a milk-transferred toxin from a poisonous plant; deaths of livestock and waterfowl from algae in water; and the loss of over 100,000 turkeys in England from aflatoxin in peanut meal. Some of the most lethal compounds known, such as the botulism toxin and aflatoxin, are natural compounds.

To keep the subject of toxicity in realistic perspective, it is also necessary to be aware of relationships between dose and effect. Virtually everything is potentially poisonous. This includes water (force-feeding about four times the daily requirement of water to an animal will kill it), protein, salt, copper, zinc, iron, vitamin A, vitamin D, etc. Thus the relationship between dose and toxicity is important. The mere presence of a toxin in a feed is not necessarily bad; what is critical is whether or not it is present at a level which will cause adverse biological effects. Biologists believe that there is a "threshold level" for toxins; at concentrations below the threshold (the non-effect level), the toxin is in fact non-toxic.

Some of the more important toxins are listed and briefly discussed below. For more information on toxins and poisonous plants, the books by Keeler et al.,[1] Kingsbury,[2] and Liener[3] are excellent sources.

GOITROGENS

Goitrogens are substances which inhibit the synthesis of the thyroid hormone, thyroxin. Their presence in feeds results in the development of an enlarged thyroid gland, called *goiter*. Goitrogens are found in members of the *Brassica* group, including cabbage, cauliflower, kale, rape, mustard, etc. Goitrogens were discovered when laboratory rabbits were fed a diet of raw cabbage, and developed goiter. Moderate amounts of cabbage or other greens will not cause problems. Varieties of rapeseed low in glucosinolates (a type of goitrogen) have been developed, so rapeseed meal can be used safely in rabbit feeding.

GOSSYPOL

Cottonseed meal contains a toxic substance called *gossypol*. It is toxic to animals, causing tissue damage, and in some animals causes male sterility. Gossypol occurs in both free and bound form in the meal. It is the level of free gossypol which is of significance. Free gossypol can be "tied up" by the addition of ferric sulfate to the feed. This procedure has been used to detoxify cottonseed meal for swine feeding. Recent studies at the OSU Rabbit Research Center indicate that cottonseed meal can be safely used in rabbit rations, at moderate levels (5–10% of the diet). The level of gossypol in cottonseed meal varies according to the variety of cotton. Because gossypol increases the resistance of the plant to pests and diseases, new varieties of cotton tend to have higher gossypol contents. Cottonseed meal is less valuable than the cotton fiber or the cottonseed oil, so the quality of the meal is a minor consideration in plant breeding.

---

[1]Keeler, R. F., K. R. Van Kampen, and L. F. James, eds. *Effects of Poisonous Plants on Livestock.* New York: Academic Press, Inc., 1978.
[2]Kingsbury, J. M. *Poisonous Plants of the United States and Canada.* Englewood Cliffs, New Jersey: Prentice-Hall, Inc., 1964.
[3]Liener, I. E., ed. *Toxic Constituents of Plant Foodstuffs,* 2nd ed. New York: Academic Press, Inc., 1980.

LECTINS (HEMAGGLUTININS)

Lectins are substances in beans that, when added to a blood sample, cause the red blood cells to agglutinate or clump together. This is why they have been called *hemagglutinins*. In the living animal, they are not absorbed, and so do not affect the red blood cells. However, in the digestive tract they cause damage to the intestinal wall, and reduce the absorption of nutrients. As a result, growth is reduced. Soybeans, broad beans, and common beans, including pinto, kidney, and navy beans, all contain lectins. Raw beans should not be fed to rabbits for this reason. Cooking destroys lectins and other toxins such as trypsin inhibitors, so heat-treated beans can be safely used.

MIMOSINE

Mimosine is a toxic amino acid found in the tropical forage plant *Leucaena leucocephala*. This plant has tremendous potential as a protein source in tropical countries (Fig. 7-1). Unfortunately, the mimosine in it causes alopecia (loss of hair) and in ruminants causes goiter. Leucaena is quite palatable to rabbits, which consume it readily (Fig. 7-2). The leaves contain over 30% protein. Leucaena, when fed along with other tropical forages, can be very effectively used by rabbits as a protein source. It should not be fed for extensive periods at more than 10% of the total dry weight of the diet, or it may cause mimosine toxicity problems. Plant breeders in Australia and Hawaii are developing low mimosine varieties of Leucaena, which should improve the feeding value of this high protein plant.

MYCOTOXINS

Mycotoxins are toxic substances produced by fungi or molds that grow on feeds. Moldy grains may be toxic. The exact consequences of feeding moldy feed to rabbits can't be precisely predicted, because there are a large number of different molds and mycotoxins that could be involved, which have varying effects.

Among the major mycotoxin groups are aflatoxins, produced by molds (*Aspergillus flavus* and *A. parasiticus*) which grow on grains

Fig. 7-1. A rabbitry in Haiti, surrounded by a Leucaena hedge which can be harvested for feeding to the rabbits. (Courtesy of OSU Rabbit Research Center)

Fig. 7-2. Rabbits eating Leucaena in a rabbitry in Haiti. (Courtesy of OSU Rabbit Research Center)

and other feeds (e.g., soybeans, cottonseed meal). Problems with aflatoxins were first observed in 1961, when more than 100,000 turkey poults died in England. This outbreak, called *Turkey X Disease,* was traced to the presence of mold toxins in peanut meal. Subsequent studies have identified numerous specific aflatoxins (aflatoxin B_1, B_2, G_1, G_2, M_1, etc.). They cause severe liver damage, and with chronic low doses, cause liver cancer. In rabbits, aflatoxins cause animals to go off feed and water, to become dehydrated and lethargic, and to develop liver damage and jaundice.

Numerous other mycotoxins which contaminate grains are known. They include citrinin, orchratoxin, T-2 toxin, and zearalenone; these toxins cause acute kidney and liver damage, adverse effects on reproduction, and death. It is believed that in some cases mycotoxins may cause enteritis in rabbits, while in other cases, feeding moldy feed does not induce enteritis.

Another important mycotoxin is *ergot.* Ergot is a substance produced by a mold *(Claviceps purpurea)* that infects the seed heads of rye, oats, wheat, triticale, and Kentucky bluegrass. Ergot affects the central nervous system and the smooth muscles. It causes the blood vessels in the feet and legs to constrict, cutting off circulation. This may cause gangrene. Ergot may also cause abortion. Rabbits may shuffle their feet continuously, suggesting pain in the extremities.

Sweet clover contains a substance called *coumarin.* If sweet clover hay becomes moldy, the mold growth converts coumarin to a substance called *dicumarol.* Dicumarol is an inhibitor of vitamin K, and causes a vitamin K deficiency. This vitamin functions in the clotting of blood, so in vitamin K deficiency, spontaneous hemorrhaging occurs. Feeding moldy sweet clover may thus cause excessive bleeding, and death. The rat poison warfarin acts in a similar manner, killing rats by internal hemorrhage.

OXALATES

Oxalic acid is found in some plants, such as amaranthus, spinach, and chard. Rhubarb leaves are poisonous because of their high oxalate content. Oxalic acid forms a complex with calcium, and renders it insoluble as calcium oxalate. If oxalic acid is absorbed, it combines with the blood calcium and precipitates it. This causes a rapid drop in serum calcium levels, and causes tetany. Greens such as amaranthus, spinach, and chard can be fed to rabbits at moderate levels with no problems from oxalate toxicity. Pigs have been poisoned by feeding on wild pigweed *(Amaranthus retroflexus)* and lamb's-quarters *(Chenopodium album)*, due to their oxalate content.

PYRROLIZIDINE ALKALOIDS

Some plants contain toxic pyrrolizidine alkaloids, which cause irreversible liver damage. In the US Pacific Northwest, the poisonous plant tansy ragwort *(Senecio jacobaea)* is widely distributed. This plant contains these alkaloids. Rabbits raisers in the Northwest might be concerned about possible contamination of alfalfa with tansy ragwort, and the effect this might have on their rabbits. Fortunately, rabbits are very resistant to the pyrrolizidine alkaloids, unlike animals such as cattle and horses. It is of interest that the forage crop comfrey *(Symphytum officinale)* also contains these alkaloids. Again, because rabbits are resistant to their effects, comfrey can be safely fed to rabbits. Because comfrey has been shown to cause cancer in rats, direct human consumption of comfrey may not be advisable. Crotalaria, which grows in the southern United States and other warm areas, is another poisonous plant which contains pyrrolizidine alkaloids.

SAPONINS

Alfalfa and other leguminous forages (e.g., clovers) contain substances called *saponins.* Saponins are bitter, and reduce the palatability of these forages. Alfalfa meal at high levels in rabbit feeds generally causes some palatability problems, resulting in excessive feed wastage. This appears to be due to the saponin content, causing the feed to be bitter. Plant breeders are developing low saponin strains of alfalfa, which should increase the value of alfalfa as a rabbit feed. An interesting side effect of saponins is that they reduce serum and tissue cholesterol levels. It is possible that the low cholesterol content of rabbit meat may be partially due to the saponin content of alfalfa meal, which is generally a major constituent of rabbit diets.

TRYPSIN INHIBITORS

Soybeans and most other beans contain proteinaceous substances (trypsin inhibitors) which interfere with the action of certain digestive enzymes, such as trypsin and chymotrypsin, in animals. They cause reduced protein digestibility, enlargement of the pancreas, and reduced growth. Raw soybeans should not be fed to rabbits. Commercial soybean meal has been cooked to destroy trypsin inhibitors, so it is a high quality feed that is safe to use.

UREA

Urea is a source of non-protein nitrogen (NPN), which is commonly fed to cattle and other ruminants. It is converted by bacteria in the rumen into protein. The bacterial action in the rabbit hindgut does not utilize much urea. Therefore, urea should not be used in rabbit feeds as a partial replacement for protein. It is converted in the rabbit gut to ammonia, which is absorbed and can cause poisoning.

WOOLLY-POD MILKWEED POISONING

The leaves and stems of the woolly-pod milkweed *(Ascelpias eriocarpa)* may be found mixed with straw or other types of roughage, and are toxic to rabbits. The leaves are classified as broad, and the undersurface is covered with a fuzzy or woolly growth. The air-dried leaves have a greenish yellow color; the stems are woody, smooth, hollow, brittle, and colored a light yellowish green. This weed grows mainly in the Pacific Southwest.

When rabbits eat the woolly-pod milkweed, they develop a paralyzed condition that rabbit breeders have designated as "head down" disease. The back of the animal becomes more arched than normal, and the head is tucked down between the front legs and rests on the tip of the nose. The neck muscles become paralyzed, the eyes seem to bulge somewhat, and the membranes in the inner corners of the eyes become inflamed. The animal is unable to raise its head from the floor or control the use of its legs. The front legs extend outward to the side, and the hind legs extend outward and forward (Fig. 7-3). In the more acute cases the hind legs extend be-

Fig. 7-3. "Head down" disease, caused by the consumption of woolly-pod milkweed. (Courtesy of USDA)

yond the front feet and the animal rests on its rump; in attempting to move, it goes backward in a nervous, unsteady manner (Fig. 7-4). Droppings are small, hard, and dark.

Fig. 7-4. "Head down" disease—a more completely paralyzed case. (Courtesy of USDA)

Apparently there is considerable variation among rabbits as to their susceptibility to the toxic properties of the milkweed, and the symptoms vary somewhat, depending on the quantity consumed or the length of time the rabbit has been eating it. Those that consume larger quantities of leaves and stems, or those that are more susceptible to the poisons, show more advanced stages of paralysis. The head is flat on the floor and the animal may or may not be able to raise it. At this stage the ears droop, and when the rabbit attempts to move, it raises and lowers its front feet in rapid succession but is unable to coordinate muscular movement so it moves in a jerky, unsteady manner. Eventually, the animal becomes completely paralyzed.

Three to four leaves of the milkweed may produce death. On autopsy the stomach and the intestines reveal small hemorrhagic areas, and the intestines may contain a catarrhal (mucous) secretion. The urinary system shows symptoms of irritation, with enlarged kidneys and small hemorrhages beneath the capsule. The liver is enlarged and of a dark reddish brown color.

As it is impossible for the paralyzed animal to eat and drink unassisted, it is necessary to place food and water in shallow utensils under its head two or three times each day. Support its head at a convenient height, by holding the tips of the ears, so it can eat and drink and consume enough feed and water to enable it to throw off the poison. Greens and succulent feeds are preferable to other feeds, and if the animal eats and drinks readily it should recover entirely in a few days after it stops eating the milkweed.

You should carefully inspect all roughage used for feed or for nest box bedding and remove all the leaves and stems of the milkweed plant.

Rabbit Diseases

One of the most devastating and discouraging aspects of rabbit production is disease. The death of a beautiful litter or doe is not only an economic loss from the standpoint of reduced income and increased expense, but it also has an emotional impact on the rabbit raiser. Hours of work and generations of breeding can be wiped out overnight by the cruel finger of disease and death. Disease and death are an integral part of any livestock operation. This is particularly true in rabbit raising. Mortality in many herds averages 20% or more of all animals born. Often, animals are found dead which looked perfectly normal a few hours before. This high rate of mortality can be so discouraging that it may cause some rabbit raisers to give up the business.

The success or failure of your rabbit operation will probably depend on your ability to keep disease at a minimum. Most diseases occur because of management mistakes or lack of knowledge. The total loss of rabbits due to disease in the United States averages 20–25%; this includes the kits born dead, the nest box deaths, the fryer deaths, and the loss of does and bucks. It is interesting that rabbit raisers in Europe have just about the same percentage loss in their industry and, as a matter of fact, have essentially the same diseases.

GENERAL CONSIDERATIONS

Disease is defined as a morbid process having a characteristic number of symptoms. A disease may affect the whole body or any of its parts, and its cause may or may not be known. Building upon this definition, you should be aware that disease comes about because of interactions between disease-producing agents and the host (the rabbit in this case). These disease-producing agents are continually in the environment of the rabbit. The logical question to ask, then, is, "Why aren't all rabbits sick?" In answer to this question, a number of factors are involved. First, rabbits differ in their genetic resistance to disease. Some animals may have more resistance to specific diseases than others. In the case of snuffles, for instance, some animals appear to be quite resistant. The disease is caused by a bacterium called *Pasteurella multocida*. Sometimes when one animal has snuffles, one in the next cage is unaffected, even though it is being exposed to *Pasteurella*. Apparently this animal has some genetic factor that makes it resistant.

Another factor to consider in disease is the concentration of the disease-producing agent. We know that viruses exist in the environmental surroundings of rabbits. But if the number of virus particles in the environment is kept low, the number actually attacking the rabbit will be relatively few. The natural defense mechanisms of the rabbit may be able to cope with a few virus particles, but if a large number are present, the defense mechanisms are overwhelmed and a disease is produced. The concentration of organisms is related to both sanitation and the density of animals in the building. As with any animal that is raised in close confinement, disease seems to increase almost proportionally with the increase in numbers of animals in a given space. The typical rabbit raiser starts an operation with a few rabbits in a barn or shed and all seems to go extremely well, with little disease, excellent conception, and beautiful rabbits. Because things are going well, he or she decides to double or triple the size of the herd. However, the space remains the same. The grower decides to double tier or reduce the space between rows or use any other combination of space-saving ideas. This results in overcrowding, and then problems begin. Another factor that compromises management when a herd is increased is a decrease in the time that you have for each individual rabbit. By doubling the herd you cut in half (approximately) the time that you have for each rabbit. Therefore there is a tendency to miss the first signs of trouble. You don't see the soft stool, the missed meal, the increased amount of hair on the cages, etc.

Ventilation, sanitation, and observation are three of the most important factors involved in disease control. Diseases are usually caused by some type of organism. It may be a bacterium, a virus, a protozoan, an arthropod, or some other kind of organism. Air dilution is a very effective method of reducing the numbers of some organisms. The numbers of the disease-producing organism may determine whether there is a disease produced. Air dilution is one of the reasons that you find less respiratory problems in well ventilated barns where the air the rabbit breathes is changed often. The other method of reducing the number of potential disease organisms is by physically or chemically removing them. This is called *sanitation*. The manure is removed, the cages and nest boxes are disinfected, and the hair on the cages is removed. All of these procedures reduce the number of harmful agents. A single rabbit hair can carry literally thousands of bacteria or viruses.

Observation, of course, refers to training yourself to look for some signs of initial discomfort in animals. A sick animal is somewhat like a sick human, except it doesn't make such a big fuss about it. It doesn't want to eat, may not drink, is lethargic (doesn't want to move much), may have a dull appearance in its eyes, may have a rough hair coat, and generally is unthrifty in appearance. If you miss these signs when they occur and you don't notice anything until there is a profuse nasal discharge or diarrhea, it's generally too late to do much about it. However, if you see the initial symptoms, a treatment of one kind or another may not only be helpful but may save the life of the animal.

QUARANTINE

All sick rabbits and those that have been exposed to contagious or infectious diseases should be isolated, and those that have been displayed at shows or new stock that has been purchased should be kept removed from the herd and held in quarantine for at least two weeks. These precautionary measures may prevent spread of infection in the rabbitry in case communicable diseases are in the incubation stage at the time the animals are isolated.

During quarantine, rabbits should be examined closely every day for signs of disease, especially signs of nasal discharge or diarrhea. The use of a broad-spectrum antibiotic (such as oxytetracycline) may be advisable if rabbits have been purchased from questionable sources. Antibiotics in the drinking water or feed can also be used to decrease the gastrointestinal microflora (bacteria, etc.). As the antibiotics are withdrawn, a new microflora population will be established from the environment near your rabbitry. This will make introduction of the animal into your herd much easier. Quarantine areas should be separate from the main herd or rabbitry. Rabbits housed in quarantine should be cared for after the husbandry of the main herd has been accomplished. This procedure reduces the chance that diseases will be spread from the quarantine area to the main rabbitry. It is always a good idea to wash and/or disinfect your hands after treating sick rabbits or rabbits in quarantine, as a number of diseases can be spread by contact. Separate clothing and foot covers for wearing in the quarantine area should also be considered.

DIAGNOSING DISEASES

Some diseases can be diagnosed by observation of clinical signs while the rabbit is living. Other diseases cannot be diagnosed without a post-mortem examination and, in some cases, special techniques. As a rabbit raiser, you should become very familiar with the normal physiological characteristics of a rabbit and the normal appearance of the internal organs. You can accomplish this by learning a few facts such as the normal temperature, 102°–103°F; the normal pulse rate, 140–150; the normal respiration rate, 50–60; and the normal general appearance of a healthy rabbit stool (manure). You can only learn the normal appearance of the internal organs by repeated examination of these organs when normal rabbits are slaughtered. Then, when a rabbit dies for some unknown reason, you will be prepared to do your own post-mortem examination. With a little practice, you may become proficient in diagnosing the more common diseases and with this information be able to take immediate measures for preventing an outbreak of a certain disease.

In making the post-mortem examination, remove the pelt to facilitate examination of the carcass. After removing the pelt, place the animal on its back and make a midline incision through the body wall. This will reveal the internal organs (Fig. 8-1). Examine the lungs and the heart in the thoracic cavity. If the lungs are normal, they will be a pale pink color. If the lungs are purple or have purple and pink splotches, or yellow or white spots, they are probably diseased. Hemorrhages and red spots in the lungs may be seen if the animal has struggled while dying. Next examine the organs in

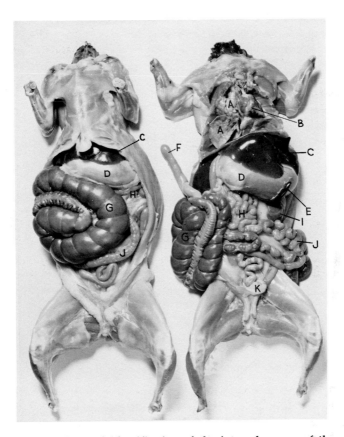

**Fig. 8-1. Location and identification of the internal organs of the rabbit.
A—lungs; B—heart; C—liver; D—stomach; E—spleen; F—appendix; G—cecum;
H—small intestine; I—kidney; J—large intestine; K—bladder.**

the abdominal cavity (the thoracic and abdominal cavities are separated by the diaphragm). The large organ closest to the diaphragm
is the liver. It should be purplish red, very smooth, and shiny. A
change in color or the presence of white spots signals disease.

Next examine the digestive tract (Fig. 8-2), starting with the
stomach. The stomach lays under the liver. It should be filled with a
very wet mix of rabbit feed and water. Occasionally you will see
fecal pellets (manure) in the stomach. This is normal, as rabbits
practice coprophagy (eating their own fecal pellets). The long tubu-
lar structure coming from the bottom of the stomach is the small
intestine. Its contents are scant and almost slimy. The small intes-

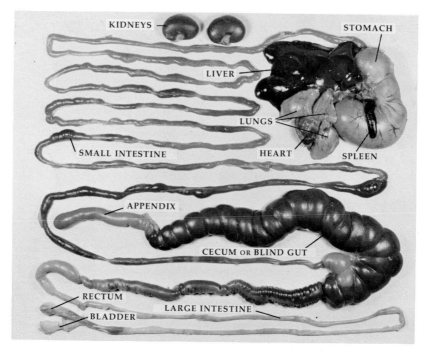

Fig. 8-2. Respiratory and digestive tracts of a healthy rabbit.

tine empties into a large organ called the *cecum*. The contents of this part of the digestive tract should be semi-solid (somewhat like putty). If you find the cecum and/or small intestine to be two or three times normal size and the contents very watery, you should suspect an enteric problem. You may also see a reddening of the walls of these organs due to hemorrhage. The cecum empties into the colon, or large intestine. This organ is smaller than the cecum and normally should contain the round fecal pellets. Diseases in this organ would be signaled by vaseline-like contents, or no fecal pellets.

After examining the digestive tract, look at the kidneys, located underneath the digestive tract and normally encased in fat. They are two walnut size organs lying on either side of the backbone. They should be brownish to purple, with a smooth surface. A rough surface, change in color, or white spots indicate disease. The bladder and reproductive organs are the last structures to be examined in an internal post-mortem examination. The bladder is located at the posterior end of the abdominal cavity. It looks like a small balloon when filled with urine. The bladder wall is normally quite thin, and the normal urine is cloudy. Because the rabbit excretes large amounts of calcium, the urine will often feel a little granular due to calcium crystals. The ovaries and uterus in females and the penis and testicles in males should be examined (Figs. 9-1 and 9-3). Each ovary is located at the end of the uterine horn near the kidneys. They are very small, about bean size. They often will have little blister-like structures on them which contain the developing eggs. The uterus should be about the same color as the body wall. An enlarged uterus containing a whitish fluid indicates disease.

If you are continuing to have a disease problem that you cannot diagnose, take both sick and dead rabbits to your local veterinarian or to a state diagnostic laboratory. Many veterinarians are becoming more experienced in rabbit diseases and are now receiving training in the treatment of special animals such as rabbits.

SPECIFIC RABBIT DISEASES

A number of specific diseases will be discussed; however, by far the most important will be pasteurellosis and enteritis. The other diseases discussed in this chapter are of importance to the rabbit raiser, but the number of diseases covered is by no means exhaustive. Diseases that are seldom seen will not be discussed.

PASTEURELLOSIS

Virtually all rabbitries are infected with *Pasteurella multocida.* Many rabbits carry this organism in their nose even when showing absolutely no signs of nasal discharge. The term "pasteurellosis" covers a multitude of clinical conditions all caused by *P. multocida.* By far the most common manifestation of pasteurellosis is the condition called *snuffles.* However, pasteurellosis is also evidenced by pneumonia, abscesses, weepy eyes, pyometra (uterine infection), orchitis (testicular infection), and wry neck.

Snuffles

There is no such thing as a cold in rabbits. Mucopurulent nasal discharges (pus) that many people attribute to colds are almost in-variably caused by *P. multocida* in conjunction with another bac-terium called *Bordetella bronchisepticum* (Fig. 8-3). The preliminary signs of sneezing and discharge have to be differentiated from dust or drinking water in the nose. Usually if the sneezing continues, and especially if you begin to feel a matting of the fur on the inside of the front feet (a rabbit uses its front feet to wipe its nose), you can be quite confident that snuffles has appeared in the rabbit herd. Snuffles is extremely contagious. Each time a rabbit sneezes it con-

Fig. 8-3. Snuffles, showing the typical nasal discharge. (Courtesy of D. J. Har-ris, Corvallis, Oregon)

taminates the surrounding area with thousands of bacteria. People themselves can spread these bacteria on their hands and clothes (the chance of rabbits contracting snuffles at a show or fair is extremely good unless you are very careful and take precautions). Rabbits can pass it to each other by contact, and equipment and cage accessories easily transmit the organism. The other forms of pasteurellosis discussed above generally begin appearing after snuffles is noticed. Strict culling or isolation of rabbits with snuffles will keep the problem from getting out of hand. Rabbits can be treated for snuffles with a number of antibiotics. This treatment at first may appear to have been successful. The sneezing stops as does the discharge, but as soon as the rabbit is stressed (often it is reproductive stress), it breaks with the disease again and this time it is very difficult to treat. Vaccination for *P. multocida* has been tried many times by both researchers and rabbit growers, with no success. By far the most important factor in controlling snuffles is prevention. Strict sanitation, good ventilation, and strict culling aid in preventing the disease. Any rabbit displaying signs of snuffles should be immediately culled. Ventilation is very important, since both humidity and air ammonia levels are involved in the transmission and development of snuffles. In environmentally controlled buildings, 10–20 air changes per hour are recommended.

Pneumonia

If snuffles is allowed to go untreated, or if the number of cases in the rabbitry continues to increase, rabbits will begin to die from pneumonia. Pneumonia is an inflammation of lung tissue, resulting in reduced oxygen uptake by the blood. It is one of the leading causes of death in rabbits. It also leads to poor weight gains, rough hair coats, and generally unthrifty rabbits. It matters little how good the feed is if the rabbits are only breathing on half of one lung.

The common signs of pneumonia are rabbits with their heads tipped back, or open-mouth breathing. In albino rabbits a change in eye color from the bright pink to a bluish pink is very suggestive of pneumonia. This is due to poor oxygenation of the blood; the bluish pink color in the eye results from capillaries on the retina becoming bluish due to lack of oxygen. The lips may also show a bluish color. Another suggestive sign of pneumonia is sudden death of fryers or does when they are stressed due to moving, breeding, etc. A post-mortem examination of dead rabbits will rapidly reveal pneumonia. The pink lung tissues will be turned a liver color (purplish), or part will be pink and part will be purplish. Often there will be fluid in the chest cavity. It may be clear or cloudy. All of these signs point toward pneumonia. Occasionally other bacteria are involved, but by far the greatest cause of pneumonia is *P. multocida*. By the time one is able to diagnose pneumonia clinically, there is very little chance of treating it. Both broad-spectrum antibiotics and sulfa drugs have been tried with little success.

Abscesses

The majority of abscesses are caused by *P. multocida*. They are a common condition in rabbitries with poor ventilation and sanitation. Abscesses are usually seen in the subcutaneous areas and occur when the *Pasteurella* organism invades a break in the skin due to a scratch, a cut, or a sore. Abscesses can also occur internally. These usually result from a septicemia (organism in the blood). Treatment involves lancing the abscess, if it is external, draining the purulent material (pus), and putting the rabbit on antibiotics. Penicillin-streptomycin is an effective antibiotic combination. Be sure that the incision made in the abscess is quite large to allow proper drainage. Ideally the abscess should heal from the inside to the outside. When a small incision is made, the outside heals first and a new abscess is soon started because of poor drainage. In the long run, however, prevention is much preferred over treatment, as treated rabbits often show a recurrence of the problem and may well act as carriers of the *Pasteurella* organism. In most rabbitries it is probably best to cull such rabbits immediately.

Metritis and Orchitis

These are problems with the reproductive system that can be caused by *P. multocida*. Metritis, an infection of the uterus, is sometimes called *pyometra*. Orchitis is an infection of the testicles. Both of these conditions are observed in rabbitries that have poor ventilation, poor sanitation, and a high incidence of snuffles.

Metritis should be considered whenever you have a doe that readily accepts the buck but will not conceive. Although there are many other causes of poor conception rates, metritis is often a factor. The *P. multocida* organism can gain entrance into the uterus by one of two methods. Either it enters during kindling (due to dirty nest boxes), or it enters with the semen from bucks with infected testicles. Metritis or pyometra is easily diagnosed if you see a yellowish white discharge from the doe's vent. However, metritis can occur without discharge. Sometimes there will be an elevation of the rabbit's rectal temperature above 103°F. If the infection is of long standing, that symptom may not readily be observed. Palpation of the uterus is helpful in diagnosing metritis. If the uterus feels enlarged or full of fluid, it is very suggestive of this infection. The only practical treatment for this condition is culling the rabbit from the herd.

Orchitis is a rare condition in male rabbits. Either one or both testicles become enlarged and sometimes feel hot to the touch. The organism *P. multocida* has gained entrance to the testicle either through the urethra in the penis or from the bloodstream (septicemia). This problem becomes extremely dangerous in a rabbit herd, because a buck will spread *P. multocida* bacteria with each ejaculation. Does bred to this buck may develop metritis. Therefore, you should frequently examine the buck's testicles for changes in size, color, or temperature. If any abnormalities are observed the buck should be isolated, and if the change persists the buck should be culled. Antibiotic treatment for this condition is of limited value, and the chances you take if it isn't cleared up are great.

Wry Neck

This condition, involving continual twisting of the head, is usually caused by *P. multocida* infection in the middle ear. This infection affects the equilibrium of the rabbit (Fig. 8-4). It is somewhat analogous to the feeling you get when there is water in your ear. Treatment is not effective, so rabbits with this condition should be culled. There is nothing wrong with the meat from these rabbits, and they can be safely eaten.

Weepy Eyes

This condition (Fig. 8-5), which is often seen in young rabbits in the nest box and sometimes in older does, can be caused by several different bacteria, including *P. multocida*. If the infection is detected early, it can easily be cleared up with ophthalmic antibiotic ointments. Ointments containing Chloromycetin are particularly ef-

Fig. 8-4. A typical case of wry neck.

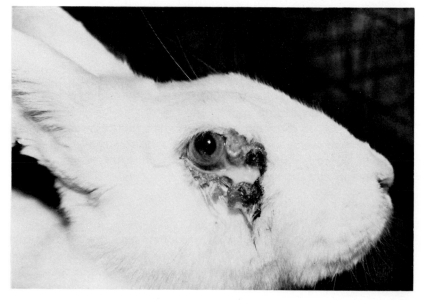

Fig. 8-5. A severe case of weepy eyes. (Courtesy of D. J. Harris, Corvallis, Oregon)

fective. If the infection persists or returns, a blocked tear duct can be anticipated. If a rabbit is valuable, it can be taken to a veterinarian who can open this duct while the rabbit is under anesthesia.

ENTERIC DISEASES

A major cause of death in fryer rabbits is the complex of diseases called *enteritis*. Many years ago it was believed that all diarrheal problems were caused by the same disease. In fact, it was primarily called *mucoid enteritis*. More recently it has been shown that enterotoxemia, Tyzzer's disease, and coccidiosis, as well as the classic mucoid enteritis, are all separate diseases.

Enterotoxemia

This disease was first described by the Rabbit Research Center at Oregon State University in 1978. The clinical signs of profuse diarrhea, dehydration, reduced feed intake, and rough hair coat are readily observed in rabbits. A typical case of enterotoxemia is shown in Fig. 8-6. Although enterotoxemia can attack rabbits of any age, it is seen most commonly in fryers four to eight weeks of age. These sick rabbits die very quickly, usually within 12 to 24 hours. On post-mortem examination of rabbits dying of this disease, an enlarged cecum and sometimes small intestine are seen. The colon is generally empty. In about 70% of these rabbits, especially junior breeding stock or does, a reddish cecum is observed. This is due to hemorrhage in the wall of the cecum.

Several bacteria have been suggested as the cause of this disease, including *Clostridium perfringens* Type E and *Escherichi coli*. Toxins have been found in rabbits dying from enterotoxemia. The iota toxin produced by *Cl. perfringens* has been detected in the luminal contents of the digestive tracts of many dead fryer rabbits. While *E. coli* placed surgically in the intestines of rabbits has been shown to produce diarrhea, neither *E. coli* nor *Cl. perfringens* has been shown to cause enterotoxemia when given orally to rabbits. It is very possible that a triggering mechanism is necessary to cause these bacteria to produce their toxins. It has been shown that enterotoxemia is more common when diets low in fiber and high in energy are fed than when high fiber diets are used. It has also been stated by "old-time" rabbit raisers that when they fed rabbits alfalfa hay and whole oats, few diarrhea-related deaths were seen. Perhaps current methods of feeding high grain diets to rabbits in order to get them to market in eight weeks is partly responsible for the increased number of cases of enterotoxemia. Successful treatment of enterotoxemia is difficult. Broad-spectrum antibiotics such as oxytetracycline in the water give short-term relief from the disease, but it often will return when the antibiotics are discontinued. The feeding of hay or straw to rabbits is of help in preventing the disease; however, outbreaks have occurred in rabbitries that routinely feed hay. Alfalfa hay may not be effective if the rabbits eat only the leaves, which are low in fiber, and leave the stems. Restricting the high energy feed to both does and fryers has helped in severe outbreaks, but there seems to be a very fine line between feeding enough to not interfere with weight gains and feeding too much, which results in enterotoxemia. Perhaps the most successful treatment is to change feeds. Preferably the change should be to a lower

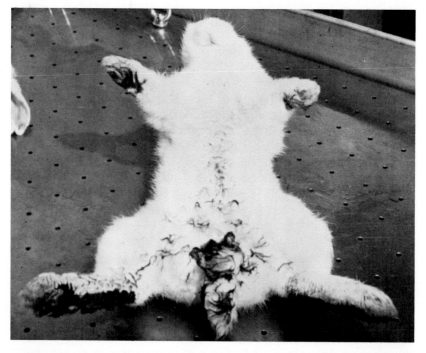

Fig. 8-6. Enterotoxemia in a rabbit, showing the typical soiling of the legs and anal area. (Courtesy of OSU Rabbit Research Center)

energy feed with a higher fiber content, but changing to any new feed may be beneficial for a short period of time.

Enterotoxemia seems to be cyclic. It strikes a rabbitry and then disappears, only to return at a later date. It is seen more often in large herds. It also is seen more often when rabbitries get overcrowded and the sanitation level decreases. It is not known if the disease is contagious. Enterotoxemia or "overeating disease" is a common problem in sheep, and a vaccine is available to prevent it. There is no effective vaccine available for rabbit enterotoxemia. Even if a vaccine for rabbit enterotoxemia were developed, it would likely be too expensive for routine use with fryers. Ultimately the best solution may be the development of diets, resistant stock, or management systems that reduce the incidence of enterotoxemia.

Tyzzer's Disease

In 1917 a man by the name of Tyzzer discovered a disease in Japanese waltzing mice. A diarrheal disease similar to the one in mice has been found in rabbits. The clinical signs of profuse diarrhea and rapid death (12–48 hours) are seen in fryer rabbits primarily. Post-mortem signs are very similar to those of enterotoxemia, except for salt grain size white spots in the liver. When special stains are used, microscope examination of these white spots often reveals the long, slender rods of the bacterium *Bacillus piliformis*. No treatment for the disease has been effective. In severe outbreaks, complete elimination of the herd, followed by thorough cleaning and disinfection of the rabbitry, has allowed repopulation.

Coccidiosis

There are two types of coccidiosis, an intestinal form and a liver form. Both forms are capable of producing a diarrheal disease that must be considered when enteritis is observed. Coccidiosis is caused by a protozoan parasite that invades the epithelial cells of either the bile duct or the intestine, depending on the species of *Eimeria* involved. There are 10 different coccidia species of the genus *Eimeria* that infect the intestine. While the damage to the digestive tract can be great when the infection is severe, generally the intestinal coccidia are of little concern. The intestinal coccidia are more of a nuisance than anything else. Most conventional rabbitries have some degree of intestinal coccidiosis, and most people must accept this as part of raising rabbits. The effect of these parasites on weight gains is not known. Not much attention is paid to the disease until enteritis outbreaks occur. The role of coccidiosis in enterotoxemia and mucoid enteritis has been questioned by a number of researchers. Some believe it is involved, while others think it is an incidental finding. Enterotoxemia has been reported in rabbits that are known to be free of coccidiosis.

From a practical point of view, liver coccidiosis, caused by *Eimeria steidae,* is a problem. The damaged bile duct epithelium causes large sawdust size white spots on the liver, thus causing its condemnation by the inspector in the slaughter plant. Severe liver coccidiosis can be fatal to rabbits.

The treatment of coccidiosis seems to be a continual battle. Sulfaquinoxaline has been the drug of choice for years. It is generally administered in the drinking water at 0.04%. However, it can be mixed in the feed at 0.025%. If it is used in the water, it is recommended that it be given continuously for two weeks. If it is used in the feed, it is given for three weeks. There are many different schemes for giving this drug, and some are more effective than others. Other sulfa drugs at various dosages and some of the newer coccidiostats such as amprolium and monensen sulfate have been used occasionally, but have not been approved in the United States for addition to rabbit food.

Mucoid Enteritis

The classic symptoms of mucoid enteritis are a jelly-like stool coming from a sick fryer rabbit (Fig. 8-7). The rabbit drinks large quantities of water (Fig. 8-8), will not eat, and wastes away over a period of several days. These sick rabbits often grind their teeth, making a unique noise. They also exhibit the "water bottle" sound if picked up and shaken. Their temperature is usually subnormal.

Post-mortem examination generally shows an impaction in the digestive tract. The most common site is at the ileocecal junction (where the cecum joins the small intestine), but it also can occur in the cecum or anywhere along the small intestine. Several studies have demonstrated the role of impaction in causing mucoid enteritis (Fig. 8-7). The causes of impaction are not known.

There is no effective treatment for mucoid enteritis. By the time the animal is observed to be affected, the disease has generally progressed to a terminal state.

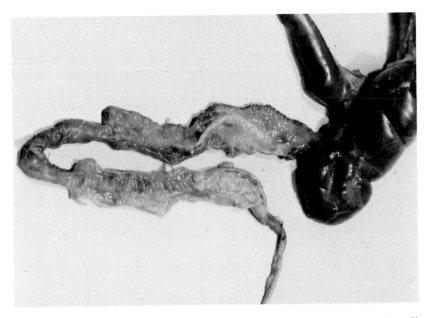

Fig. 8-7. Mucoid enteritis. This is an experimental case, produced by tying off (ligating) the colon, to mimic an impaction. Note the profuse accumulation of jelly-like mucus. (Courtesy of G. Sinkovics, Hodmezovasarhely, Hungary)

Fig. 8-8. A rabbit with mucoid enteritis. (Courtesy of USDA)

MASTITIS

Mastitis is an infection of the mammary glands of the doe. It is also called *blue bag, caked breast,* and *caked udder.* It is often caused by the bacterium *Staphylococcus aureus* but can also be caused by *P. multocida* and several other bacteria. The mammary glands swell up, turn red, and become very painful. Does will not let the young nurse, and the lactating glands become more swollen. The bacteria gain entrance into the mammary gland through the teat canal, a wound, or the bloodstream (septicemia).

Any time a nursing doe goes off feed, mastitis should be considered and her mammary glands checked. If you are not sure if the glands are swollen, take the doe's rectal temperature. Does with mastitis often have increased temperatures of 104°F and above. Antibiotic therapy at this early stage often reverses the condition, and the doe is able to continue to nurse her litter. If too many days pass without treatment, the glands will become bluish, abscessed, and very hard. The litter will die, and the doe may also. If the doe dies, never foster the litter to a new doe. The infected young will spread the bacterial agent to the mammary glands of the new doe.

Treatment of mastitis is best accomplished with injectable antibiotics. If the condition is detected early, 200,000 units of penicillin and ¼ gram of streptomycin per day injected into the muscle of a rabbit for three days are quite effective. The question as to whether to save a doe that has had mastitis is best answered on an individual basis. If the infection occurs again in the next lactation, cull the doe. If mastitis is not seen again, you can retain the doe. Disinfecting nest boxes, cages, and ancillary equipment is extremely important in reducing the number of cases of mastitis. One ounce of sodium hypochlorite bleach per quart of water is a very effective disinfectant against both bacteria and viruses.

RABBIT SYPHILIS

This disease has many names, including *vent disease* and *spirochetosis.* Whatever it is called, it can become a major problem in a rabbitry if left untreated. The disease is characterized by small blisters or reddish-raw sores on the external genitalia of both does and bucks. In severe cases, crusty scabs and sores will appear on the nose and lips of rabbits (due to their practice of coprophagy).

Another noticeable sign is a decrease in conception rate and a reluctance on the part of the doe and the buck to mate. Rabbit syphilis must be differentiated from "hutch burn" due to dirty cages and bacterial infection of the genitalia. Rabbit syphilis is caused by the organism *Treponema cuniculi*. This organism, a spirochete, is quite easily seen in scrapings of the syphilis lesions (sores) with a dark-field microscope. If rabbit syphilis is suspected, an infected rabbit with lesions should be taken to a laboratory with dark-field microscopy capabilities. There is also a blood serum test for this disease. The test is a "Rapid Plasma Reagent" Test, or R.P.R. The problem with this test is that it detects antibodies and tells only that the rabbit has been exposed to the *Treponema* organism but does not tell if it has an active case. Dark-field microscopy is by far the most conclusive test. Rabbits that have been treated with antibiotics will not show the spirochete in the scrapings.

Once a proper diagnosis of rabbit syphilis has been made, it is quite easily treated. Penicillin is the drug of choice. One treatment of 200,000 units of penicillin will cause the spirochete to disappear from the lesions. However, it is recommended that a long-acting penicillin be used at weekly intervals. Another problem that is just being recognized is that syphilis can be passed to the young from the doe by contact. Therefore, if syphilis is in the herd, all rabbits including the junior virgin breeding stock and nursing kits must be treated to completely eradicate the disease.

Another point that should be discussed is the loaning out of a buck to service someone else's rabbits. This is a good way to bring syphilis back to your herd. If you want to develop a rabbit stud service, keep a separate buck just for this purpose, and do not use it in your rabbitry. Check its genitalia frequently.

SORE HOCKS

The scientific name for this disease is *pododermatitis*. However, the name "sore hocks" is much more descriptive in that what you see is a loss of hair on the foot pads and a big sore on the hocks (Fig. 8-9). This disease should be suspected whenever you see a rabbit sitting with more weight on the front feet than normal. Also, the rabbit will walk with an unusual motion, as if walking on eggs. An inspection of the feet quickly reveals sore hocks. It can affect all four feet but it is usually first observed on the hind feet. There

Fig. 8-9. Sore hocks. (Courtesy of OSU Rabbit Research Center)

seems to be a genetic predisposition for this disease. Certain strains of rabbits within a breed will show a higher incidence of sore hocks than other strains. Generally the more susceptible rabbits show a lack of dense fur on the pad itself. Poor body condition may also increase susceptibility. Other factors that are involved in this disease are the type of wire on the cage floor, the cleanliness of the cage floor, and the condition of the cage floor (rusty or rough, etc.).

Once sore hocks occurs, it is extremely difficult to rid the rabbit of the problem. Recurrence of the disease is very common. Placing boards or mats in the cage is helpful, but increases your sanitation problems. Removing the rabbit from its cage and placing it in a pen on the floor with sawdust or hay helps the feet to heal, but soon after you return the rabbit to a cage it may develop sore hocks again. Salves, ointments, sprays, and many other medications have been tried, and with diligence you can sometimes get the sores to heal. However, it is generally much more economical to cull the rabbit, and by all means, do not save any breeding stock from this animal. Sore hocks seems to be a major problem in Rex rabbits. This is due to the short guard hair on the feet. Perhaps through selection this problem can be eliminated, even in the Rex. It is also a problem in giant breeds, such as the Flemish Giant.

MALOCCLUSION

Malocclusion (buckteeth) in rabbits (Figs. 8-10 and 8-11) is generally considered to be a heritable disease. It has been described by some geneticists as a genetic recessive, although its exact mode of inheritance is controversial. Parents with normal teeth can both be

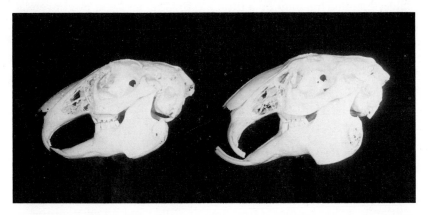

Fig. 8-10. Rabbit skulls showing normal teeth (left) and malocclusion (right). (Courtesy of USDA)

Fig. 8-11. A rabbit with malocclusion. (Photo by S. D. Lukefahr)

carrying a recessive gene for malocclusion, and 25% of their off-spring may have the disease. It should also be pointed out that rabbits can injure their mouths especially by biting or pulling on cage wire and show evidence of malocclusion but never pass it on genetically. The problem is in being able to tell if it came from an injury or if it is inherited. To be safe, most rabbit raisers simply cull all animals with malocclusion, including the parents that produce the malocclusion. This may be a little too drastic, and you might repeat the breeding of parents producing malocclusion to see if it repeats before culling a particularly good line of rabbits. Testing the parents by inbreeding, by breeding a buck to his daughter, for instance, will determine if the animals are carriers of the trait.

YOUNG DOE SYNDROME

A new disease has recently appeared in rabbitries (or at least has been recently diagnosed). The term "young doe syndrome" came about because the disease seems to be more prevalent in first and second litter does but can occur in does of any parity (number of litters). A doe kindles a fine, healthy litter and when the litter is 4–10 days of age the doe dies. Sometimes diarrhea is observed. Sometimes it is noted that the doe is off feed for a day or two. In other cases nothing out of the ordinary is noticed except a dead doe.

Enterotoxemia is the major cause, but staphylococcal mastitis can also cause this syndrome. When enterotoxemia is the cause, a post-mortem examination will almost always show an inflamed cecum with increased amounts of fluid in the upper digestive tract. Because the toxin from *Clostridium perfringens* Type E is so potent, the rabbit will die in 12–24 hours. If the cause is mastitis, the death may be somewhat slower. If the initial signs of being off feed and having a high temperature are missed, it will appear that a normal doe has died suddenly. The toxins from the bacteria invading the mammary glands go into the blood system, overwhelm the defenses, and kill the doe.

While careful observation and immediate attention to does off feed may save a doe from the mastitis phase of young doe syndrome, the enterotoxemia phase can be prevented. It is becoming common to restrict the feeding of does during gestation and then to put them on full feed or double the feed when they have kindled. This may lead to enterotoxemia. If you are going to use restricted feeding, then a more gradual increase in the feed will completely eliminate young doe syndrome due to enterotoxemia. Gradually increase the feed by an ounce a day or every other day until full feed is reached.

PREGNANCY TOXEMIA

This condition, also called *ketosis,* occurs much more often in some rabbitries than in others. Female rabbits suddenly die shortly before or shortly after kindling. On post-mortem examination the most obvious lesion is a yellow or orange liver. If you were to examine the liver under a microscope, you would find a tremendous amount of fat in the liver cells. This infiltrating fat causes two problems. It interferes with the normal metabolic processes of the liver and the breakdown of the fat into metabolizable energy, causing ketone bodies to be produced. Thus the name "ketosis." The exact cause of this disease has never been found, but the feeding of high energy diets may be involved. As far as treatment goes, the disease strikes so quickly that very few cases have ever been successfully treated. In cattle having a similar disease, injections of glucose have been found to be helpful.

ENCEPHALITOZOONOSIS

Encephalitozoonosis, also called *nosema,* is caused by a protozoan parasite called *Encephalitozoon cuniculi.* This disease is seldom noted except during post-mortem examinations. It is believed by many veterinarians that it is much more common in rabbitries than most people realize. Occasionally rabbits will exhibit neurological symptoms such as convulsions, tremors, and even partial paralysis. Generally, no symptoms at all are observed. Post-mortem examination of rabbits affected with encephalitozoonosis reveals the kidney's surface to be pitted (like someone stepped on it with hobnail boots), and in some cases the entire kidney is shrunken. This parasite also attacks the brain (resulting in neurological signs), but this is not readily observable unless a post-mortem examination is done. The disease organism is shed from infected rabbits through the urinary tract. The urine from infected rabbits then becomes the means of transmission. No treatment is known. It should be noted that the meat from infected rabbits is safe to eat.

RINGWORM

Favus, or ringworm, as it is commonly called, is a fungal disease of rabbits. It is characterized by crusty, shallow sores on the face or feet that increase in size if not treated. Hair is often lost in a circular pattern over the lesions (thus the name "ringworm"). This disease is caused primarily by two genera of fungi: *Microsporum* and *Trichophyton*. There are several species of fungi in each group capable of infecting rabbits. Some of these are also transmissible from rabbits to humans and vice versa. Ringworm is very contagious, so take precautionary measures when handling affected animals. Gloves are essential, and you should wear clothing that can be boiled or disposed of. Disinfect cages used by infected animals. Ringworm lesions are most common on young rabbits, especially the nursing young, but can also occur on adult rabbits. In European countries ringworm is a major problem. Confirming the diagnosis of a suspect case of ringworm is generally done by a microbiology laboratory. Hair or skin scrapings are taken, and placed on culture medium. The fungal spores grow slowly, often taking two weeks or more to reach the vegetative stage necessary for diagnosis. The treatment of ringworm depends on whether it is an individual or herd outbreak. Several topical medications are available. By far the least expensive is ordinary iodine. An ointment containing hexetidine is very helpful in treating isolated cases of ringworm. If a herd problem is encountered, the drug griseofulvin is the best choice. The drug can be put on the feed at the rate of 20 milligrams per kilogram of feed and fed for 25 days. This treatment is effective, but the drug is quite expensive.

MYXOMATOSIS

Myxomatosis is a devastating viral disease of rabbits. The virus was purposely introduced into Australia to kill wild rabbits. In the United States, it has been observed in wild rabbits in California and Oregon. Myxomatosis is transmitted from wild rabbits to domestic rabbits primarily by mosquitoes. In the Pacific Northwest, the virus which causes this disease is carried in the wild by the brush rabbit, *Sylvilagus bachmoni.* This rabbit acts as a reservoir for the virus and does not seem to be affected by it. It may develop skin tumors that soon regress. However, when a mosquito transmits the virus to a domestic rabbit, a severe fatal disease occurs.

There are two forms of the disease, an acute or rapid killing form, and a long-term, chronic form. In the acute phase of the disease very little is observed except dead rabbits. Rabbits of all ages are affected. If you are very observant, you may see a slight redness of the eye a day or two prior to death. At this point, the rectal temperature will be elevated to 105°–106°F. You may also note that the rabbit does not eat well. In the chronic form of the disease, the eyelids, lips, face, and sometimes ears swell up to gigantic proportions (Fig. 8-12). Hence it is sometimes called "big head disease." Characteristic lesions are shown in Fig. 8-13. Another sign which will almost always confirm myxomatosis is the swelling of the vent area in does, and the scrotum and prepuce in bucks. If this is observed along with swollen eyelids, you can be sure that the disease is myxomatosis. Another point to consider in trying to diagnose the

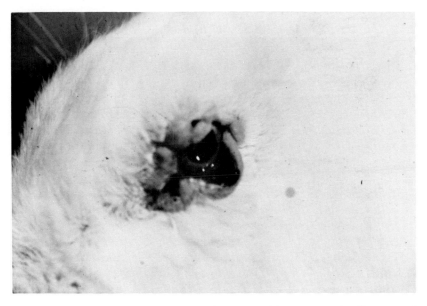

Fig. 8-12. The swollen conjunctiva of a rabbit with myxomatosis. (Courtesy of OSU Rabbit Research Center)

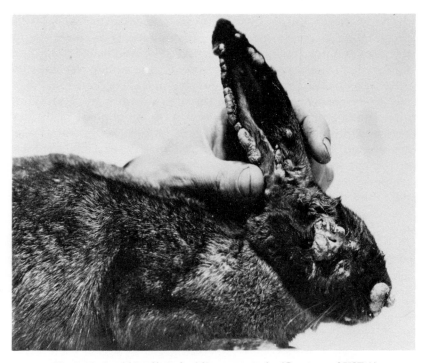

Fig. 8-13. A rabbit affected with myxomatosis. (Courtesy of USDA)

disease is the time of year. Myxomatosis is generally seen in late summer and early autumn (the bad mosquito time).

So far the disease has been limited in the United States to those areas where the wild brush rabbit lives. Its normal range is from the Pacific Ocean to the Sierra Nevada and the Cascade mountains, and from the Columbia River in Oregon down to California. There is no treatment. Antibiotics are not effective against viruses. A vaccine is used in Europe, where this disease is common, but it is not approved for use in the United States. The only method of combatting the disease is to immediately destroy affected rabbits. If you kill and burn or bury diseased rabbits, you can keep the disease in check. If you suspect myxomatosis, take a rabbit to a diagnostic laboratory for confirmation of the disease. Microscopic examination of cells of the eyelids will disclose the large cytoplasmic inclusion bodies. Once the disease has been confirmed, immediately kill all sick rabbits. Whenever a rabbit goes off feed or appears abnormal, take its rectal temperature. If the temperature is elevated above

103.5°F, kill the rabbit and burn or bury the carcass. Because the disease is so deadly, it is better to make a mistake and kill a rabbit that doesn't have myxomatosis than to allow one to live that does have it. Keeping flying insects out of the rabbitry is helpful in preventing the disease; however, the disease can also be transmitted by direct contact and by your hands. People living in Oregon and California should be very careful about sending rabbits to shows and fairs in the late summer and fall. Any sick rabbit should be immediately removed in order to protect the others at the show.

BROKEN BACK

Although not a disease, broken back is a condition that occurs fairly regularly in rabbitries. A rabbit (usually a doe but occasionally a buck) is observed dragging its hind feet. The rabbit may have partial feeling in the feet but does not seem to have control of them. Radiographs of the vertebrae of this rabbit will disclose a fracture or dislocation. The nerves in the spinal cord are damaged, and the rabbit loses motor control of the hind legs. If it is a severe case the rabbit will also lose control of the bladder and bowels. There is no realistic treatment, and the animal should be eliminated from the herd.

MANGE

Many rabbits are infested with mites. These minute external parasites live in the fur and cause very little trouble. Occasionally the population gets too large and this skin condition results. The hair coat may look unthrifty, or loss of hair may occur in a number of places, most commonly on the back of the neck. The two most common fur mites are *Cheyletiella parasitovorax* and *Listraphorus gibbus*. If only a few rabbits are involved, a cat flea powder is very effective in ridding them of mites. If many animals are affected, then the entire herd should be treated. A 0.5% malathion dip works well. Dipping should be done on a warm day. All of the rabbits are completely submerged (one at a time) in a dipping vat, and then placed in the sun or a warm room to dry off. Ten days later the procedure is repeated.

EAR MITES

Ear canker is a common malady in most rabbitries. It is caused by an external parasite, *Psoroptes cuniculi,* that establishes a home in the external ear canal. This parasite causes damage to the external ear canal, and the ear produces a brownish exudate (Fig. 8-14). The irritation caused by the mites elicits a reaction from the rabbits. They scratch their ears with their hind feet and introduce bacteria into the ear, quickly setting up an infection. Ear mite infestations can become so severe that rabbits lose condition and reproductive performance is impaired.

Ear mites are easily detected by close inspection of the external ear canal. The mites are readily seen under a microscope (Fig. 8-15) but usually are not visible to the naked eye. Ear mites are readily treated by using any number of ear mite medications. Most have a mineral oil base, with some parasiticide such as malathion added. The 3 × 3 × 3 scheme of treatment is very effective in treating ear mites. Apply several drops of the medication with an eyedropper to the ear canal. Be sure to massage the base of the ear with your thumb and finger to spread the medication over the entire inner

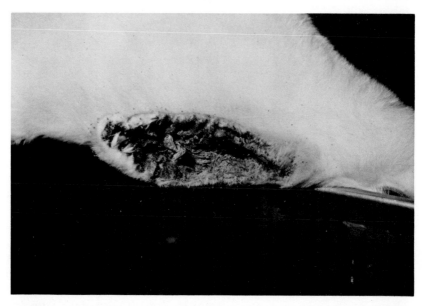

Fig. 8-14. Severe infestation with ear mites. (Courtesy of OSU Rabbit Research Center)

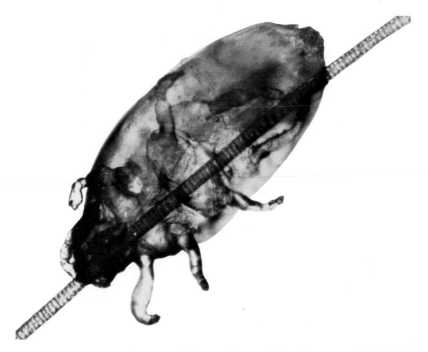

Fig. 8-15. A magnified view of an ear mite on a hair. (Courtesy of OSU Rabbit Research Center)

surface of the ear. This should be repeated for three days in a row, then every other day for three treatments, and then once a week for three weeks. Thus, this is the 3 × 3 × 3 treatment schedule. In rabbitries with a continuous ear mite problem, a routine treatment of every animal in the rabbitry one day a month will soon rid the rabbitry of this parasite.

FUR CHEWING

In some rabbitries fur chewing is a major problem, while in others it never occurs. Hair loss around the muzzle can be due to sharp edges on the feeder causing irritation. The chewing of fur from the body is generally caused by another rabbit, either one in the same cage or one reaching through the wire from an adjoining cage. There are several causes of fur chewing. Sometimes it is a vice developed by a rabbit or rabbits. One rabbit or several in a cage will start to pull hair out of their cage mates. They seem to do it from boredom. One rabbit will be fully furred and the others almost naked. The one without a mark is generally the offender. The addition of a round can (something to play with), or removal of the offender, or reduction of the number of rabbits in the cage may stop this vice.

Rabbits also pull hair when the diet is inadequate. Low fiber diets provoke hair pulling. Either increasing the fiber level or providing free choice hay or staw will stop this problem. The addition of 5 pounds of magnesium oxide per ton of feed will sometimes be effective in preventing hair chewing.

RED URINE

Rabbit urine is somewhat unusual compared to that of other livestock. It often contains large amounts of calcium carbonate, which forms deposits on cages (Fig. 4-19), walls, and floors. A rabbit absorbs calcium efficiently and excretes the excess in the urine. A red coloration of the urine is often seen. This seems to be a nor-

Fig. 8-16. Rabbit urine that is highly colored with a red pigment (left), and normal urine (right). The pigmented urine was collected from animals being fed a diet containing Leucaena meal. A reddish orange pigment is often seen in the urine of apparently healthy rabbits.

mal phenomenon in the rabbit, and does not indicate a disease problem. The pigment is especially apparent when the urine is alkaline. Certain types of feeds, such as alfalfa and Leucaena (Fig. 8-16) seem to increase the intensity of the pigmentation of the urine.

Rabbit Reproduction

Co-authored by James I. McNitt

Reproduction is a complex process which requires hormonal coordination between the male and the female. The primary means of such coordination is through the nervous system and by hormones, which are substances carried in the blood from special glands to the organs upon which the hormones have their effects. These effects may be changes in the organs themselves (such as stimulating ovulation), or one hormone may stimulate the target organ to secrete a second hormone which in turn is carried to another organ where it has an effect.

Due to such complexity, it is difficult to completely describe rabbit reproduction in a single chapter. The aim in writing this chapter has therefore been to provide an overview of the processes and the major hormones involved in reproduction. Special emphasis has been placed on those aspects which are of direct concern to the rabbit producer. Readers wishing more detailed information regarding this topic are directed to books which deal specifically with reproductive physiology.

THE MALE

Organs of Reproduction

The reproductive organs of the male fall into four basic categories: the primary sex organs, accessory sex glands, ducts, and external genitalia (Fig. 9-1).

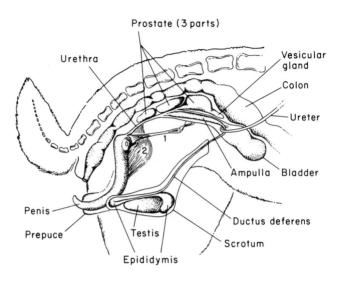

1 - Pelvic symphysis
2 - Ischiocavernosus muscle

Fig. 9-1. The reproductive system of the male rabbit.

The testes are the primary organs of reproduction of the male. They produce spermatozoa (sperm) and hormones (androgens), which affect reproductive function and behavior. The paired testes are ovoid structures measuring about 35 × 15 millimeters and weighing approximately 2 grams. The testes are essentially sacs of coiled tubules within which the sperm are formed. This process, known as *spermatogenesis*, involves changes from a rather normal-looking circular cell into the highly specialized spermatozoon, which has transmission of genetic information from the male to the female as its only function. Development begins in the walls of the tubules, and as the spermatozoa develop, they move toward the center or lumen of the tubule. Between the cells of the tubule walls are sustentacular or Sertoli cells which nourish the developing spermatozoa. Once the sperm reach the lumen of the tubule, they are transported through the tubule by fluid pressure. This transport takes the sperm to the top of the testis and out into the epididymides.

Androgens are produced by Leydig (interstitial) cells which are found between the tubules. These cells are under the control of hormones from the anterior pituitary, which is located at the base of the brain. These controlling hormones regulate the blood levels of the androgens which, in turn, control spermatogenesis and sexual activity of the buck. It is the lack of androgens which makes the castrated male disinterested in females or in fighting with other bucks.

The accessory sex glands of the male include the vesicular, prostate, and bulbourethral glands. All these glands produce secretions which are added to the spermatozoa to form the ejaculated fluid known as *semen*. The functions of these secretions include adding fluid volume to the ejaculate to facilitate movement of semen through the male and female reproductive tracts, providing nutrients and buffers for the spermatozoa, providing a gelatinous plug to seal the female tract, and providing substances which stimulate contractions of the vagina and uterus of the female to enhance movement of spermatozoa through the tract.

The ducts through which the sperm move after leaving the testes proper include the epididymides, deferent ducts, and urethra. The epididymides lie close to the top of the testes and function as a place of maturation of the spermatozoa. It has been found that spermatozoa which have not undergone a period of maturation in the epididymides are incapable of fertilizing eggs. The epididymides also serve as a place of storage for spermatozoa; fertile spermatozoa have been recovered from epididymides after eight weeks of storage. The normal time required for movement of sperm through the epididymides is 8 to 10 days.

The deferent ducts carry the sperm from the epididymides to the urethra and also function to some extent in sperm storage. The accessory sex glands normally add their secretions to the semen at or near the junction of the deferent ducts and the urethra.

The urethra is the common passageway for semen and urine. It carries semen from the junction with the deferent ducts to the end of the penis, from which the semen is ejaculated into the vagina of the female. The bladder joins the urethra just beyond the point of junction of the urethra and deferent ducts.

The external genitalia of the male include the penis, the scrotum, and the prepuce. The penis is an erectile organ that is used for insertion of the ejaculate into the female tract. The penis is normally flaccid and rests in the prepuce as shown in Fig. 9-1. It becomes rigid at the time of breeding due to constriction of the penile veins. The erect penis is held forward along the abdomen. Since arterial blood continues to flow into the organ, it becomes turgid and can thus penetrate the vulva and vagina of the doe. There is a sensitive tip on the penis known as the *glans penis*. Stimulation of the glans penis by the vagina of the female (or by a properly prepared artificial vagina) results in ejaculation. This is due to a reflex contraction of the duct system which forces out spermatozoa stored in the deferent ducts and the last third of the epididymis. Fluids from the accessory glands are also released into the ductus deferens and urethra at the time of ejaculation. After subsidence of erection, the penis is pulled back into the prepuce by muscular contraction.

The scrotum of the rabbit consists of two relatively hairless sacs which contain the testes. These function to protect the testes and to provide an area with a lower temperature than the body cavity, since spermatogenesis cannot occur at body temperature. The testes of the rabbit can move freely in and out of the abdomen and so are not always found in the scrotal sacs.

The prepuce is a fold of skin on the abdomen which protects the penis.

Spermatozoa

Spermatozoa are highly specialized cells which carry genetic information from the male through the female reproductive tract to fertilize the ova of the female. For this purpose, the spermatozoon has a head which carries the genetic information and a tail which provides propulsion by its whiplike movements (Fig. 9-2). The portion of the tail nearest the head is known as the *midpiece* and contains organelles which function in metabolism and provide energy for movement of the tail. Spermatozoa do not begin to swim (become motile) until they are ejaculated into the vagina of the doe, where there is a higher concentration of oxygen than in the male tract.

The testes produce 50 to 250 million sperm each day. The numbers of sperm produced may be affected by breed, age of the buck, and nutrition. Production of spermatozoa begins at puberty and is continuous throughout the reproductive life of the buck. Most unejaculated sperm degenerate in the epididymides, and the components are resorbed into the blood. Some sperm may be passed in the urine.

Reproductive Activity of Bucks

Bucks reach sexual maturity between four and eight months of

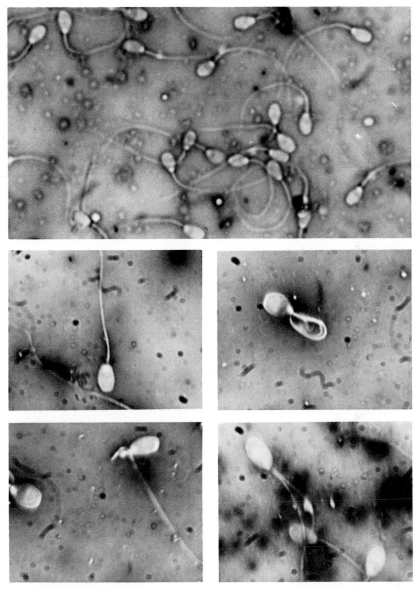

Fig. 9-2. Rabbit spermatozoa. Top: normal rabbit spermatozoa. Note the proto-plasmic droplets on the tails of some sperm. The granular material in the back-ground is normal in rabbit semen. Center left: normal rabbit spermatozoa. Center right: defective sperm, showing a coiled tail. Bottom left: defective sperm, with a broken midpiece (right) and with a round, enlarged head (left). Bottom right: defec-tive sperm, with two tails. (Courtesy of OSU Rabbit Research Center)

age, depending on breed and level of nutrition. In a study of New Zealand White bucks, daily sperm output was found to increase from 20 weeks of age to a mature level at about 31 weeks of age. The normal ejaculate volume for mature bucks will range from 0.4 to 1.5 milliliters, with an average of about 0.7. Sperm per ejaculate is highly variable between bucks as well as between successive ejaculates from the same buck. The range is between 10 and 300 million spermatozoa per milliliter, with an average around 150 million. The number of spermatozoa ejaculated depends on the breed of the buck, recent use, and level of stimulation. There is also indication that there may be short cycles of three to eight days' duration in some of the semen characteristics such as sperm concentration.

The number of sperm and volume of ejaculate required for fertilization are unknown, but studies using artificial insemination have shown that sperm concentrations of less than 1 million sperm per milliliter result in pregnancy. It is thus likely that most ejaculates will contain sufficient sperm for fertilization unless, as sometimes happens, an ejaculate is produced which is totally devoid of sperm (aspermic or "dry" ejaculate).

THE FEMALE

Organs of Reproduction

The organs of reproduction of the female include the ovaries, oviducts, uterus, cervices, vagina, and external genitalia (Fig. 9-3).

The ovary, the primary organ of reproduction of the female, produces the eggs, or ova, and hormones (primarily estrogens and progesterone). The ovaries lie within the abdominal cavity, with one on each side near the kidneys. The ovaries are ovoid structures about 20 × 10 millimeters which weigh 0.5 to 0.75 gram, depending on the activity of the ovarian structures. The central portion or medulla of the ovary consists of connective tissue containing nerves and blood vessels. The outer layer or cortex contains the ova in various stages of development as well as various other types of tissue including blood vessels, nerves, and muscle tissue. At the time of a doe's birth, thousands of undeveloped ova are contained in the cortex. From the time of puberty until death or the end of the reproductive life of the female, these undeveloped ova undergo development and are shed (ovulated), or degenerate.

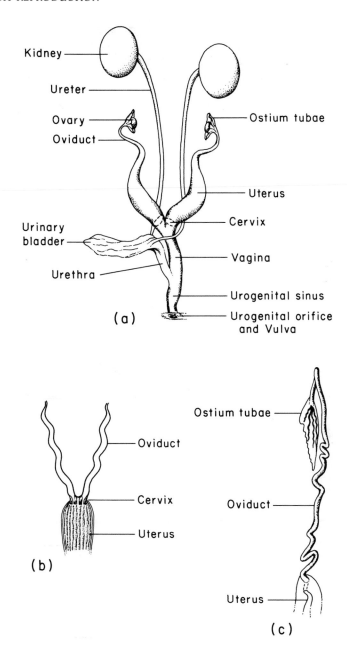

Fig. 9-3. The reproductive tract of the female rabbit (a), with expanded views of the cervices (b) and oviduct (c).

The oviduct is the site of fertilization, functions in a maturation process of spermatozoa known as *capacitation,* and is the location where early embryonic development occurs. The upper end of the oviduct is spread into the ostium tubae, which partially surrounds the ovary. On the edges of the ostium tubae are numerous small projections known as the *fimbria.* These nearly cover the ovary. Beating of the fimbria causes waves of movement of fluid toward the opening of the oviduct and, at the time of ovulation, sweeps the ova into the oviduct. The uterus is the organ in which most of the embryonic development occurs and which provides muscular force for expulsion of the fetuses at birth. The uterus of the rabbit is formed of two distinct horns which do not join to form a body. Each horn of the uterus connects into a cervix which opens into the common vagina. The cervices function as muscular plugs to keep the uterine horns closed except at the time of mating and parturition (birth or kindling).

The vagina is the site of sperm deposition at mating and acts as a channel for the young at parturition.

The external genitalia of the rabbit include the urogenital sinus, which is continuous with the vagina and is the chamber into which the urethra empties urine. The external lips of the urogenital sinus form the vulva, which can be used as an indicator of sexual receptivity of the doe. The clitoris lies within the urogenital sinus with the sensitive portion, the glans clitoris, projecting into the urogenital opening. Because of the location of the urethra (Fig. 9-3), urination by the doe following breeding does not necessarily prevent fertilization.

Estrus and Ovulation

Does become receptive to bucks at about 3½ months of age and become capable of conception at 4 or 4½ months. These ages will vary with the breed of rabbit, the smaller breeds generally reaching puberty earlier than the larger breeds. The level of nutrition will also affect the age of onset of reproduction function. It is generally not advisable to breed does during the first month or two that they are capable of reproduction, as they are still growing and the attainment of mature size may be prevented or delayed if the doe is also expected to produce and feed a litter at this time.

Rabbits do not have a precise estrus cycle as is found in many other animals. At the time of puberty, follicle-stimulating hormone

(FSH) from the anterior pituitary gland (located at the base of the brain) begins inducing growth of follicles, with corresponding development of ova within them. The ova begin development with a single layer of follicle cells surrounding them. The number of follicular cells gradually increases until numerous layers are present. As the follicle develops further, a fluid-filled cavity forms with the ova located in the center upon a hillock of cells. By this time, the follicle has enlarged to such an extent that it bulges from the surface of the ovary. At ovulation the outer layer of the follicle ruptures, and the ovum is expelled along with the fluid.

The follicles produce estrogens, which are the hormones that cause the female to be receptive to the male. Follicular development generally occurs in waves, with 5 to 10 follicles on each ovary at the same stage of development at any one time. Follicles continually commence development, so follicles at several stages of development are continually present. When follicles reach mature size, they remain active in producing estrogens for about 12 to 14 days. After this period, if ovulation has not occurred, these follicles will degenerate with a corresponding reduction in the estrogen level and receptivity. After about 4 days a new wave of follicles will begin producing estrogen, and the doe will become receptive once again. The doe thus has a cycle of 16 to 18 days, with about 12 to 14 days of receptivity and 4 days when the doe will refuse to mate. This timing is extremely variable due to individual differences, sexual stimulation, and environmental factors such as nutrition, light, and temperature.

Ovulation in the rabbit occurs only after induction by an external stimulus such as mating. Intense sexual excitement or mounting of the doe by other rabbits may also induce ovulation. This may result in a condition known as *pseudopregnancy*, which will be discussed below. An ovulatory stimulus results in the release of luteinizing hormone (LH) from the anterior pituitary. This hormone causes rupture of the mature follicles approximately 10 hours after the stimulus occurs. After appropriate stimulus, a number of follicles on one or both ovaries will rupture. The number of ova shed from each ovary is one factor which determines the ultimate litter size. Other factors include the number of shed ova which are fertilized by the sperm and the number of fertilized eggs which go through the entire intrauterine development process. For clarity, the remainder of this discussion refers to a single ovum and its development, but it should be borne in mind that similar processes are simultaneously occurring with up to 20 other ova.

When the ovum has been shed from the ovary, LH stimulates changes in the follicular cells and the follicle rapidly develops into a corpus luteum (yellow body), which produces hormones known as *progestins*. These are necessary throughout pregnancy for development of the embryo. The primary action of the progestins is to stop muscular contractions of the uterus and to stimulate production of nutrients for the embryo.

The corpus luteum begins actively secreting within three days of ovulation and continues throughout pregnancy. The hormone output increases until about the fifteenth day of pregnancy and remains at a high level until the last week, when the hormone level begins to fall. The progestins control uterine function, especially inhibition of muscular activity, so the embryo can remain in the uterus and be nourished throughout pregnancy. The progestins also inhibit sexual receptivity in the pregnant female, although follicles continue to develop and produce estrogen throughout pregnancy. Since follicles are present at the end of pregnancy, the doe is sexually receptive and capable of ovulation immediately after parturition.

Pseudopregnancy

If ovulation does not result in pregnancy, either due to lack of fertilization by the spermatozoa or because the stimulus was due to abnormal stimuli such as mounting by other does, or excitement, the doe may become pseudopregnant. In this condition a corpus luteum is formed with the subsequent production of progestins. The doe is thus generally not receptive during the period of pseudopregnancy, which lasts 16–18 days. If mating does occur during pseudopregnancy, it often is not fertile, since the hormones of the corpus luteum interfere with capacitation of the sperm and movement of the spermatozoa through the female tract. At the end of pseudopregnancy, the doe may engage in behavior normally seen at or near kindling, such as nest building and lactation.

Fertilization, Implantation, and Pregnancy

At the time of mating the buck deposits several million spermatozoa in the vagina of the doe. These move by contractions of the female tract and by swimming to the middle portion of the oviduct, where fertilization occurs. The first sperm are found in the oviduct within 15 to 20 minutes of mating, although the majority are not found there for several hours. Of the millions deposited into the vagina, only a few thousand actually reach the site of fertilization.

Before the sperm are capable of fertilizing the egg, they must undergo a series of changes known as *capacitation*. These changes require approximately 6 hours. Since ovulation occurs 10 hours after mating and the ova remain viable for only 6–8 hours, it can be seen that, at the time the freshly ovulated ova move into the oviduct, the sperm are just reaching a stage when fertilization can occur. This is important, as it has been shown that as the sperm or ova age, the proportion of ova which are fertilized declines and the proportion of abnormal embryos increases.

When the ovum is released from the follicle, it is swept into the oviduct and moves to the middle third of the oviduct, where fertilization occurs. This movement generally takes less than 10 minutes. "Fertilization" refers to the entry of a spermatozoon into the egg and fusion of the genetic material of the male and the female (syngamy). Once one sperm has entered the ovum, changes occur in the egg membrane which generally prevent entry of additional sperm. Cellular division and development of the embryo begins almost immediately after syngamy. The developing embryo remains in the oviduct until the 8- or 16-cell stage is reached. This takes 72 hours, after which the embryo migrates to the uterus, where it floats in the uterine fluid and is nourished by it. During this period, nutrients enter the embryo by diffusion through the cell membranes. After seven days the embryo becomes too large to be properly nourished solely by diffusion, so it attaches to the wall of the uterus, and the placenta (afterbirth) begins to form. This process is known as *implantation*. The placenta provides protection for the embryo and a close connection between the embryonic and maternal circulatory systems. There is no direct connection between these two systems, although the two blood supplies pass very close to each other in their respective vessels. In this fashion, oxygen and nutrients can diffuse through the vessel walls from the doe to the young, and the wastes from the young can diffuse out to the circulatory system of the doe. Transport of oxygen and nutrients within the embryo is carried out by the embryonic circulatory system.

It should be noted that, since the doe has two entirely separate uterine horns and two cervices, there is no opportunity for movement of embryos from one horn to the other. Such movement is often seen in litter-bearing species such as the pig, in which there is a common body of the uterus and a single cervix, allowing balancing of the numbers of embryos in the two horns. No such balancing is possible in the rabbits, so the embryos in one horn result from fertilization of ova shed from the ovary on that side only.

Pregnancy in rabbits lasts an average of 31 to 32 days, but may be as short as 29 days or as long as 35 days. The longer gestation periods are generally seen when there are only a few young in the litter. These young are generally heavier at birth (as high as 100 grams) than those from larger litters which are carried for a shorter period of time.

Embryonic growth is not constant. At the sixteenth day of pregnancy, the embryos of New Zealand White does average 0.5 to 1 gram; at day 20, about 5 grams; and at birth, about 60 grams. Birth weights vary from 25 to 90 grams, depending on the age and breed of the doe and the number of young in the litter.

Parturition and Maternal Care

During the last week of pregnancy the progestin secretion by the corpus luteum declines markedly. This results in a change in the ratio of progestins and estrogens which may, in some manner, stimulate the behavior known as *nest building*. This is seen a few days before parturition and involves building a "material nest" of hay, straw, or whatever nest material is provided (Fig. 4-13). In the day or so prior to kindling there is a loosening of the hair on the belly, thighs, and dewlap. The doe pulls this hair (Fig. 4-14) and interweaves it with the material nest to form the "maternal nest" (Fig. 3-14). The quality of the maternal nest and the time at which the nest building occurs depend on the breed of the doe, her previous experience (the quality of the nest tends to improve with successive litters), the nesting material available, and the season of the year.

Parturition occurs in response to a decrease of the progestin levels (which maintain the uterine muscles in a quiet state during pregnancy) and the sudden release of the hormone oxytocin from the posterior pituitary. The exact stimulus for this release is not known. Oxytocin stimulates contractions of the uterine musculature which force out the fetuses. Reflex contractions of the abdominal musculature also assist in the birth process.

Parturition in the rabbit normally occurs in the early morning, taking about 30 minutes, with individual kits born at intervals of 1 to 5 minutes. The doe crouches in the nest and licks each of the young as it is delivered. This dries the kits, removes blood and tissue debris, and stimulates blood circulation. The firstborn kits generally begin nursing before the rest of the litter is born. This may assist in the birth process, since the suckling stimulus will result in further release of oxytocin. The entire litter is generally delivered at one time, although it may be spread over one to two days. Occasionally a single fetus will be delivered a day or more before the remainder of the litter. The kits are hairless (Fig. 9-4), blind, and deaf at birth.

When parturition is complete, the doe eats the placenta and dead kits. This is common behavior among animals, even noncarnivores like the rabbit. Since the waste material may attract predators or act as a substrate for the growth of bacteria, such behavior increases the chances of survival of the young.

The number of young in the litter and their total and individual weights depend on the breed of the doe, her nutritional status, her age, and her environment. The small breeds such as the Polish generally produce less than 4 young, whereas the larger breeds such as the New Zealand White, Californian, and Flemish Giant average 8 to 10 kits in each litter. Litters of up to 18 kits are occasionally seen. Poor nutrition may result in production of small, weak, or dead kits, or may result in resorption of the entire litter. Similarly, overly

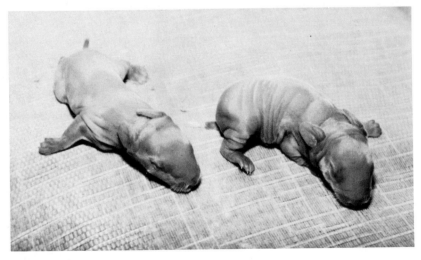

Fig. 9-4. Newborn rabbits. (Courtesy of OSU Rabbit Research Center)

fat does may not carry their litters through the entire gestation period. First litters are generally smaller than second and subsequent litters.

Kits will begin to develop hair within about 4 days after birth, and the eyes will open at about 10 days. During the early period after birth the doe licks the young to stimulate defecation. The doe will then eat the feces to keep the nest clean. The young urinate in the nest material, however, which is the reason for having a thick layer of nest material under the nest as well as drainage in the bottom of the box.

Some does, especially those that are young or exceptionally nervous, or those that are disturbed during kindling, may give birth outside the nest (scattering) or may eat some or all of the young (cannibalism). The causes of these abnormal behaviors are not known, although they are most often seen with does which build poor nests. A doe which persists in either behavior for several successive litters should be culled. Scattering of the litter often results in loss of the kits because rabbits, unlike other species such as cats, do not return kits to the nest.

During the nesting period the doe spends little time with the litter. Nursing generally only occurs once each day, for a period of five minutes or less. Though the doe may sit in the nest at other times, she pays little attention to the kits. In fact, does often seem oblivious to the squeals of young upon which they happen to be standing. Some does may be defensive about their young and jump into the nest if they are disturbed. This may cause injury to the kits and should be prevented if possible. More aggressive does may stomp when upset, or may attack by biting or scratching if the litter is disturbed.

Lactation

The growth of the young during the suckling period, especially during the first three weeks, greatly affects their later performance. For this reason, lactation can be considered as much a part of the reproductive process as ovulation, pregnancy, or parturition.

The mammary glands of the doe generally consist of eight physiologically distinct sections, four along each side of the abdomen (Fig. 9-5). The glandular tissue of the rabbit is similar to that of other species and consists of hollow, ball-shaped structures known as *alveoli* where the milk is actually formed. The milk moves from

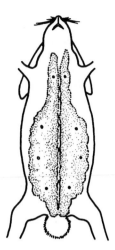

Fig. 9-5. Location of mammary tissue in the rabbit. Shaded areas represent mammary tissue, and circles are the nipples.

the alveoli through a series of ducts to the gland and teat cisterns. The teat itself is the external opening of the gland and consists of the external protuberance (nipple), with five to eight central canals through which the milk flows during suckling. The mammary gland also contains blood and nerve supplies, and variable amounts of fat.

Milk is formed in the alveoli by direct diffusion of constituents from the blood, by modification of substances from the blood, or by synthesis within the cells of the alveoli using materials which diffuse into the cells from the blood. Milk formation is a continuous process. As the milk is formed, it is stored in the alveoli and upper parts of the duct system until a suckling stimulus causes let-down of the milk and it enters the lower duct system.

The mammary glands of the doe begin forming when she is still an embryo. After birth, development is arrested until puberty, when the increased levels of estrogen associated with that period result in partial development of the duct system. The elevated progestin levels of pregnancy stimulate development of the alveoli. The release of the hormone prolactin at the time of parturition initiates milk production. Continued stimulation by this hormone due to its release caused by the suckling stimulus is responsible for the continued production during the lactation period.

Although milk production is a continuous process, the milk is unavailable to the young until a suckling stimulus causes the release of oxytocin. This hormone causes the contraction of the muscles around the alveoli and forces the milk down the duct system to the gland and teat cisterns. Suckling by the young forces the milk past the teat sphincter and into the mouths of the young.

The quantity and composition of the milk produced by the doe vary throughout lactation, as shown in Table 9-1. It will be noted

Table 9-1. Approximate Quantity and Composition of Milk Produced at Various Stages of Lactation in Fauve de Bourgogne Does

	Day After Birth					
	1	7	14	21	24	30
Milk yield (g/day)	50	160	220	240	220	160
Water (%)	69	74	74	73	67	63
Protein (%)	14	14	13	13	16	17
Fat (%)	15	9	9	10	14	18
Lactose (%)	1.6	0.9	1.0	0.9	0.8	0.2
Ash (%)	1.6	2.1	2.2	2.4	2.6	2.8

Source for quantity data: Lebas, F., *Annales de Zootechnie*, vol. 17 (1968), pp. 169–182.
Source for composition data: Lebas, F., *Annales de Zootechnie*, vol. 20 (1971), pp. 185–191.

that the quantity of milk produced increases until the end of the third week of lactation and declines thereafter. At this point the kits generally start eating solid food, and the milk of the doe becomes less important in affecting the performance of the young. The milk composition also changes at this time, with a decrease in the water and lactose (milk sugar) contents and an increase in the contents of protein, fat, and ash (which represents the mineral matter such as calcium) found in the milk. A typical lactation curve is shown in Fig. 9-6.

Table 9-2 is a compilation of approximate milk composition figures for various species and has been included for comparison purposes. The milk of the rabbit is higher in protein, fat, and ash than the milk of other species except the rat. The lactose level is lower. The milk of the rat is, in many respects, similar to that of the rabbit, although rat milk has a much higher level of fat.

When the litter is weaned, there is a decreased stimulus for the secretion of prolactin, so there is a decline in the amount of milk

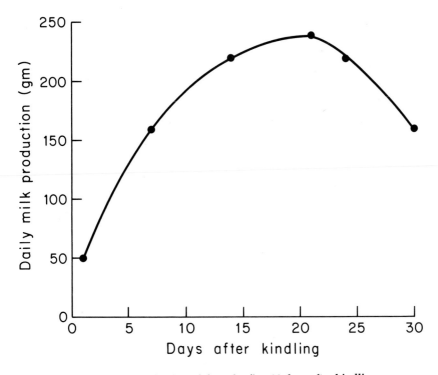

Fig. 9-6. Milk production of does the first 30 days after kindling.

Table 9-2. Approximate Milk Composition of Various Species

	Percent Composition				
	Water	Protein	Fat	Lactose	Ash
Rabbit	74	13	9	1	2.2
Cow	88	3	4	5	0.8
Goat	87	4	4	5	0.8
Human	87	2	4	7	0.3
Cat	82	9	3	5	0.5
Rat	68	12	15	3	1.5

produced. Since no suckling occurs, the alveoli will also fill with milk, and further milk formation will be inhibited. The combination of decreased stimulus and filling of the alveoli results in a phenomenon known as *drying off*. Once milk production has ceased, the milk in the alveoli will gradually be resorbed into the blood, and the mammary gland will return to its non-lactating size.

10

Rabbit Breeding and Genetics

Co-authored by Steven D. Lukefahr

BASIC GENETIC TERMINOLOGY

Successful rabbit breeders who consistently produce superior stock, whether for fancy or commercial purposes, generally have acquired a basic knowledge of applied genetics. It is on the basis of this knowledge that the rabbit raiser can most effectively select to improve herd performance for the traits of interest.

An effective way of introducing genetics is to define relevant terms involved in inheritance, the fertilization process, and the expression of genetic material.

Inheritance of Genetic Material

1. *Nucleus*—a cellular organelle found in all body cells, such as those in bone, muscle, skin, etc.

2. *Chromosome*—the largest unit of inheritance that is found in the nucleus, is made of DNA (deoxyribonucleic acid), contains genes, and is inherited in pairs.

3. *Gene*—the basic unit of inheritance that carries information to control the production of specific protein products such as fur, enzymes, muscle, and glandular products. It is composed of substances called *nucleotides* which "code" for specific amino acids. A gene located on a particular chromosome may code for the synthesis of pigmented fur. In the case of an albino rabbit, the albino gene actually inhibits the synthesis of colored fur. The known genes for coat color of the rabbit are shown in Table 10-1.

Table 10-1. Major Genes for Coat Color in Rabbits

Locus	Color	Locus	Color
A	Agouti (gray-brown)	En	Dominant white-spotting
a^t	Tan	en	Self-colored
a	Black		
		V	Self-colored
B	Black	v	Blue-eyed white
b	Brown or chocolate		
		W	Normal agouti band
C	Full color	w	Agouti with yellow pigment
C^{chd}	Dark chinchilla		band doubled in width
C^{chm}	Medium chinchilla		
c^{chl}	Light chinchilla	Si	Normal
c^H	Himalayan	si	Silver
c	Albino		
D	Black	**Locus**	**Hair Structure**
d	Blue dilution		
		R	Normal
E	Agouti	r	Rex fur[1]
E^D	Black extension of agouti band		
E^S	To produce steel-colored fur; steel—weaker form of E^D	Sa	Normal fur
		sa	Satin fur
e^j	Japanese brindling		
e	Yellow	L	Normal
		l	Angora wool
Du	Self-colored		
du^d	Dark dutch-spotting		
du^w	White dutch-spotting		

[1]Three pairs of Rex genes found on different loci have been reported.

   4. *Locus*—the specific region or point on a chromosome where a particular gene is found. The plural of "locus" is "loci."
   5. *Alleles*—two or more genes at a locus. For example, three alleles are known for the *A* loci affecting coat color in rabbits. The *A* allele codes for agouti-type (wild type) fur, the *a* allele codes for non-agouti black fur (self), and the *a^t* allele codes for tan fur on specific regions of the body.
   6. *Mutation*—a spontaneous change in the structure of a gene. The result is a sudden, heritable change in the offspring. Mutations

are exceedingly rare, with only 1 mutation for each 100,000 to 1,000,000 gametes/locus/generation in a population. Most mutations are lost in a few generations. Generally, mutations are lethal, due to detrimental physical or nervous conditions. Occasionally, a desirable mutation is observed. A desirable mutation in rabbits that occurred centuries ago was albinism. Today, premium prices are paid for white fryers, since their pelts can be dyed.

When a simply inherited trait suddenly appears in a herd, most likely it is due to a pair of recessive genes that have become fixed (homozygous) and fully expressed in a rabbit, and not due to a mutation.

7. *Mitosis*—a form of division in somatic cells (body cells). In mitosis a cell divides, producing two identical daughter cells with the same genetic make-up as the parent cell. This is how a rabbit grows.

8. *Meiosis*—a form of cell division that results in the formation of the sex cells (sperm and ova). During meiosis a separation occurs between paired chromosomes (called *segregation*), forming the sex cells. As a consequence, only one chromosome of each chromosome pair is found in the sex cell or gamete.

Gametogenesis and Fertilization

1. *Gametogenesis*—formation of sex cells in the testes and ovaries. Sex cells are also called *gametes.*

2. *Independent assortment*—the random union of the gametes involved in fertilization. Independent assortment of gametes with subsequent development into zygotes (fertilized ova) enhances genetic variability in a rabbit herd.

3. *Somatic cell*—a body cell (muscle, bone, glandular cell, etc.) containing a complete set of paired chromosomes (diploid number). The numbers of chromosome pairs for humans and several livestock species are listed in Table 10-2.

4. *Sex cell*—a sperm or ovum that contains only one member from each chromosome pair (haploid number). A sex cell from a rabbit has 22 chromosomes, whereas a body cell contains 44 chromosomes. Upon fertilization, similar members of chromosome pairs unite, restoring the chromosome number to 44 (22 from sperm + 22 from ova = 44). In other words, for a given chromosome pair, one chromosome was inherited from the sire and the other was inherited from the dam.

Table 10-2. Number of Chromosomes of Man and Livestock Species

Species	Pairs of Chromosomes	Total Number
Cattle	30	60
Horse	32	64
Man	23	46
Rabbit	22	44
Sheep	19	38

5. *Sex chromosomes*—the one pair of chromosomes determining the sex at fertilization. A normal sperm cell contains either an X or a Y sex chromosome, whereas a normal ovum contains only an X chromosome. Females are XX and males are XY. Fig. 10-1 displays this phenomenon.

6. *Autosomal chromosomes*—all chromosomes other than the sex chromosomes. In the rabbit, 21 autosomal chromosome pairs and 1 sex chromosome pair exist (Fig. 10-2).

7. *Sex-linked trait*—a trait controlled by genes located on the X chromosome. The classic example of a sex-linked trait is that of the calico cat, which is always female *(XX)*. On one X chromosome there is a gene for black fur color, while on the other X chromosome there is a gene for orange fur color. A female cat with this inherited condition will be black and orange (calico). Sex linkage for fur color traits in rabbits is unknown.

8. *Sex-limited trait*—a trait that can be expressed by only one sex, such as milk production or sperm production. Genes involved in expression of sex-limited traits are generally located on autosomal chromosomes. Therefore, nearly equal contributions come

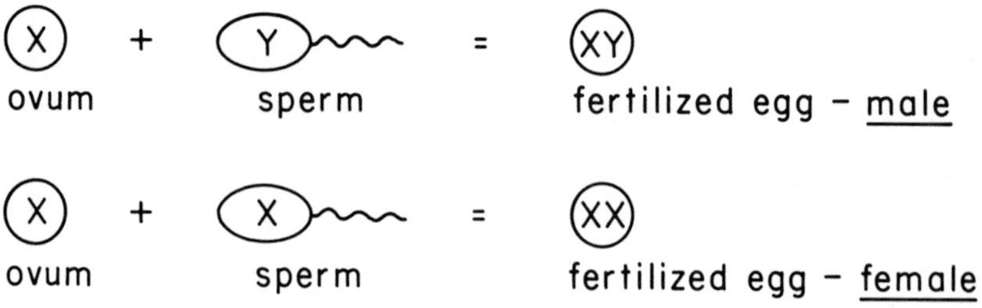

Fig. 10-1. Determination of sex at fertilization.

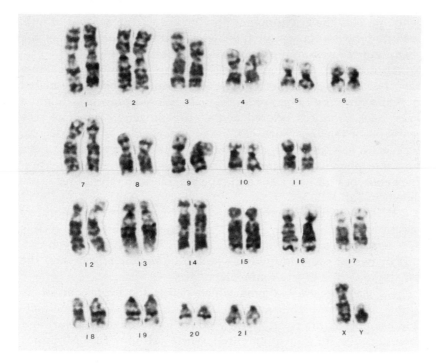

Fig. 10-2. A karyotype of the domestic rabbit, showing the 21 chromosome pairs and the X and Y sex chromosomes. (Courtesy of Richard Fox, Bar Harbor, Maine, and S. Karger, AG, publisher, *Cytogenetics and Cell Genetics*)

from the sire and the dam, so the ability of a doe to produce milk, for example, depends on the genes transmitted from both her dam and her sire.

Gene Expression

Since chromosomes are inherited in pairs, half the chromosomes of an individual are inherited from its sire and the other half from its dam. Thus half of the total number of genes are likewise inherited from the sire and the other half from the dam. Genes are also inherited in paired units (one gene from each parent for each locus). One gene pair, several pairs, or hundreds of pairs may be involved in the expression of a given trait.

1. *Phenotype*—the observed expression of a trait due to combined environmental and genetic influences. At fertilization, a rabbit's genetic potential for growth rate is determined. However, its

genotype plus the environment provided (e.g., the amount of milk produced by its dam, and the diet it receives) will regulate the phenotypic expression for growth of the rabbit.

2. *Genotype*—the total genetic make-up of a rabbit. To illustrate, two bucks are colored. However, when both bucks are mated to albino does, one buck produces only colored progeny while the other buck produces colored and albino progeny. Therefore, the genotype of the first buck is CC and the genotype of the second buck is Cc (C—full color, c—albinism). Although both bucks have the same phenotype (colored fur), they have different genotypes. The genotypes for hair color and type of American rabbit breeds are shown in Table 10-3.

3. *Heritability*—the proportion of total observed (phenotypic) variation of a trait within a herd that is due to genetics. If a trait is 50% heritable, one-half of the phenotypic difference between records of two or more individuals is due to genetic effects, and the remainder is due to environmental effects.

4. *Dominant gene*—a gene which masks the expression of its paired allele. Some traits are only influenced by a single gene pair. One example is fur color. Gene C codes for normal fur color, and gene c codes for non-pigmented white (albino) fur. Mating a homozygous colored rabbit to an albino rabbit would produce colored offspring as shown in Fig. 10-3. Since the colored rabbit can only transmit C genes and the albino rabbit can only transmit c genes, all of their offspring will have one C gene and one c gene, with the result that all offspring will have colored fur, as shown in Fig. 10-3. For fur color, color is thus dominant to no color (albinism). The expression of colored fur over albinism when both genes are present in the individual is called *dominance*. Dominant genes are usually capitalized, while recessive genes are not.

		Gametes from sire	
		C	C
Gametes	c	Cc	Cc
from			
dam	c	Cc	Cc

Fig. 10-3. Illustration of the genotype of the progeny produced by mating a homozygous colored buck with an albino doe.

Table 10-3. Genotypes of American Breeds of Rabbits

Breed	Genotype	Breed	Genotype
American White	cc	Flemish Giant	
American Blue	aa dd	Steel gray	E^SE
American Sable	aa $c^{chp}c^{chp}$	Light gray	(unknown)
American Standard		Sandy	ww
chinchilla	$c^{chd}c^{chd}$	Black	aa
American chinchilla	$c^{chd}c^{chd}$	Blue	aa dd
American Giant		White	cc
chinchilla	$c^{chd}c^{chd}$	Fawn	ee
English Angora		Florida White	cc
White	ll cc	Havana	
Black	ll aa	Chocolate	aa bb
Blue	ll aa dd	Blue	aa dd
Fawn	ll ee	Harlequin	e^je^j
French Angora		Himalayan	aa c^Hc^H
White	ll cc	Lop (French) varied	
Black	ll aa	+ white	Enen
Blue	ll aa dd	Lop (English) varied	
Fawn	ll ee	+ white	Enen
Belgian Hare	ww	Lilac	aa bb dd
Beveren		New Zealand	
White	vv	Red	ee
Blue	aa dd	White	cc
Black	aa	Black	aa
Californian	aa c^Hc^H	Palomino	
Champagne d'Argent	aa sisi	Golden	ee^1
Creme d'Argent	ee sisi	Lynx	bbdd
American Checkered		Polish	
Giant	aa EnEn	White	cc
American Dutch		Black	aa
Black	du^ddu^waa	Chocolate	aa bb
Blue	du^ddu^waa dd	Rex	
Chocolate	du^ddu^waa bb	White	rr cc
Tortoise	du^ddu^waa ee	Black	rr aa
Steel gray	$du^ddu^wE^S$e	Blue	rr aa dd
English Spot		Castor	rr
Black	Enen aa	Chinchilla	rr c^{chd}
Blue	Enen aa dd	Opal	rr dd
Chocolate	Enen aa bb	Lynx	rr bb dd
Gray	Enen	Sable	rr aa $c^{chl}c^{chl}$
Tortoise	Enen aa ee	Seal	rr $c^{chm}c^{chm}$
Lilac	Enen aa bb dd	Red	rr ee
		Lilac	rr aa bb dd
		Havana	rr aa bb
		Californian	rr aa c^Hc^H

(Continued)

Table 10-3 (Continued)

Breed	Genotype	Breed	Genotype
Satin		Silver Fox	
Black	sasa aa	Blue	sisi aa dd
Blue	sasa aa dd	Black	sisi aa
Chocolate	sasa aa bb	Silver Marten	
Red	sasa ee	Black	$a^ta^tc^{chd}$
Chinchilla	sasa c^{chd}	Blue	$a^ta^tc^{chd}dd$
Copper	sasa bb	Chocolate	$a^ta^tc^{chd}bb$
Siamese	sasa aa $c^{chl}c^{chl}$	Sable	$a^ta^tc^{chp}c^{chl}$
White	sasa cc	Tan	
Californian	sasa aa c^Hc^H	Black	a^ta^t
Siamese Sable	aa $c^{chl}c^{chl}$	Blue	a^ta^tdd
Silver		Chocolate	a^ta^tbb
Gray	sisi aa	Lilac	$a^ta^tbb\ dd$
Fawn	sisi ee		
Brown	sisi ww		

[1]Presumed genotype of the Golden Palomino.

5. *Recessive gene*—a gene whose observed expression is masked by its dominant allele when both are present. Using the above example, the only possible way for a rabbit to be an albino is if it has two *c* genes *(cc)*. Albinism is therefore called a *recessive trait*. Recessiveness is expressed only when both recessive genes are present.

6. *Homozygote*—an individual having identical alleles at a specific locus. When both genes for a given gene pair are similar (in the last example—*cc*), the rabbit would be considered a *homozygote*. If a colored rabbit is *CC* it is homozygous dominant, and an albino rabbit *(cc)* is homozygous recessive, for coat color.

7. *Heterozygote*—an individual having dissimilar alleles at a specific locus. When the genes of a given pair are dissimilar, the rabbit would be termed *heterozygous*. Mating a colored heterozygote *(Cc)* to an albino rabbit would produce on the average half albino *(cc)* and half colored *(Cc)* offspring.

8. *Incomplete dominance*—dominance that is not complete between two different alleles of the same gene pair or locus. Mating a Californian *(cHcH)* to a New Zealand White *(cc)* will produce heterozygotes *(cHc)* which are intermediate in color on the extremities between the parental breeds (Fig. 10-4). This is called *incomplete dominance*, since the c^H is expressed but not as strongly as in the homozygote.

Fig. 10-4. Incomplete dominance. The middle rabbit is a cross between a New Zealand White (left) and a Californian (right). The crossbred animal shows coloration of the extremities that is intermediate between the parental breeds. (Courtesy of OSU Rabbit Research Center)

9. *Epistasis*—the combined effect of an interaction between different pairs of genes found at different loci. Mating a blue rabbit (*aaBBdd*) to a chocolate rabbit (*aabbDD*), where *a* = non-agouti black, *B* = black, *b* = chocolate, *D* = black, and *d* = blue fur, will produce all black offspring which are genetically *aaBbDd*. Epistasis is demonstrated when two black rabbits of this genotype are mated. The results of such a mating are shown in Fig. 10-5.

Thus this mating will produce, on the average, nine black, three blue, three chocolate, and one lilac (blue-dove) colored offspring. A probability of 1/16 exists for producing a lilac from this double heterozygous mating. The two homozygous-recessive gene pairs (*bb* and *dd*) are involved in coding for lilac colored fur, due to an interaction between both pairs of genes, producing a unique color.

Another type of epistasis is *recessive epistasis*. If an albino rabbit with black ancestors (*aaccEE*) is mated to a tortoise-shell rabbit (*aaCCee*), where *a* = non-agouti black, *c* = albino, *C* = color, *E* = agouti, and *e* = red fur, the offspring will be black with the genotype *aaCcEe*. The tortoise-shell colored rabbit has yellow or red fur with black points. Whether a rabbit has red or yellow fur de-

Gametes produced by sire

Gametes produced by dam	aBD	aBd	abD	abd
aBD	aaBBDD black	aaBBDd black	aaBbDD black	aaBbDd black
aBd	aaBBDd black	aaBBdd blue	aaBbDd black	aaBbdd blue
abD	aaBbDD black	aaBbDd black	aabbDD chocolate	aabbDd chocolate
abd	aaBbDd black	aaBbdd blue	aabbDd chocolate	aabbdd lilac

Fig. 10-5. Illustration of epistasis with a 9:3:3:1 phenotypic ratio of offspring, where both the sire and the dam have the genotype *aaBbDd*.

pends on the presence of rufus (rich red pigment) polygenes and other modifier genes. Mating two black rabbits of this genotype will yield the results shown in Fig. 10-6.

This mating will produce, on the average, nine black, three tortoise-shell, and four albino rabbits. Albinism is therefore a recessive-epistatic trait; any rabbit that is homozygous-recessive for the albino alleles *(cc)* is albino white, regardless of the genotype at

Gametes produced by sire

Gametes produced by dam	aCE	aCe	acE	ace
aCE	aaCCEE black	aaCCEe black	aaCcEE black	aaCcEe black
aCe	aaCCEe black	aaCCee tortoise-shell	aaCcEe black	aaCcee tortoise-shell
acE	aaCcEE black	aaCcEe black	aaccEE white	aaccEe white
ace	aaCcEe black	aaCcee tortoise-shell	aaccEe white	aaccee white

Fig. 10-6. Illustration of recessive epistasis with a 9:3:4 phenotypic ratio of offspring, where both the sire and the dam have the genotype *aaCcEe*.

any other loci. For this reason, all New Zealand White rabbits are albino, since they have the *cc* genotype. The tortoise-shell color is also an epistatic condition, since both gene pairs *(aa* and *ee)* code for black and yellow or red fur, although on different regions of the body.

Several books which provide more information on coat color inheritance in the rabbit are available. Some examples of these are:

Robinson, Roy. *Color Inheritance in Small Livestock.* Bradford, England: Watmoughs Limited, 1978.

Sanford, J. C. *The Domestic Rabbit,* 3rd ed. New York: John Wiley & Sons, Inc., 1979.

Searle, A. G. *Comparative Genetics of Coat Colour in Mammals.* New York: Academic Press, Inc., 1968.

Weisbroth, S. H., R. E. Flatt, and A. L. Kraus, eds. *The Biology of the Laboratory Rabbit.* New York: Academic Press, Inc., 1974.

BREEDING SYSTEMS

Breeding systems are useful in establishing and maintaining genetic variation in a specific state for a trait or traits of interest. Linebreeding, outcrossing, crossbreeding, and inbreeding are breeding systems often used by rabbit raisers. The best breeding system or systems for any particular rabbit producer will depend on many factors. Initial quality of the base herd, purpose or goal of the producer (fancy vs. meat production or dual-purpose), and intended management of genetic variation in the established herd are a few such factors.

A pedigree is a description of the ancestry of an individual. The most common pedigree is the bracket style, as shown in Fig. 10-7. This is the sort of pedigree used for registration papers (Fig. 10-8). In this style, the upper ancestor for each bracket is the sire for that particular mating and the lower, the dam. Each ancestor is shown separately for every mating in which it was involved. For example, in Fig. 10-8, Caesar was involved in four matings so is shown four times on the pedigree. He is thus an ancestor of both the dam and the sire of Caesar V.

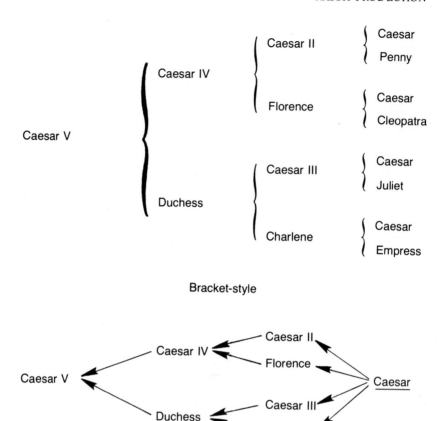

Bracket-style

Arrow-style*

*The common ancestor is underlined.

Fig. 10-7. Illustration of linebreeding with bracket- and arrow-style pedigrees.

For studying relationships, an arrow-style pedigree is often more convenient. In this style, each individual is included only once. An arrow pointing toward an individual indicates movement of genes from an ancestor, while arrows pointing away indicate gene flow from the individual. Note that the four matings of Caesar in the ancestry of Caesar V are indicated by four arrows pointing away from him. The arrow-style pedigree includes only common

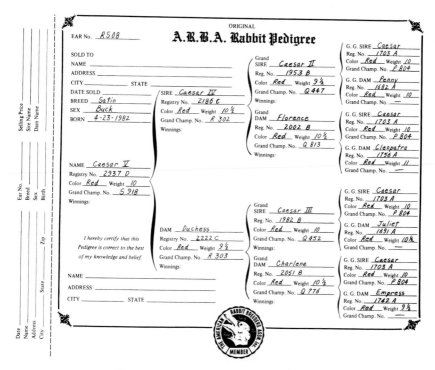

Fig. 10-8. An example of a typical pedigree.

ancestors and ancestors on the direct line from the common ancestors.

In the discussion of breeding systems, the relationship of two individuals is expressed numerically as the percentage of genes the two have in common. Table 10-4 shows the relationships between specific relatives. These relationships are affected by the breeding system used and may vary from 0 (totally unrelated) to 100% (identical twins). Relationships of 25% or greater are generally considered close in rabbit breeding.

The genetic relationship is the percentage of genes that an individual has in common with its relative(s). A rabbit would have 50% of its genes in common with its dam, since it received half of its inheritance from its dam at the time of fertilization. As the number of generations between a rabbit and its ancestor increases, the percentage of genes in common with that ancestor decreases at the rate of one-half per generation. First cousins share the inherit-

Table 10-4. Genetic Relationships Between Specific Relatives

Type of Family Relationship	Genetic Relationship
1. Parent – offspring Brother – sister (full-sibs) Quadruple great-grand-parent – great-grand-offspring (e.g., Caesar, Fig. 10-7)	50%
2. Half brother – half sister (half-sibs) Uncle – niece, nephew Aunt – niece, nephew Double first cousins Grand-parent – grand-offspring	25%
3. First cousins	12.5%

ance from one set of grand-parents. The relationship between grand-parents and grand-offspring is 25%, and between cousins, 12.5%.

Linebreeding

Linebreeding is the mating of less closely related individuals in a herd in an attempt to preserve or increase the genetic influence of a superior common ancestor. A common ancestor appears on both sides of a pedigree (sire and dam sides). Examples of less closely related matings would be individuals with a common grand-sire, grand-dam, uncle, etc. A superior rabbit might be a grand-champion with excellent show table qualities, or a commercial herd sire with a progeny average of 4.5 pounds at eight weeks of age. Linebreeding is most valuable after the superior ancestor is dead, since its genes can still be concentrated through the matings of its relatives. The purebred pedigrees in Fig. 10-7 illustrate the use of linebreeding with pedigree styles commonly used by geneticists.

In this pedigree, Caesar is a grand-champion buck as well as a common ancestor. Caesar, the great-grand-sire of Caesar V, appears four times in the pedigree. Caesar could be called the "quadruple great-grand-sire" of Caesar V. The parents of Caesar V likewise have Caesar as their double grand-sire. The genetic relationship between Caesar and Caesar V is nearly 50%, which is equivalent to stating that, on the average, one out of every two genes was transmitted indirectly from Caesar to Caesar V. If, on the other hand,

Caesar had appeared only once in this pedigree (as a single great-grand-sire), his average genetic influence on Caesar V would have only been 12.5%. Caesar V's genes have been concentrated without causing intense inbreeding.

The next pedigree represents the use of linebreeding in a commercial herd (Fig. 10-9). In this pedigree, three common ancestors appear; they are A10, B02, and C22. In the arrow-style pedigree it can be observed that arrows point away from the common ancestors for more than one path direction of gene transmission from ancestor to progeny. Ancestors that appear on both sides of a bracket-style pedigree but not in an arrow-style pedigree are not common ancestors.

If commercial herd sires A10 and C22 and dam B02 are proven superior for economically important traits, their genes can be concentrated by use of a linebreeding system, as shown in Fig. 10-9. In this pedigree, three common ancestors make up the linebred family. It should be stressed that in a linebred family, strict culling meas-

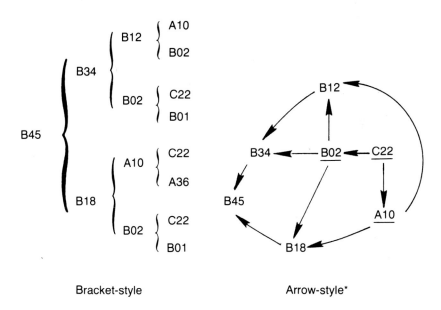

Bracket-style   Arrow-style*

*Common ancestors (e.g., A10, B02, C22) are underlined.

Fig. 10-9. Illustration of the usage of linebreeding with bracket- and arrow-style pedigrees.

ures should be maintained each generation to concentrate only the genes with favorable effects.

The genes of a superior common ancestor can be maintained or increased through the mating of its relatives. Since linebreeding is actually a mild form of inbreeding, inbreeding itself is differentiated by the mating of closely related individuals in a herd (e.g., brother-sister, sire-daughter, son-dam). Most commercial breeders prefer linebreeding over inbreeding, since depression in growth rate and reproductive performance may be observed when intense inbreeding is practiced. This depression occurs since undesirable genes (usually recessive) become homozygous or concentrated quite rapidly and, as a result, overall vigor is reduced. Linebreeding lessens this effect, although it still occurs at a milder rate. Strict culling of undesirable individuals is critical to prevent the spread of undesirable genes whenever inbreeding or linebreeding is used.

It is imperative that the common ancestry or "family lineage" is indeed superior, as proven by sound records, if it is to be preserved genetically through linebreeding. A relatively moderate to large number of breeding animals (50 or more) within a linebred strain is essential to avoid intense inbreeding and/or to maintain genetic variation for traits of economic importance. It is wise to use many sires in a line in order to secure genetic variation. Genetic variation and strict culling are key components that will ensure the breeding merit of a linebred strain.

Outcrossing

Outcrossing or outbreeding is the mating of unrelated individuals or lines within the same breed. Under several conditions outcrossing is a breeding option to consider. A few examples are:

1) When a genetic defect appears (e.g., malocclusion or hydrocephalus).

2) When the overall fitness or vigor of a line declines due to mild or intense inbreeding.

3) When the genetic merit of a trait or traits becomes limited or restricted in a line.

Point #1 is more or less a special case when a line of rabbits is known to transmit defective genes in a herd. It is generally advised that offspring from this line should not be saved as replacements (which is a most effective way of "weeding the genetic garden"). Often it is economically desirable to keep the "genetic carrier" parent breeders in the herd until their productivity declines. Through outcrossing, both objectives are met; the probability of increasing the incidence of the abnormality is avoided, and the breeders remain in the herd until productivity declines. To reiterate, no offspring should be saved from carriers of detrimental genes, whether the progeny are linebred or outcrossed. A further discussion on selecting against deleterious recessive traits is presented in the section on the selection of qualitative traits.

Overall fitness or vigor declines (thus affecting commercial performance) as a result of increasing the proportion of homozygous-recessive genes in a line or inbred strain through mild or intensive inbreeding. Outcrossing reduces the proportion of homozygous gene pairs in the progeny. This effect will in itself restore physical vigor. It should be clearly recognized that undesirable genes affect not only qualitative traits such as hydrocephalus, but quantitative traits such as fertility and growth, as well.

Genetic merit of a line may become restricted for one or several traits through linebreeding or intense inbreeding, and/or limited numbers in a line and poor genetic quality. Flat shoulders, protruding hipbones (evidence of a narrow loin), and poor flesh covering over the rump or hindquarters may be a consistent weakness in a line. Selection gives extremely slow improvement for these characteristics within a line if genetic merit is poor and limited numbers are involved. By outcrossing several members of such a line to an unrelated line which exhibits excellent qualities for these traits, the line weaknesses can be overcome most effectively. Once an improved state has been reached, the line can be re-established if desired. It is good practice to combine both outcrossing and linebreeding alternatively between two or more generations to introduce and concentrate superior genes systematically.

The pedigree shown in Fig. 10-10 is representative of an outcrossed mating. Note that both the sire and the dam of rabbit XY01 are linebred, although to different ancestors (X10 and Y42). This is, of course, an outbred mating, since no relatives of rabbit XY01 are found on both sides of its pedigree (sire and dam sides). Suppose that this pedigree came from a commercial herd in which line X possesses excellent growth characteristics but has poor texture and density of fur and thin foot pads, and so is more susceptible to sore

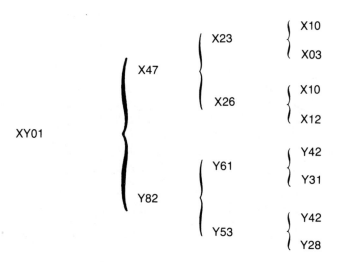

Fig. 10-10. A bracket-style pedigree of an outcrossed rabbit. An arrow-style pedigree cannot be drawn, since no ancestor of XY01 appears on both sire and dam sides of the pedigree.

hocks. Line Y does not have the genetic growth potential of line X, but it possesses excellent texture and density of fur, and thick foot pads. By crossing lines X and Y (outcrossing), the growth characteristics and fur qualities of the progeny should be above the average of the parents.

Outcrossing may be the best breeding system for commercial producers who raise only one breed. Since masking of undesirable recessive genes and improved genetic merit may occur when outcrossing is properly practiced, improved breeding and growth vigor should increase performance and profits. A commercial breeder can expect to see a noticeable improvement in vigor and performance of outcrossed compared to linebred or inbred stock, especially for fertility-related traits, since these are in general more affected by undesirable recessives.

Crossbreeding

Crossbreeding is the mating of individuals of two or more different breeds. It differs from outcrossing, which is the mating of unrelated individuals within the same breed. Although the genetic effects are similar for the two systems, the effects are more extreme when crossbreeding is practiced. The major genetic effects of crossbreeding are:

1) To increase the level of heterozygosity.

2) To mask the expression of detrimental recessive genes.

"Heterozygosity" is the term given to the degree to which one or several gene pairs contain dissimilar members. Since half the inheritance is derived from each parent, the level of heterozygosity of the offspring increases as the genetic relationship between the parents decreases. This concept applies to individuals of the same breed or of different breeds. Logically, a crossbred individual would have on the average a higher level of heterozygosity than a purebred, since individuals of the same breed have more genes in common. Hybrid vigor (heterosis) is the increase in fitness or productivity of crossbred or outcrossed offspring above the average of the parental breeds or lines, because of the increased heterozygosity of the offspring. The term "vigor" is used to refer to all health and production traits.

Traits that may be significantly affected due to this higher state of fitness are litter size, conception rates, and growth traits. Numerous studies in Europe, where crossbreeding of rabbits is extensively practiced, have demonstrated crossbred superiority above the average of parental breeds (hybrid vigor) for many commercially important traits. Rabbit-breeding farms producing commercial hybrid stock are found in Europe.

Crossbreeding and outcrossing increase the level of heterozygosity, thus masking the expression of detrimental recessive genes. This alone is the means by which gene pairs that may have been previously homozygous in the purebred parental generation become heterozygous in the crossbred generation (F_1 generation). Many traits are deleteriously affected by homozygous-recessive genes. Crossbreeding tends to prevent their expression by substituting a favorable dominant gene for an undesirable recessive gene, thus altering gene pairs from the homozygous to the heterozygous state. Because hybrids show increased vigor, greater uniformity in performance is usually expected in crossbred animals in the F_1 generation. As a consequence, vigor, especially fertility, is improved. Growth-related trait performances are improved in the hybrid progeny.

To optimize economically on hybrid vigor in a commercial herd, several stringent guidelines should be followed:

1) Obtain the best purebreds to produce hybrids.

2) Combine breed strengths systematically in a crossbreeding program.

3) Maximize the level of hybrid vigor expressed by the dam and offspring.

Logically, the best commercial hybrids are derived through the planned mating of the best purebreds. Indiscriminate matings of unproven parental breed members to produce crossbreds is a way to generate poor quality stock (appropriately called *mongrels*). Unfortunately, this statement has been true for many commerical producers who have attempted to pursue a crossbreeding program. The best purebreds would be rabbits from a productive line with proven records for traits such as fertility, milking ability (estimated by recording 21-day total litter weights), litter health, or pounds of rabbit marketed.

An example of optimal utilization of the breeds involved in a crossbreeding program would be to mate crossbred does of excellent maternal breeds (which produce large litters and a good supply of milk) to bucks of another breed known for superior post-weaning gains, feed efficiency, and carcass merit. Whatever breed combinations are employed, the end goal should be to produce marketable rabbits of good quality by eight to nine weeks of age.

To maximize the level of hybrid vigor expressed by commercial dams and offspring, the doe as well as the offspring should be crossbred. A crossbred doe should produce larger litters and more milk, and should last longer in the herd than the average of the parental purebreds involved in the cross. Such an added effect expressed by hybrid does is called *maternal heterosis*. Offspring benefit from this effect through more rapid gains through increased milk production of their dam, as an example. If one superior breed exists that is even better than the crossbreds it produces for fertility and maternal traits, outcrossing of lines within the superior breed would be recommended.

To produce does which are crossbred, it is best to choose two breeds known for excellent fertility and mothering ability. Such a crossbred doe should then be mated to a buck of a third breed, preferably a fast growing and thrifty breed (Fig. 10-11). To capitalize on the resulting near-maximal hybrid vigor, it is best to

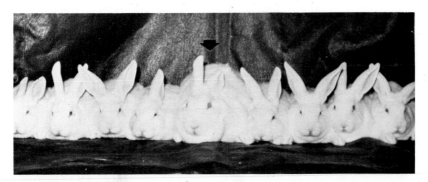

Fig. 10-11. A three-breed terminal cross. The doe (arrow), a Florida White ×
New Zealand White cross, was bred to a white Flemish Giant to produce the terminal cross litter. (Courtesy of OSU Rabbit Research Center)

market all of the three-breed cross offspring since uniformity of
production is greatest. Such a crossbreeding system is called a
three-breed terminal cross. If the best maternal source available is a
purebred, mating to a terminal sire of another breed would produce
two-breed terminal crosses (Fig. 10-12). Replacements are generated
through the mating of purebred parental lines. Actually, only a
small proportion of the breeding rabbits in a herd would need to be
purebred in order to sustain a predominantly crossbred operation.
The producer must consider the material and financial resources
available before engaging in such an endeavor.

Fig. 10-12. A two-breed terminal cross. The offspring were produced by mating
a Californian buck to a New Zealand White doe (arrow). (Courtesy of OSU Rabbit
Research Center)

Inbreeding

Inbreeding is the mating of individuals more closely related than the average of the population. Brother-sister and sire-daughter matings are examples of close inbreeding. Matings of lesser related relatives such as grand-sire–grand-daughter or first cousins in an attempt to concentrate the genes of a superior ancestor is a mild form of inbreeding called *linebreeding*. The genetic effects of inbreeding and linebreeding are similar, although more extreme in the case of inbreeding. Under certain conditions, inbreeding can be invaluable to the breeder of commercial and fancy rabbits alike. The genetic effects of inbreeding are:

1) To increase the level of homozygosity.

2) To aid as a test for screening carriers of detrimental recessive genes.

In increasing the level of homozygosity, members within each gene pair (one member is derived from each parent) become concentrated through inbreeding. For example, by mating a sire to his daughter, the same genes become concentrated or homozygous as paired units. Dominant and recessive genes alike become homozygous or fixed as a consequence of inbreeding.

The value of increasing the level of homozygosity is that through inbreeding, a family that is superior for one or several traits has its superior genes concentrated. Strict culling of poorly performing individuals for a few generations will result in selected inbred individuals that are an excellent source of superior genes. Individuals possessing a preponderance of unfavorable homozygous-recessive genes will be less vigorous. Such individuals should be culled, and only the best individuals should be saved as potential breeding stock. Even the best inbred individuals may show less vigor than non-inbred rabbits of the same breed. By mating inbred bucks to unrelated does, vigor is restored in the offspring. More vigor can be expected of the offspring through such a mating than through random, linebred, or possibly even simple outcrossed matings. This vigor could benefit the producer in terms of profits.

As a means of screening for carriers of detrimental recessive genes, inbreeding is most effective. In any herd the presence of a detrimental recessive trait such as hydrocephalus is a genetic calamity. Since through inbreeding, gene members become concentrated in the homozygous state, detrimental recessive genes as a consequence become exposed through trait expression. A brother and a sister (full-sibs) may both be carriers of the hydrocephalus gene (*hy*), but each may never produce a defective offspring when unrelated or outcrossed matings occur. This is because expression of the deleterious recessive is masked by the dominant allele. However, when these carriers are mated together, 25% of their offspring on the average will be affected. Such planned matings are most useful to producers of reputable breeding stock who want to ensure that their stock remains free of defects. Inbreeding therefore can be used as a tool to detect carriers of undesirable genes.

In producing meat rabbits, systematic use of inbreeding and outcrossing could be incorporated into a large commercial herd. Such a system is called *topcrossing*. The success of such a breeding system has not been conclusively verified. Since a high state of vigor is desirable in breeding does, it is best that they be crossbred or outcrossed through the mating of superior parental breeds or lines. However, since bucks represent a smaller proportion of the breeding herd, it may be economically feasible to create inbred lines to produce inbred herd bucks to mate to crossbred or outcrossed does, preferably of a different breed or line. Selected inbred sires should produce more uniform and higher quality market rabbits than non-inbred sires. This is expected for two reasons:

1) Masking of undesirable recessive genes by desirable dominant genes transmitted from the inbred sire to the offspring.

2) Transmission of superior genes from the inbred sire to the offspring.

Masking of undesirable recessive genes is a function of increased heterozygosity of the progeny. Consistent transmission of superior genes from the inbred sire is a function of increased homozygosity of the sire (also called *prepotency*). Inbreeding increases the rate of homozygosity of superior genes when intense selection is practiced. Therefore, the genetic merit (also called *breeding value*) of an inbred individual as a sire should be recognizable. An inbred line consisting of a minimum of 50 breeders (40 does and 10 bucks) may have adequate genetic diversity to produce superior inbred herd sires. Only experienced rabbit breeders with a knowledge of genetics, a large herd, and an excellent recordkeeping system should consider this type of breeding program. Furthermore, breeding performance of inbred rabbits may be low. In laboratory animals, 20 or more consecutive generations of full-sib matings have eventually produced isogenic lines (individuals within a line having the same genotype) of high quality stock. This success is usually recognized only after many lines were established and only one or a few lines survived the test of inbreeding, which exposed detrimental recessive genes.

To maintain a high level of herd vigor and uniformity, all offspring from an inbreeding-outcrossing mating system should be marketed. However, if several inbred lines exist in a herd, outcrossed does may be saved as breeders and mated to inbred sires of a different line.

Growth and carcass traits should be selected for within an inbred line with only low to moderate selection intensity placed upon fertility-related traits. Highly heritable traits such as growth and carcass characteristics are less affected by changes in environmental and/or managerial conditions than are fertility-related traits, and therefore a more accurate account of true genetic merit for such traits is expressed. An invaluable asset for line production is a sound system of recordkeeping.

In summary, crossbreeding and inbreeding are essentially opposites in their respective genetic effects and consequences. Linebreeding has effects similar to, but less intense than, inbreeding. Outcrossing, like crossbreeding, increases heterozygosity but occurs within a breed. Since there is not and may never be a perfect breed for all traits, crossbreeding is most useful in combining breed strengths to optimize herd productivity. When a producer prefers a purebred operation, inbreeding is useful in screening carriers of detrimental recessive genes, and also in concentrating genes from superior lines. It is up to the individual rabbit raiser to employ his or her knowledge of genetics and rabbit husbandry to recognize when a change in breeding system is needed, and how to best pursue improvement and/or maintenance of the genetic integrity of the stock in future generations. Ultimately, economic decisions are necessary to monitor which breeding system is most applicable to the producer's own set of resources.

SELECTION AND RECORDKEEPING

A rabbit breeder's reputation is based on the performance level, uniformity, and rate of improvement of the stock. To improve the genetic quality of a herd, selection of young stock is perhaps the most important phase of rabbit breeding. Generally, improved genetic quality results in improved herd performance measured by total meat production. Success in advancing genetic improvement through selection depends on the heritability of the trait or traits to be selected, as well as the genetic relationship between the traits. The term "heritability" refers to the proportion of observed variation of a trait expressed within a herd or population of rabbits that is due to genetics. When a trait expressed by the rabbit is heritable, selection of superior individuals should correspond to improvement of the trait in subsequent generations. Further discussion of heritability will be provided following the sections on selection of traits.

Traits or characters expressed by the rabbit can be either qualitative or quantitative. Qualitative traits (e.g., fur color and structure, blood type) are usually influenced by one or a few pairs of genes, while quantitative traits (e.g., fertility, carcass quality) are usually influenced by many pairs of genes, perhaps hundreds.

Selection for Qualitative Traits

Selection for a qualitative trait is a simpler process than selection for a quantitative trait. To illustrate using a commercially important coat color trait, white fur can easily be incorporated and maintained in a colored herd through the introduction of a white buck. The albino white buck (genetically cc) is mated to several homozygous colored does (genetically CC), where c is recessive for absence of color and C is dominant for full color. All progeny from the above matings are heterozygous (genetically Cc) and are colored. If white progeny appear in a litter from this cross (F_1), then the dam is heterozygous for albinism. If all F_1 progeny are colored, brother-sister matings will result in progeny (F_2 generation) of which an average of 25% will be albino white. Thereafter, mating albinos to albinos should always result in albino progeny (Fig. 10-13).

After several such matings are made and selection for only albino whites occurs, the herd will very soon consist of all white rabbits. If a rabbit raiser should apply qualitative selection for a simply inherited trait, it is recommended that several breeding animals with the preferred trait or phenotype be introduced into the herd to avoid subsequent inbreeding depression of reproductive and growth traits in later generations.

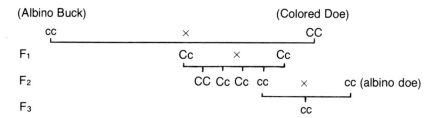

Fig. 10-13. Illustration of the incorporation of a qualitative, simply inherited trait into a herd.

In the above example it can be visualized that such traits are discrete in expression. A discrete trait is observed in general when a "yes" or "no" condition arises, and there are no intermediates. A rabbit is either colored or non-colored (albino) phenotypically. Another qualitative trait, hydrocephalus (water on the brain), affects newborn rabbits. Hydrocephalus is characterized by enlargement of the head due to excess fluid accumulation (Fig. 10-14). Hy-

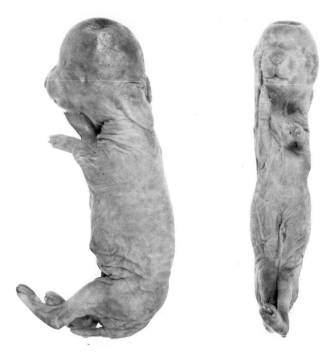

Fig. 10-14. Hydrocephalus in a rabbit kit. Left, side view. Right, front view. (Photos by S. D. Lukefahr)

drocephalus is a recessive character *(hy)*. The question could be asked, "Does a rabbit have hydrocephalus at birth?" Assuming that newborn rabbits can easily be scored as normal vs. hydrocephalic, there are no intermediates. To select against this undesirable trait, proven carriers *(Hyhy)* can be mated to suspected carriers. If no kits with hydrocephalus appear (out of at least eight young born), it is highly probable that the suspect does not carry the deleterious gene. If the suspect rabbit is in fact a carrier of hydrocephalus, a 25% occurrence of the disorder on the average should appear in the litter.

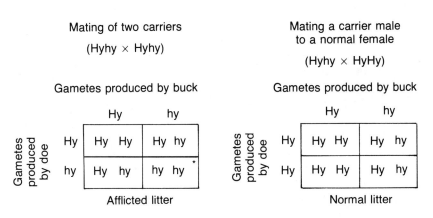

*Offspring are genetically afflicted with hydrocephalus.

Fig. 10-15. Two examples of the transmission of hydrocephalus.

Hydrocephalus is not always a genetic defect. It can occur when pregnant does are fed a diet deficient in vitamin A. Diets containing moderate (20% or more) levels of alfalfa, or which are supplemented with vitamin A, should be adequate in vitamin A status to prevent hydrocephalus.

When one is considering selecting for qualitative genes at several loci, the situation becomes more complex. Any rabbit raiser who has bred for specific rare coat colors is amazed (and oftentimes frustrated) at the complexity and outcomes of coat color inheritance. The following example illustrates this phenomenon:

Red Satin (AA CC ee sasa) × Siamese Satin (aa $c^{chl}c^{chl}$ EE sasa)

where   A = agouti

a   = non-agouti black
C   = full color
c^{chl} = light chinchilla
E   = agouti
e   = red
sa   = satin fur

The progeny (F_1) will all be agouti satins ($AaCc^{chl}Eesasa$). This occurs because A and E alleles are dominant for agouti fur, C is dominant to c^{chl}, and $sasa$ is homozygous-recessive. If these animals are intermated, the offspring (F_2) will also be satins. Because the F_2 generation (second cross) allows a complete genotypic array in the offspring (due to genetic recombination), recessive colors (often called "hidden colors") are exposed and, in addition, some may not resemble the colors of the original parental generation (Red Satin and Siamese Satin). This occurs because of exchange of genes between chromosomes during gametogenesis. The genetic and phenotypic outcomes are presented in Fig. 10-16. Since the three pairs of genes are all heterozygous, eight different allelic arrangements are possible from each parent through segregation (Fig. 10-16). Thus, if two triple heterozygotes are mated together, 64 (8 × 8) independent genetic outcomes are possible.

In this particular mating, progeny of different colors (phenotypes) are produced. They are:

Ratio	Color
27	Agouti satin
9	Red satin
9	Light chinchilla satin
9	Black satin
3	Siamese satin
3	"White" satin
3	Tortoise-shell satin
1	Seal point satin
64	

Specifically, three "white," brown-eyed progeny appear because the $c^{chl}c^{chl}$ genes (when homozygous) remove yellow from the agouti intermediate band (A-), and the ee genes (when homozygous) remove black from the agouti terminal band (A-), so that color is absent for the most part. Sometimes black ticking on the head, flanks, and lower hips of the "white" rabbit is present.

Gametes produced by sire

Gametes produced by dam	ACE	ACe	$Ac^{chl}E$	$Ac^{chl}e$	aCE	aCe	$ac^{chl}E$	$ac^{chl}e$
ACE	AACCEE agouti	AACCEe agouti	$AACc^{chl}EE$ agouti	$AACc^{chl}Ee$ agouti	AaCCEE agouti	AaCCEe agouti	$AaCc^{chl}EE$ agouti	$AaCc^{chl}Ee$ agouti
ACe	AACCEe agouti	AACCee red	$AACc^{chl}Ee$ agouti	$AACc^{chl}ee$ red	AaCCEe agouti	AaCCee red	$AaCc^{chl}Ee$ agouti	$AaCc^{chl}ee$ red
$Ac^{chl}E$	$AACc^{chl}EE$ agouti	$AACc^{chl}Ee$ agouti	$AAc^{chl}c^{chl}EE$ light chinchilla	$AAc^{chl}c^{chl}Ee$ light chinchilla	$AaCc^{chl}EE$ agouti	$AaCc^{chl}Ee$ agouti	$Aac^{chl}c^{chl}EE$ light chinchilla	$Aac^{chl}c^{chl}Ee$ light chinchilla
$Ac^{chl}e$	$AACc^{chl}Ee$ agouti	$AACc^{chl}ee$ red	$AAc^{chl}c^{chl}Ee$ light chinchilla	$AAc^{chl}c^{chl}ee$ "white"	$AaCc^{chl}Ee$ agouti	$AaCc^{chl}ee$ red	$Aac^{chl}c^{chl}Ee$ light chinchilla	$Aac^{chl}c^{chl}ee$ "white"
aCE	AaCCEE agouti	AaCCEe agouti	$AaCc^{chl}EE$ agouti	$AaCc^{chl}Ee$ agouti	aaCCEE black	aaCCEe black	$aaCc^{chl}EE$ black	$aaCc^{chl}Ee$ black
aCe	AaCCEe agouti	AaCCee red	$AaCc^{chl}Ee$ agouti	$AaCc^{chl}ee$ red	aaCCEe black	aaCCee tortoise-shell	$aaCc^{chl}Ee$ black	$aaCc^{chl}ee$ tortoise-shell
$ac^{chl}E$	$AaCc^{chl}EE$ agouti	$AaCc^{chl}Ee$ agouti	$Aac^{chl}c^{chl}EE$ light chinchilla	$Aac^{chl}c^{chl}Ee$ light chinchilla	$aaCc^{chl}EE$ black	$aaCc^{chl}Ee$ black	$aac^{chl}c^{chl}EE$ siamese	$aac^{chl}c^{chl}Ee$ siamese
$ac^{chl}e$	$AaCc^{chl}Ee$ agouti	$AaCc^{chl}ee$ red	$Aac^{chl}c^{chl}Ee$ light chinchilla	$Aac^{chl}c^{chl}ee$ "white"	$aaCc^{chl}Ee$ black	$aaCc^{chl}ee$ tortoise-shell	$aac^{chl}c^{chl}Ee$ siamese	$aac^{chl}c^{chl}ee$ seal point

Fig. 10-16. Illustration of 64 independent outcomes from a triple-heterozygous mating.

The rarest phenotype ($^1/_{64}$ occurrence), $aac^{chl}c^{chl}ee$ is a seal point or a seal Siamese, and is characterized by faded dark points and blackish ticking of fur over a predominantly white body. Another type of epistasis observed in this mating is the tortoise-shell (*aaCCee* or *aaCcee*). The *aa* and *ee* homozygous-recessive pairs of genes interact, producing non-agouti black points and red or yellow fur throughout the body.

It can be appreciated how much time and patience is required to produce specific coat colors that may be "hidden" in the herd. Large numbers of matings and offspring are necessary to enhance the likelihood of uncovering such recessive traits.

Selection for Quantitative Traits

Unlike qualitative traits, quantitative traits are non-discrete (continuous). Since quantitative traits are continuously distributed, plotting the weights of many rabbits in a herd at 56 days of age should give a normal bell-shaped curve (Fig. 10-17).

The vertical line in the center of the curve represents the average weight of all rabbits weighed. The area under the curve represents the proportion of all rabbit weights between 2 and 5 pounds. Thus quantitative traits are continuously distributed as a function

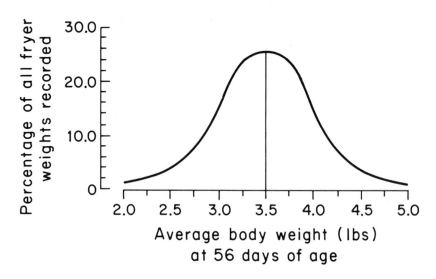

Fig. 10-17. Bell-shaped distribution characterizing a quantitative trait.

of many genes with small cumulative effects on the trait of concern. For example, assume that 100 genes contribute toward the body weight at 56 days. If each gene contributes 0.04 pound, then cumulatively 0.04 pound times 100 genes results in a 4-pound rabbit.

Quantitative traits include such important characteristics as fertility, growth and feed efficiency, milk production, density of fur, disease resistance, and carcass quality. How does heritability affect quantitative traits? Heritability is the proportion of total observed variation of a trait within a herd that is due to the expression of genes affecting the trait. Theoretically, if a trait is 100% heritable, all observed variation detected among all the rabbits in a herd would be due solely to genetic expression. Any observed difference between rabbits for the same trait would then be due to genetic differences. In Table 10-5, heritabilities are given for several eco-

Table 10-5. Heritabilities (h^2) of Quantitative Traits in Rabbits

Trait	Percent Heritability (h^2)	Source
Fertility traits		
Litter size born alive	2.1	Lampo and Van Den Broeck (1975)
Litter size born alive	3.0	Rollins et al. (1963)
Disease-related traits		
Diarrhea and pneumonia deaths to 56 days of age	12	Rollins and Casady (1967)
Survival to 56 days	6	Harvey et al. (1961)
Growth traits		
Birth weight	40	Bogdan (1970)
Daily gain: 22–43 days	58	Varela-Alvarez (1976)
29–70 days	61	Poujardieu et al. (1974)
Body weight: 56 days	35	Leplege (1970)
Litter weight: 56 days	22	Lukefahr et al. (1981)
56 days	0	Rollins et al. (1963)
Litter weight at 56 days adjusted for litter size	69	Lukefahr et al. (1981)
Loin width: 56 days	60	Bogdan (1970)
Carcass traits		
Hot carcass weight: 70 days	61	Poujardieu et al. (1974)
Dressing percent	60	Fl'ak et al. (1978)
Weight of leg meat	60	Fl'ak et al. (1978)

nomically important traits. In general, traits related to fertility are lowly heritable, growth and feed efficiency traits are moderately to highly heritable, and carcass traits are highly heritable. Degree of heritability does not reflect the number of genes involved in the expression of the trait. Since the estimate of heritability is a function of genetic variation for the trait, fertility traits are lowly heritable, because natural selection in the wild has favored rabbits that were above average genetically for fertility. After centuries of natural selection for fertility traits, genetic variation has probably been reduced. Alternatively, natural selection has given little or no advantage to rabbits with above average dressing percentage. Because of little intervention from natural selection, genetic variation for carcass traits is generally considerable.

To improve herd performance for traits of low heritability, providing a good management system (quality commercial diets, artificial barn lighting, etc.) may be more effective than selection alone. However, it should not be inferred from the last statement that a herd genetically inferior for a given trait (e.g., litter size born) could always surpass performance of a genetically superior herd for the same trait if environmental quality were improved in the first herd but not in the second.

Quantitative traits are normally distributed (on a bell-shaped curve) as a consequence of many genes that contribute additively to total genetic expression of a trait. Based on the magnitude of the heritability estimate (range from 0–100%), rate of genetic improvement following selection is usually proportional to the magnitude of the heritability estimate. If a trait is not heritable, genetic improvement following selection will be negligible. Since the goal of the breeder is to improve herd performance in consecutive generations through genetic selection of superior stock, it is desirable to select for traits that are moderately to highly heritable or are highly related to total pounds of rabbits produced. The next section will discuss this subject.

Recordkeeping

A systematic use of records kept on average herd production and individual rabbit performance is essential in developing a profitable business.

Cage cards are useful in recording litter weights, fertility, kindling performance, etc., but permanent records for all breeding stock that are compiled and easily accessible are essential in projecting herd performance and in making economic decisions. An organized recordkeeping system may also be an asset when bank loans are sought.

Performance records should be kept on all does and bucks. Important doe traits include conception rate, litter size born and reared to weaning, growth rate of the litter, milking ability, disease resistance, fur quality, and longevity of production. To evaluate and compare does for all these traits (by direct or indirect methods), a relatively simple and effective system of recordkeeping is needed. This is necessary because selection should be carried out by comparison with the herd average for the trait in question.

Effective trait selection for doe evaluation can be accomplished through the recording of 21- and 56-day total litter weights. Several scientific studies have demonstrated the strong positive relationship between total milk production of does for the first 21 days following kindling and the total litter weight at 21 days of age. It has been reported that observed variation between litters (range in litter size of 3 to 11 kits) for total 21-day litter weight was mainly related to the total 1–21 day milk yield of the doe (97% of total variation). By 21 days after kindling the does' lactation curve is beginning to decline (Fig. 9-6). Therefore, selecting does indirectly for superior milking ability (through recording 21-day total litter weights) should be an effective means of improving maternal performance. Does with several records have a more accurate account of true genetic merit than does with fewer records, and thus should be more disease-resistant, having remained in the herd longer. Since gross profits are derived through sales of total pounds of rabbit and not total average pounds of rabbit, the rabbit raiser should strive to increase total production of marketable fryers. Although average rabbit weights at 56 days of age are generally reduced as litter size increases, selection for superior breeding stock for total litter market weight should also result in selection for heavier fryers, regardless of litter size. In such litters, excellent milking ability of the dam and high genetic merit for rapid weight gains attributable to both parents are important. Fertility traits are generally of low heritability, whereas growth traits are at least moderately heritable. In commercial herds in which litter size born is satisfactory, selection of does from rapidly gaining litters should result in genetic progress in terms of total meat production. This is the case because selection of replacements on the basis of total 21-day litter weight will provide simultaneous selection for milk production, genetic growth potential, and, to some extent, litter size.

Since 21-day litter weight is largely influenced by milk production of the doe and only partially by size of the litter, fostering kits between litters should not interfere with accuracy of selection. Fostered kits should be identified by some permanent mark (e.g., ear tag, tattoo, chick toe punch mark in ear) if replacements are to be chosen from the litter. If 56-day litter weights are to be used as a basis of selection, weights of fostered kits should not be included. A doe record sheet suitable for selection purposes is shown in Fig. 10-18.

It is also desirable to select sires on the basis of their genetic worth or breeding value. Since a buck's genes are transmitted widely in the herd, accurate and valid selection of sires is a very important task. Important sire traits are fertility, including libido (sex drive); percent fertile matings and litter size born; rate and efficiency of growth to market weight; disease resistance; and fur and carcass quality. In general, traits related to fertility are lowly heritable (less than 15%), and growth and carcass traits are moderately to highly heritable. For sire selection, it would appear most efficient to choose young bucks from dams that are superior for maternal characters and from sires that excel in market weights of their offspring of the same age. A sire record sheet is shown in Fig. 10-19.

Efficiency of feed conversion is another important sire trait. Individual potential sire selection for feed efficiency may improve economy of gains by the progeny. However, because of the labor involved, and because of a positive genetic correlation between rate and efficiency of gain, selection for superior market weights is perhaps the most important means of herd sire selection.

Since fertility traits are in general lowly heritable, it is recommended that sires should not be selected for fertility per se but rather should be culled if average litter size born (after several matings) drops below seven, and/or if average number of deaths from birth to marketing exceeds two. These are arbitrary values which may be changed to suit the needs of the rabbit raiser. This method of selection is called the *independent culling technique*. The term refers to culling of sires below a specified value for litter size born, regardless of their merit for other traits. Thus, the recommended trait to select for intensively in sires is total litter market weight at 56 days of age. Ranking sires can be done by calculation of each sire's average litter market weight. Although more complicated indices for sire genetic evaluation are available (utilization of genetic

Doe Breeding Record

Cage Location _____

Ear # _____
Born _____
Breed _____

Sire _____
Dam _____

Dam Performance

	Fertility			Litter Growth	
Buck	Service Date	Conception Score*	Date Kindled	Litter Size Born	Litter Size Born Alive	21-Day Litter Milk Weight	56-Day Litter Market Weight

*Conception score: 0 = infertile mating; 1 = fertile mating.

Fig. 10-18. An example of a doe performance record sheet.

Buck Breeding Record

Cage Location _____

Ear # _____

Born _____

Breed _____

Sire _____

Dam _____

Sire Performance

Doe	Cage Location	Date of Service	Fertility			Mortality	Litter Growth
			Conception Score*	Number Born	Number Born Alive	Number of Kits That Died from 1 to 56 Days	Total Litter Weight at 56 Days of Age

*Conception score: 0 = infertile mating; 1 = fertile mating.

Fig. 10-19. An example of a buck performance record sheet.

parameters, information from relatives, repeated records, etc.), this is a simple but still useful selection tool for determining genetic merit for total 56-day litter weights.

After a sufficient number (a minimum of 20) of litters are produced from sires that are proven to be superior for this trait (to balance the effect of litter size), young bucks—from outstanding dams—that are heaviest at 56 days of age should be chosen as potential herd sires. Such bucks at the time of selection should be carefully inspected for thick foot pads, dense fur with good texture, and normal teeth. Only the best young bucks should be chosen, since their genetic contribution for many important economic characters will be widespread compared to does.

Rabbit pedigrees can be a useful guide in planning matings when supplemented with performance records, notes on undesirable characteristics (e.g., genetic carrier of hydrocephalus), disease incidence and/or longevity, show winnings, etc.

In conclusion, recordkeeping and the subsequent selection process are vital factors in maintaining accurate records and in improving herd performance. Computer packages programmed for

Fig. 10-20. A home computer unit used by Noel Berkeley, Marcola, Oregon, to provide a daily chore sheet, to aid in genetic selection, and to provide periodic financial statements. (Courtesy of D. J. Harris, Corvallis, Oregon)

utilization in rabbit production enterprises would certainly aid in making more accurate evaluation of herd breeders and in substantially less time. These computer program packages can be used to provide daily work sheets (e.g., matings to make, nest box entries, palpations, litters to be weighed, etc.) in a matter of a few seconds. The computer can also be used to rank the top breeders and to select replacements from superior parents. A home mini-computer (Fig. 10-20) generally will pay for itself, by reducing errors (forgetting to put in nest boxes, etc.) and by releasing time so the producer can spend more time looking after rabbits and less time keeping records. Several commercial computer programs for rabbit raisers are available.

11

Rabbit Shows

All rabbit shows, whether they be specialty club, local, state, national, those held at county or state fairs, or the American Rabbit Breeders Association Annual Convention Show, are excellent for informing the public of the development and extent of the rabbit industry (Fig. 11-1). They offer splendid opportunities for beginners and others interested in rabbit raising to acquaint themselves with

Fig. 11-1. American Rabbit Breeders Association Show. (Courtesy of *The National Rabbit Raiser*)

the characteristics of the various breeds and varieties, and are especially beneficial to established breeders because the shows make it possible for them to contact other rabbit raisers and compare their results with their own rabbit breeding operations.

At the shows, the meat classes bring together the commercial breeds and create much interest. To further this interest, demonstrations are staged to emphasize skill and speed in slaughtering, together with the proper procedure for handling the skins, and the highlight is the judging of the meat animals, on foot and then in the carcass. The shows offer an opportunity for displaying cooked rabbit meat and for serving rabbit sandwiches, salads, etc., as samples in order to acquaint people with the excellent qualities of rabbit meat.

The fur classes place special emphasis on the density and quality of the rabbit coat, and by carefully studying the winning animals in these classes, breeders become familiar with the standards to reach for in their own operations. Exhibits of dressed skins, garments of rabbit fur and wool, and fur craft novelties create interest and add variety.

PREPARATION OF RABBITS FOR SHOWS

Probably the most important decision to be made in preparing a show entry is the selection of outstanding prospects for type, breed character, density and quality of fur, and proper age for the particular class in which each animal will be entered. When possible, choose several rabbits for each class for conditioning for the show, because some will not come up to expectations, and the larger the number you have available for making a final selection, the greater your chances for winning a class. Preparation of the animals for the show must be started in plenty of time so they will be properly developed, have firm flesh, and be at the peak of condition at judging time. The breeding date for the does should be so regulated that the resulting show entries will have full advantage of the age limit for the class.

Most breeders feed their show rabbits on the ration that is fed to the herd at large, but in many instances it is a good practice to feed small quantities of green feed or root crops daily to stimulate the appetite and to keep the digestive system in good tone, with the quantity of all of the feeds being regulated to meet each individual animal's requirements. Bread and milk are excellent supplements, especially for young rabbits that are being prepared for exhibition.

Primeness of pelt is always important in connection with show rabbits but is a rather difficult problem to handle with mature rabbits, for at certain seasons of the year they are in various stages of molt. The judge may overlook slight molting in an older rabbit if the individual animal is outstanding in other characteristics.

You must handle the prospective show rabbit to help it overcome any fright and to teach it to "pose" so it will show the breed type to the best advantage, for when the animal is alert, fresh, and well trained it makes its best appearance.

In some cases a rabbit may be handled as many as 20 or more times at a show, so it is especially important that the handling be done in such a manner that the skin over the shoulders and muscles will not be bruised and become tender to the touch, for then the rabbit will flinch when being examined by the judge and not show to the best advantage. Carriers at the show should be instructed to use every precaution to guard against such bruising.

Grooming the rabbit before the show and at the show, by rubbing its coat with your hands, proceeding from the head to the tail, removes loose hair and gives the coat a good sheen. When the rab-

Fig. 11-2. Judging at an ARBA convention. (Courtesy of *Rabbits* magazine)

bit is shedding, moistening your hands will facilitate removal of the dead hairs.

Colored breeds should not be subjected to strong sunlight, because it has a tendency to fade the coat and to give it a dull appearance.

Hutch stains detract from the appearance of an animal. These can be removed from white rabbits and from the white spots on the spotted breeds with hydrogen peroxide or a similar bleaching agent. Small quantities of talc may be also applied.

Every possible means should be taken to protect the show rabbits. Often they are subjected to a lot of jostling around in transit, to extreme fluctuations in temperature, and to sudden and radical changes in feed that cause them to go "off feed." These factors may cause them to become listless and make a poor showing, so it is a good plan to have them arrive at the show in plenty of time so they will have quieted down and become accustomed to their new surroundings before going on the show table. Exhibitors may wish to furnish a supply of the feed the animals have been accustomed to, for feeding during the time they are at the show.

A rabbit should never be shown if there is any symptom of disease, for subjecting the sick rabbit to changes in temperature, feed, etc., will lower its vitality and make it easily susceptible to additional infections. Sick animals will be disqualified and will not be allowed to compete in the classes; but in the meantime they may expose other rabbits, and as a matter of fair play it is not ethical to jeopardize the health of rabbits belonging to other exhibitors.

SHIPPING SHOW RABBITS

Neat carrying cases and shipping crates are good advertising media and should be properly labeled with the name and address of the rabbit breeder. The container should be large enough so the rabbits will be comfortable and able to stretch out. If the animals are to be shipped long distances, a hardware cloth platform may be fitted inside and above the bottom of the container and, when properly bedded with straw, will assist in keeping the rabbit's coat in clean condition. A supply of the regular feed and carrots should be provided, and instructions on the proper method for feeding and watering while in transit should be attached to the crate.

EQUIPMENT FOR JUDGING

When the weather permits, one-day table shows can be held in a park or in other outdoor surroundings. Usually show cages are not available for these small shows, so the carrying cases can be used to take care of the exhibition animals, and about the only equipment required will be a table for judging the rabbits and a small table for the use of the secretary in making records. During the seasons of the year when the weather may be inclement, a show room convenient to the public should be provided for the judging. For the larger rabbit shows, a comfortable judging room with good lighting and ventilation, and when possible, seating facilities for those who are interested in watching the judging of each class, should be provided.

The table used for the judging should be covered with carpeting or burlap to prevent the rabbits from slipping and to make them feel secure. The holding cages should be of the type that will make it possible for all the animals to be in full view of the judge, and these cages should be secured to the table in such a manner that they may be tipped back and the rabbits easily brought out onto the

Fig. 11-3. 4-H rabbit judging. (Courtesy of D. J. Harris, Corvallis, Oregon)

table for inspection and comparisons. When moving the medium and heavy weight breeds from the cages to the judging table, it is preferable to support their body weight with an arm rather than to lift them by a fold of skin over the shoulders.

Much pleasure and camaraderie can accompany participation in shows. To facilitate this camaraderie, the opinions of the judges should be respected. For the most part, the judges are selected because of their knowledge of the standard requirements for the different breeds and varieties, their aptitude for handling rabbits, their fairness in making decisions, their desire to be helpful to the exhibitors and to interested spectators, and their willingness to put in long hours to expedite the show. After a class has been placed, they take pleasure in answering questions and explaining their reasons for making certain placings.

12

Marketing Rabbits and Their Products

RABBIT MEAT

In some areas rabbit meat is a well established food served regularly at restaurants, hotels, clubs, and hospitals, and available throughout the year in stores and meat markets. The general marketing procedure in large rabbit-raising centers is for collection trucks (Fig. 12-1) to cover regularly scheduled routes within a radius of 100 to 200 miles, pick up the live animals at the rabbitries, and deliver them to a central processing plant. Some of these processing plants have a capacity of 2000 to 5000 rabbits per day (Fig. 12-2). Where there is no established market, or in small towns, a person may develop an outlet for the rabbit meat through sales to neighbors and friends. Very satisfactory roadside markets have also been established.

With any marketing system, the problems involved are those of supply and demand, producing a choice quality product, merchandising it in a form that will appeal to the consumer, and using such methods of advertising as will be most effective in the immediate area where it is to be offered. Under all circumstances, the rabbit meat should be handled in a sanitary manner. Contact the proper health authorities to determine if there are any rules or laws covering the inspection of the slaughtering process, the equipment, or the meat.

The 1¾- to 2¼-pound fryer carcass lends itself to quick preparation for the table. It may be cut into seven pieces (Fig. 12-3) to meet the requirements of the average family. The larger carcass can be made into 12 servings if you cut the hind legs into two pieces,

Fig. 12-1. A collection trailer used to haul fryers to market. Note the scales for weighing each cage of rabbits. (Courtesy of D. J. Harris, Corvallis, Oregon)

the loins and back portion of the ribs into five pieces, and the front portion of the ribs and each of the front legs into one serving each. Presentation of meat products in the most convenient form for the consumer to use is rapidly gaining favor, with the cut-up rabbit

Fig. 12-2. A large processing plant. (Courtesy of Richard Popik)

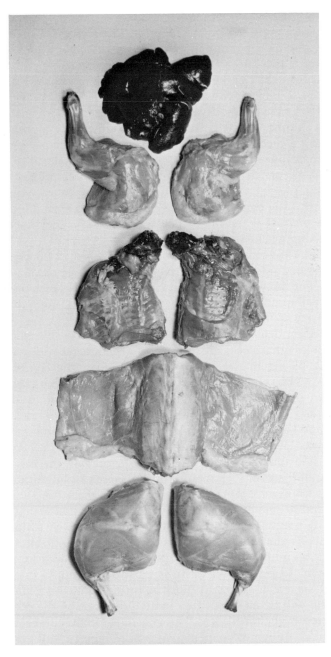

Fig. 12-3. A method for cutting up fryers.

carcass in the package becoming more and more popular and usually bringing more per pound than the whole carcass. The cuts may
be arranged in a paraffined box with a cellophane window (Fig.
12-4), but if the cartons are to be handled extensively or the contents frozen, a box without the cellophane window should be used
(Fig. 12-5). A box 9 inches long, 4 inches wide, and 2½ inches deep
is a suitable size for the fryer carcasses.

The cartons for the cut-up fryers may be made more attractive
by having a picture of cooked rabbit meat and recipes printed on
them. Some producers include the name of their rabbitry or some
other means of identification to stimulate repeat orders. It is extremely important that the supply be kept in balance with the demand, for if the consumers make purchases and then are unable to
find the product when they wish to use it again, they may discontinue asking or looking for it.

Quick-freeze units may be placed in a store and packaged rabbits delivered once or twice a week, with the proprietor paying on
the basis of the number sold. In contacting stores, restaurants, and
hotels, you may stimulate business by giving the proprietor a sample package of meat for his or her own use.

Freezing dries out the meat and causes it to lose some of its
flavor unless the pieces are arranged in cellophane and sealed prior
to being placed in the carton and frozen; or, the carton may be
wrapped with a sheet of moisture-proof, self-sealing cellophane
paper. In either case, the package should be sealed in order to shut
out the air. The liver, heart, and kidneys should be put in a small
cellophane bag before being placed with the rest of the meat, for if
these parts touch the other meat they may cause it to become dis-
colored and unappealing. For home use, prepare the carcasses for
freezing and storing by wrapping the pieces in aluminum foil or
other appropriate wrapping material to keep them from sticking together and to prevent the meat from drying out and losing flavor.

With the self-service stores no personal sales skills are involved; consequently each item is on its own, and rabbit meat is in
competition with all other types of meat being offered for sale. If it
is to be marketed to advantage, it must be presented in a manner
that will have eye appeal. It must be priced right, for if the price is
too low it will be unsatisfactory to the producer; on the other hand,
if it is too high it will deter the consumer from purchasing it. In
many areas, daily newspapers give market reports, and generally in
those regions where there is a large rabbit population, marketing

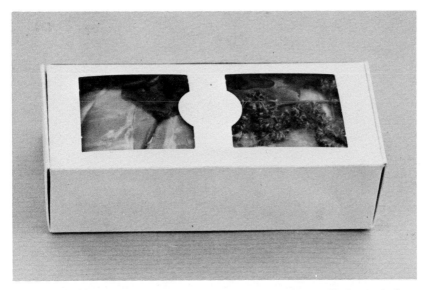

Fig. 12-4. A cut-up fryer carcass arranged in a box with a cellophane window. (Courtesy of USDA)

Fig. 12-5. An attractive box of frozen rabbit. (Courtesy of D. J. Harris, Corvallis, Oregon)

Fig. 12-6. A rabbit carcass attractively arranged on a paper plate.

services may give market reports of the price for live rabbits and often the retail and wholesale prices for the meat. In arriving at a price, it is a good plan to consider the price of beef, for often it is used as a measuring stick for evaluating other kinds of meat.

When individual members of rabbit clubs do not wish to devote the time and effort necessary to market their product, an excellent opportunity is presented for starting a cooperative similar to those that handle other agricultural commodities. By pooling their products, the members of the clubs will have a fair supply of rabbit meat available for sale, and generally arrangements can be made with one of the members to do the processing and selling for all. If this person has time, he or she can pick up the rabbits from the individual rabbitries; otherwise they are delivered to the person. Many cooperatives that have begun on a modest scale have developed into sizeable plants.

During the spring and early summer when the supply is in excess of the demand, the storing of rabbit carcasses may be a problem, but usually arrangements may be made with a cold storage plant to store the surplus; thus it can be made available later in the year when the supply is more limited. You can overcome this problem of seasonal distribution by using management practices to ensure steady year-round production and by promoting the demand for rabbit meat (e.g., for barbecues) during the summer when production is highest.

BREEDING STOCK

The business of selling registered or commercial stock requires considerable ability on the part of the producer, for the animals must be superior in type and production and must appeal to other breeders. It will be necessary to expend considerable time and expense to build up a reputation by maintaining detailed records; exhibiting rabbits at local, county, and state rabbit shows; and advertising in rabbit journals or farm periodicals.

Some commercial rabbit raisers produce registered stock, sell their best animals to other breeders, and depend on the meat market as an outlet for those individual rabbits that do not come up to breeding stock standards. The initial investment in registered breeding stock is greater than that in non-registered, and more time and labor are required to keep the breeding and production records, etc., but the asking price for the registered animals that are to be sold for breeding purposes may more than offset these extra costs.

Other commercial breeders devote their entire time and effort to producing meat for the market. For improving their herd they buy their breeding stock from those who have developed superior meat-producing animals. Adequate records and evidence of selection for performance traits are essential for the commercial seed stock producer who raises these replacement animals. As the rabbit industry expands, superior hybrid breeding stock may be available to commercial producers, who would not raise their own replacements.

LABORATORY STOCK

Rabbits are used for a variety of medical research and scientific studies for the benefit of humanity. Many laboratories, hospitals, and universities use them for studying problems relating to nutrition, disease, inheritance of malformations, and effects of new drugs; for diagnostic purposes; and for producing antisera. Anyone interested in selling rabbits to these institutions should contact the technician in charge to determine the type of animal preferred, the number used, the prices paid, etc. The requirements will depend on the nature of the problem. For certain types of research work a specific color of coat is preferred; when laboratory space is limited or the ration to be used is expensive, small breeds or young rabbits are generally desired. In producing antisera, the preference is for large breeds because large quantities of blood are used. As it usually is not economical to ship live rabbits long distances, local institutions should be contacted. Medical research is carefully monitored to ensure that humane animal treatment is carried out. Most research and medical laboratories in the United States will only buy rabbits from producers who have a federal license. Licensing procedures are available from the United States Department of Agriculture.

SKINS

Approximately 125 to 130 million rabbit skins are normally used annually in the United States. A small percent of these are domestic skins, but the bulk are imported from Australia and New Zealand, where wild rabbits are trapped to conserve forage for sheep and cattle. A majority of these skins are fully prime.

In raising commercial meat rabbits, it is more economical to market the carcasses when they meet the trade demands, regardless of the primeness of the pelt. As about 85% of the rabbits that are sold for meat are fryers that go to the market at about two months of age, the skins are small; the leather lacks strength; and frequently the fur mats, appears flat, and does not have wearing qualities comparable to skins from older rabbits.

Grades of Rabbit Skins

Skins from white domestic rabbits are frequently purchased without being graded (known as *butcher run*), but they may be classified into three or four quality grades according to size. Some firms re-sort them into many grades according to their ultimate use. In general, the quality grade of raw skins are as follows:

Grade 1—Pluckers and shearers. These are skins that have dense, uniform fur, and are free from shedding marks. They may be either plucked or sheared to simulate more expensive furs. Rabbit fur of this quality returns promptly to its original position when the skin is rubbed against the direction of the fur.

Grade 2—Long hairs (Fig. 12-7). These skins are thinner in fur than those in Grade 1, and have small shedding marks. The guard hairs are not plucked or sheared in this grade of skin. The defects are covered up to a large extent by the long guard hairs, or the defective parts are cut out and the skin is sewed up again. The poorer quality "long hairs" may be used for making toys or novelties.

Grade 3—Hatters. These skins are unsuitable for furrier use because of very thin fur and molting marks. The fur can be cut and used in making hats.

Factors That Affect Grades of Skin

Rabbit skins are taken in all seasons of the year, while other fur-bearing animals are pelted when they are approaching maturity or are mature and the skins prime. In the case of 6-pound rabbits,

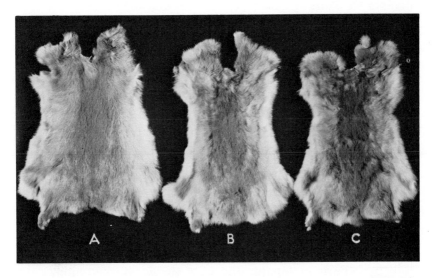

Fig. 12-7. Skins dressed "long hair." A—Fully prime. B—Prime on back only. C—All areas unprime. Note the rough appearance of the sides on B and C, indicative of unprimeness due to shedding or molting. (Courtesy of USDA)

the older, slower developing ones produce better quality skins than younger rabbits. Those that are developed rapidly by the full feeding of properly balanced rations from the time they are weaned may produce the poorest quality skins at about 7- to 9-pound weights. Most skins taken from animals up to four months of age are rough and uneven in appearance due to the contrast of old fur that has not been shed and to patches of ingrowing new coat. On the whole, the best quality skins will be those pelted from the older animals during the cold months of the year. The quality of the fryer skins is usually little affected by climate or season.

Judging Primeness

Unprimeness of skins is characterized by shedding, and the rate of growth of new hairs is clearly evident on the flesh side of the colored skins by the extent and intensity of the pigment. White skins show this discoloration on the flesh side only faintly. By blowing into the coat, you can identify unprime areas by the short fibers of the ingrowing coat. Poorest quality skins do not have the "fly back." They feel soft, and the fur mats easily (Fig. 12-7).

Markets for Skins

Good skins are in demand if they are available in large numbers, but many of the raw skin buyers do not purchase them in small quantities. It is, therefore, necessary for the breeder producing good quality pelts to pool them with other breeders in order to make up a large enough collection to justify shipment to the raw skin buyer if the pelts are to be marketed to the best advantage. If they are to be stored in order to obtain a sufficient quantity for a shipment, they should be kept in a closed container and protected with mothballs or moth crystals.

One may make inquiry regarding an outlet for the skins by contacting local raw fur buyers or rabbit clubs in the vicinity to ascertain where the members have been selling their rabbit skins. The American Rabbit Breeders Association may be contacted for a list of buyers.

Small shipments of skins may be made by parcel post, larger ones by express or freight. The pelts should be thoroughly dried and then packaged flat in cardboard cartons or wrapped in burlap.

The price received for a shipment of raw skins depends on the number and quality. Skin prices have increased considerably in the last few years, so proper care and handling of them will be economically important.

The Rex rabbit produces a very attractive pelt. Efforts are being made to develop a commercial Rex industry, to produce Rex furs of apparel quality. With reductions in the availability of wild fur, the demand for quality rabbit fur has increased. If large numbers of Rex pelts can be produced, this non-shedding type of rabbit fur may be able to compete in the fur market.

ANGORA WOOL

In the preparation of Angora wool for shipment, each grade should be placed in a separate paper bag which should be tied and placed in a corrugated box for shipping by parcel post, express, or freight. A bag about 12 inches high will hold a pound of wool without being packed too tightly. If the wool is to be stored for any length of time, mothballs or moth crystals in cloth sacks should be placed in the container.

Some rabbit breeders prefer to spin the wool that they produce to be made into yarn and knitted garments, either for their own use or for sale (Fig. 12-8). Others prefer to sell their Angora wool to organizations or individuals acting as agents and collecting large

Fig. 12-8. An Angora rabbit and lightweight, warm garments made from the wool. (Courtesy of USDA)

quantities to be sold to woolen mills. Some of these sell the wool on a commission basis. Cooperative organizations collect the wool from the members, grade it, and sell it to the mills. The movement of the product is somewhat seasonal. Some of these cooperatives make an advance when they receive the wool from the producer, and as this advance helps to pay the feed bill when Angora wool is not moving readily, the arrangement proves quite satisfactory.

FUR CRAFT

Some people may have a "knack" for making various products from fur and skins, and enjoy making coats; slippers; gloves; toys such as balls, rabbits, and teddy bears; and a variety of novelties and articles from rabbit fur. This fur craft utilizes a variety of sizes and colors of normal-coated and Rex pelts, and lends itself nicely to occupational therapy. It is especially attractive to individuals who enjoy sewing and working with patterns.

FERTILIZER

Some rabbit breeders may be so located that they can market the manure from the rabbitry to nurseries and to individuals for use as fertilizer on flowers, shrubs, fruit trees, lawns, etc. It is especially easy to incorporate into the soil, is relatively free of obnoxious weed seeds, and does not burn the plants. When larger quantities are available, it is usually sold by the cubic yard or by the ton; for retail trade in small amounts, the clean fertilizer is dried, ground or pulverized, and sacked. With attractive packaging, a product that may be sold in garden stores and supermarkets may be profitably marketed.

Rabbit manure contains about 3.7% nitrogen, 1.3% phosphorus, and 3.5% potassium. The nutrient value of manure from three species is shown in Table 12-1. It should be recognized that these are not fixed values; the composition of manure depends more on the type of ration fed than on the type of animal. It should also be recognized that nutrients in the manure are a waste as far as the animal is concerned. The nitrogen in manure comes from dietary protein that the animal didn't utilize. For example, if a sample of rabbit manure has a high nitrogen content, there is something

Table 12-1. Average Composition of Manure

Animal	Percent Nitrogen	Percent Phosphorus	Percent Potassium
Cow	2.9	0.7	2.1
Poultry	4.7	1.6	1.0
Rabbit	3.7	1.3	3.5

wrong with the ration, causing the rabbit to excrete excessive (and expensive) amounts of nitrogen. Poultry manure is high in nitrogen because chickens excrete uric acid, a very concentrated source of nitrogen. Rabbit manure is high in potassium, because alfalfa, a major ingredient in rabbit rations, is very high in potassium.

WORMS

Many rabbit raisers grow earthworms in beds of rabbit manure (Fig. 12-9). This is a way of supplementing the income of the rab-

Fig. 12-9. Worms growing in rabbit manure. (Courtesy of D. J. Harris, Corvallis, Oregon)

bitry, through the sale of worms for use as fishing bait, and sometimes for soil enrichment. The beds should not be located beneath
the rabbit cages, because digging to harvest worms will cause release of ammonia and other noxious gases into the rabbitry. The
optimal moisture conditions for raising worms are quite different
from those for raising rabbits. Therefore, it is not advisable to put
the worm beds in the rabbit building. The high moisture required
by the worms may raise the humidity of the rabbitry, causing increased *Pasteurella* problems.

13

Meat Production

Rabbits are raised throughout the world for meat, and the trend in commercial production is toward larger units. In the United States, rabbits are slaughtered when they have attained the desired market weight and condition without regard to the primeness or value of the pelt. In other countries where feed costs and labor conditions are quite different, rabbits are sometimes fed rations that will cause them to gain at a much slower rate, and each animal is kept until its combined value for carcass and pelt will bring the highest returns.

FRYERS

Fryers comprise more than 85% of the rabbits marketed for meat. Those of the medium and heavy weight breeds that are properly developed and conditioned will average 3¾ to 4½ pounds when marketed at approximately two months of age.

Carcass yield or dressing percent is determined by dividing the weight of the dressed carcass by the weight of the live rabbit. As an example, a 4-pound fryer yielding a carcass of 2¼ pounds would give a dressing percent of 56¼ (2.25 ÷ 4.00 = 0.5625). Fryer yields of carcasses vary from 50–60% of the live weight, 75–80% of which is edible.

There are several factors that affect the dressing percent. Those rabbits that are mature and that have been properly conditioned for market yield a higher dressing percent than the younger ones. Those with well sprung ribs and deep chest, carrying the width and depth of the body uniformly from the shoulders to the hips, give a higher carcass yield than narrow, rangy animals. A long, well developed loin is desirable. When rabbits are properly finished for the market, fat will be deposited over the ribs, along the backbone, in the flanks, and around the tailhead and the kidneys, increasing the dressing percent over that of the thin rabbit. In Europe, the head and feet are left on the carcass, so dressing percents are higher than in the United States. The amount of ingested material in the digestive tract also has a bearing on dressing percent. If the animal has been without food and water for several hours before being slaughtered, with a consequent smaller quantity of material in the digestive tract, the dressing percent will be higher. The breed of rabbit may also influence carcass quality. New Zealand Whites in general are superior to other breeds. Californians tend to finish out at a lighter weight than New Zealand Whites.

Some fryers are purchased on the basis of the grades such as prime, choice, or commercial. For comparable samples of these

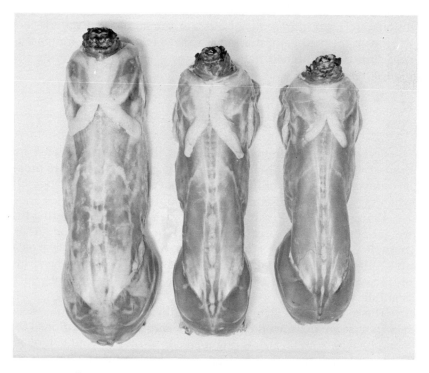

Fig. 13-1. Fryer carcasses. Prime, choice, and commercial.

three grades, prime fryers would give an average carcass yield of 57.7%; choice, 55.9%; and commercial, 52.2%. This system of grading should make it possible to obtain more per pound for the top grades and should act as an incentive for the rabbit breeder to produce a superior quality product (Fig. 13-1).

White pelts are worth more than colored pelts, so processors usually pay less for colored fryers than for white animals. Another reason for this is that dark hairs show up on the carcass, whereas white hairs don't, so more labor is required to produce an acceptable fryer carcass from a colored rabbit. Thus commercial rabbit producers should raise a white breed, such as the New Zealand White.

For maximum production, the doe must be properly handled, because as she is confined in a cage and is not able to obtain food for herself, she must depend entirely on the rabbit raiser. The level of production is in direct proportion to the quantity and quality of the ration. However, as the ability of the doe to produce is an inherited condition, no amount of increased feeding can increase production beyond the limit of that inheritance.

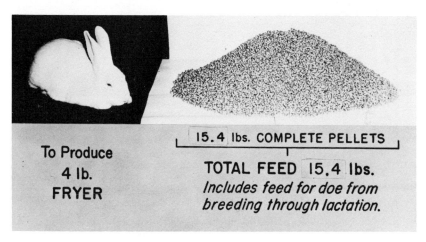

To Produce
4 lb.
FRYER

15.4 lbs. COMPLETE PELLETS

TOTAL FEED 15.4 lbs.
Includes feed for doe from breeding through lactation.

Fig. 13-2. Feed to produce a 4-pound fryer—complete pellets. (Courtesy of USDA)

When does and litters are full fed a well balanced ration, approximately 3¼ to 4½ pounds of feed will be required to produce a pound of weaned fryer at two months of age, counting all feed from mating of the doe until the litter is weaned (Fig. 13-2). The type of ration has a direct bearing on the quantity needed to produce a pound of gain. The lower the energy content of the diet, the greater the amount of feed that will be required per unit of gain.

Current commercial practice when intensive breeding is used is to wean the fryers at about four weeks of age. This allows a period of recovery for the doe before the birth of her next litter. Milk production has begun to decline by this time (Fig. 9-6), and the feed is used more efficiently when it is consumed directly by the fryers

Fig. 13-3. An 11-pound doe and her annual production of four litters, totaling 120 pounds, which is over 1000% of her live weight. With earlier breed-back to produce five or six litters per year, even greater productivity can be realized. (Courtesy of USDA)

than when converted to milk by the doe. To reduce the shock of weaning, it may be advisable to leave the litter in the cage in which they were born, and remove the doe. Much of the stress of weaning is actually the result of moving fryers to a new cage and new surroundings.

STEWERS

Most rabbits weighing more than 6 pounds live weight are graded as *stewers*. In most markets, the price paid for these heavier rabbits is generally considerably less than for fryers. They may not require any conditioning when they are culled from the breeding herd early in, or at the end of, their period of usefulness, and should yield a carcass of 55–65% of their live weight. Whether it is economically sound to condition these larger culled rabbits that are not carrying the proper amount of flesh will depend on the relative cost of feed and the market value. Many producers prefer to market them as soon as they are culled from the herd, for it saves labor, cage space, and feed.

14

Angora Wool Production

For the most part, Angora rabbits are cared for in the same manner as the normal-coated breeds, but there are a few special features for producing wool that must be taken into consideration.

The rations and methods for feeding other breeds will meet the requirements for maintenance, development, reproduction, and wool production, but as there is a tendency for the average caretaker to overfeed Angoras, take caution to prevent them from putting on excess flesh. Handle them occasionally and note the amount of flesh over the ribs and back to make sure that they are in the desired condition; then adjust the amount of ration accordingly. The young may be left with the doe until eight weeks, but only four to six young per litter should be left with the doe, depending on her capacity for nursing and taking care of them. The doe can be rebred 42 days after kindling.

The bucks that are to be used as woollers (rabbits maintained primarily for wool production) should be castrated at the time they are weaned. Although the breeding and herd bucks must be maintained in individual hutches, several woollers (both does and bucks) can be housed together in a pen to save labor in feeding and caring for them.

Because of possible contamination of the wool with hay, dust, etc., Angora rabbits should not be fed hay. They should receive a complete pelleted diet.

WOOL GROWTH

The better types of Angoras will produce from 2 to 2½ inches of wool in approximately 11 weeks, or an annual growth of 8 to 10 inches. This represents 12 to 16 ounces of wool. When properly balanced rations are fed, 100 pounds of feed is required on the average to produce 1 pound of wool.

RETARDED WOOL GROWTH

Areas where the growth of the wool is retarded become evident following removal of the baby coat at weaning age, and the patches that appear on the thighs of the rabbit may escape notice, although they may be more or less persistent and may remain for 8 to 10 months. They do not affect the wool yield materially because they cover small surfaces. There is considerable variation in the extent of the areas of retarded wool growth on other parts of the body. Most cases affect the coat only slightly and do not produce persistent spots but will cause areas of uneven growth that may escape detec-

Fig. 14-1. An Angora rabbit showing an extreme case of retarded wool growth. (Courtesy of USDA)

tion unless one makes a special effort to locate the patches. It is not the result of a nutritional deficiency.

The patches of retarded wool growth reappear on individual animals at the same season annually. Usually the extreme cases reduce the yield of wool materially for one shearing each year, and in an extreme case about five-sixths of the body area may be involved. Over the thigh, the side, and spots along the back there may be so little growth of wool since the previous shearing that the marks from the shearing may still be visible; the region just back of the neck and the shoulders may be affected to a lesser extent, with some wool covering the shear marks (Fig. 14-1). The tufts of wool over the rump, the chest, and the cheek, and along the underline, indicate the length of the wool where growth has not been retarded on the animal in Fig. 14-1. In this particular case, the wool yield for the shearing period was 1 ounce, and the next two shearings produced 3 ounces each. It is evident, therefore, that where rabbits have extensive areas of retarded wool growth the yield is reduced materially.

It is absolutely essential that records be kept of the quality and yields of wool, for these records are indispensable when matings for improving the herd are being planned and when rabbits are being culled.

WOOL BLOCK

Wool block is caused by the rabbit licking its coat and swallowing some of the fibers. These are indigestible, and they collect in the stomach and form a matted mass. The rabbit fails to eat and becomes listless, and in a well advanced case the stomach will be firm and hard to the touch. As food cannot pass from the stomach into the intestines, the animal generally dies of starvation within a few days. No effective treatment is possible for advanced cases. If you observe an Angora to be off feed, palpate the stomach through the abdominal wall. If a wool block is detected, changing the ration to green feed, root crops, or good quality hay, and massaging the stomach two or three times a day may prove beneficial. Regularly shearing or clipping the Angora and allowing access to a good quality hay and some green feed or root crops will act as a preventative. Pelleted rations should contain at least 15% crude fiber and 17% crude protein. Deficiencies of fiber or protein may result in fur chewing.

EQUIPMENT FOR GROOMING AND FOR
REMOVAL OF ANGORA WOOL

The following equipment is necessary for grooming the rabbit and for removing and collecting the wool:

A table, waist high, with a top 12 × 24 inches. It should have casters so it can be turned easily, and should be covered with a feed sack or carpeting to prevent the rabbit from slipping. *A brush,* or "hairbrush," with single steel bristles set in rubber—for brushing and removing foreign material from the wool. *A pair of sharp scissors* similar to those used by barbers. *Electric clippers.* These are especially desirable where wool is to be removed from a large number of animals. *A ruler*—to measure the length of the wool. *Containers.* A container for each grade should be within easy reach so the wool may be graded and placed in the proper one for storage at the time it is removed from the animal.

GROOMING

Commercial woollers require little grooming, provided they are properly cared for and the wool is removed every 10 to 12 weeks. If the coat is allowed to grow for a longer period, the fibers are likely to become webbed or slightly tangled, and to form mats.

For grooming, place the rabbit on the table, part the wool down the middle of the back, and brush one side, making the strokes downward. As the end of the wool is reached, brush upward and outward to remove all foreign matter. Make another parting in the wool about half an inch farther down the side and repeat until that side is completed; then groom the other side in the same way. For brushing the neck, front legs, and belly, place the rabbit on its back in your lap with the hindquarters held gently but firmly between your knees. Separate small areas of the wool and brush as with the sides; then place the rabbit on its back in your lap with its head and front feet under your arm, and hold and groom the hind legs. Cut off all stained ends of wool.

REMOVAL OF WOOL

The young Angoras should be sheared or clipped at weaning

and subsequently every 10 to 12 weeks. The wool should also be removed from the doe following breeding; by the time she kindles it should again be long enough so she can pull enough to cover her litter.

There are three methods for removal of the wool: plucking, shearing, and clipping. Each method has its proponents. The annual yield will not be influenced by the method used. The novice may prefer to remove the wool by shearing, although as he or she develops a larger herd, removal of the wool by clipping may save time.

Plucking

In the European countries, especially in France, the wool is plucked to a greater extent than it is in the United States. This plucked wool brings the highest price on the market, but it is necessary to handle the rabbit two or three times in order to remove the entire coat unless the animal happens to be in complete molt. In gaining experience in plucking, you should practice with the older does first. Test the long fibers on the different parts of the body, and if they come out easily, pluck them with the thumb and index finger, using the other hand to hold the skin against the rabbit's body. Remove only the long fibers, and do not attempt to pluck them unless they are loose.

Shearing or Clipping

There are several methods for restraining the rabbit. Some prefer to use a device for tying it, while others hold the animal in such a way that struggling can be prevented without tying it. As you gain experience, you will become proficient and devise your own methods for restraining the animal and eventually should be able to remove the wool from a rabbit in 10 to 15 minutes.

In preparing the rabbit for shearing or clipping, part the wool along the backbone (Fig. 14-2). Grasp the hind legs of the animal with one hand and begin removing the wool by shearing or clipping narrow swaths from the rump to the head, following the contour of the body (Fig. 14-3, upper) until all the wool is removed from one side. Repeat the procedure on the other side (Fig. 14-3, lower).

Fig. 14-2. Shearing an Angora rabbit—preparation. (Courtesy of USDA)

For removing the wool from under the neck and from the forelegs, restrain the rabbit by holding its ears and raising its body so that the front feet just touch the table (Fig. 14-4, upper). Then turn the rabbit over on its back on the table, and securely hold it by the ears and a fold of skin on the back of the neck to remove the coat on the thighs and on the belly (Fig. 14-4, lower). Care must be taken not to injure the teats. This precaution is especially important in the case of breeding does.

Give the rabbit a light brushing to straighten out the fibers and to prevent mats from forming with the new coat. Fig. 14-5 shows the sheared rabbit and the wool removed.

Chemical Shearing

Administration of certain chemicals causes the wool to fall out. Chemical shearing has been investigated with sheep. The tropical forage plant *Leucaena leucocephala* contains an amino acid, mimosine, that causes hair to fall out. Feeding this forage to sheep has been used as a defleecing procedure. These treatments have not

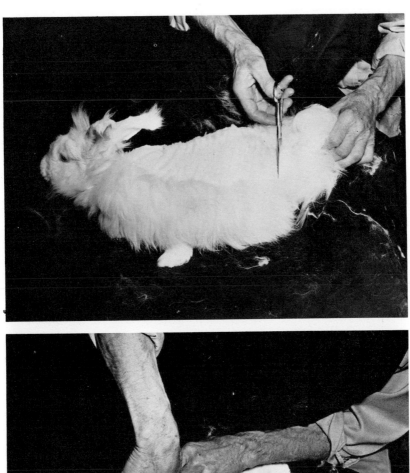

Fig. 14-3. Shearing an Angora rabbit. (Courtesy of USDA)

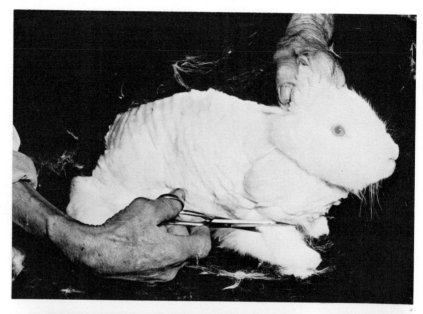

Fig. 14-4. Shearing an Angora rabbit—continued. (Courtesy of USDA)

Fig. 14-5. Shearing completed and quantity of wool removed. (Courtesy of USDA)

been studied with Angora rabbits, but would seem to offer a good means of reducing the labor requirements of obtaining wool.

CARE OF SHEARED OR CLIPPED RABBITS

The sheared or clipped rabbit will need protection from low temperatures, so ¼ to ½ inch of wool should be left on its body. You can accomplish this easily when shearing the rabbit; when electric clippers are used, a specially designed blade is available for this purpose. If the temperature drops to around 35°F, give the rabbit warm quarters until the wool has grown out at least to 1 inch in length, and provide a nest box with bedding for additional protection.

In regions where the winters are especially severe, the program should be so scheduled that the animals will not be sheared during the coldest months.

GRADING AND STORING ANGORA WOOL

Following are the commercial grades of Angora wool:

No. 1—Pure white, absolutely clean wool, free of all mats and foreign matter; staple length, 2¼ to 3 inches.

No. 2—Pure white, absolutely clean wool, free of all mats and foreign matter; staple length, 1½ to 2 inches.

No. 3—Pure white, absolutely clean wool, free of all mats and foreign matter; staple length, 1 to 1½ inches. Baby wool will grade as No. 3 because the fibers lack tensile strength. "Shorts"—Pure white and absolutely clean, but may contain slightly webbed wool.

No. 4—Pure white, clean, matted wool.

No. 5—All stained and unclean wool, matted or unmatted. If it is to be stored, mothballs or moth crystals in cloth sacks should be placed with the wool in tightly covered containers.

15

Slaughtering and Preparation
of Meat and Skins

The first step in slaughtering a rabbit is to render it unconscious. This should be done quickly in order to prevent suffering and struggling. One of two methods is generally used—either stunning the animal or dislocating its neck. For the most part, the former method is used by persons with little experience and when speed is not as important as it would be if large numbers of rabbits were to be processed. It consists of grasping the rabbit across the loin with one hand and suspending it head down, then stunning it by a heavy blow at the base of the skull between the ears with the butt end of a skinning knife, a stick, or a small iron rod. In the other method, you would hold the rabbit by its hind legs in one hand and place the thumb of the other hand on the neck just back of the ears, with the four fingers extended under the chin; then stretch the animal by pushing down on the neck with the hand. Press down with the thumb and with a quick movement raise the animal's head and dislocate the neck (Fig. 15-1). Immediately suspend the animal on a hook and cut the head off in order to prevent a blood clot forming on the neck and to ensure bleeding so the meat will have good color. A skinning knife with a 5-inch blade is a convenient size for dressing out the rabbit.

In slaughtering and dressing out the first few rabbits, it will take the novice longer than it will after he or she has developed the technique through experience. Commercial butchers can catch the rabbits out of the holding pen, render them unconscious, hang them on a hook, cut off the heads, and skin and eviscerate them at the rate of 100 or more per hour.

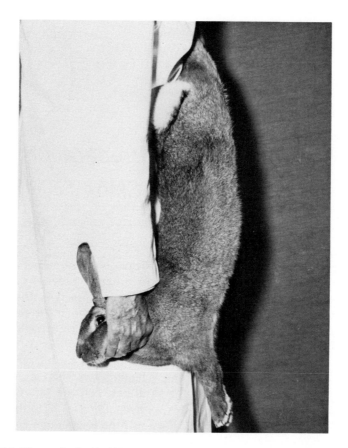

Fig. 15-1. The method of holding a rabbit for dislocating its neck in slaughtering.

In suspending the rabbit, insert the hook between the tendon and the bone of the right hind leg, just above the hock. Remove the tail and cut off the free hind leg at the hock joint. Cut off the front feet, then slit the skin just below the hock of the suspended leg, and insert the skinning knife under the skin on the inside of the leg and open it up to the root of the tail. Continue to the hock of the other leg. Carefully separate the edges of the skin from the carcass and pull the skin down over the animal, using the knife to separate the fat from the skin (Fig. 15-2) so the fat will be left on the carcass. When the skin is removed by this method it is known as a *cased skin.* Care must be taken to avoid cutting it, for even small cuts lower its value.

Fig. 15-2. Steps in skinning and removing internal organs of a rabbit. (Courtesy of USDA)

While the skin is still warm, secure it on a stretcher with the flesh side out (Fig. 15-3). A No. 9 galvanized wire can be shaped for the stretcher, and two sizes should be available, one for fryer skins and a larger size for mature and medium size skins. Place the skin on the stretcher with the two front legs on one side and pull the ends of the skin down over the stretcher to remove all wrinkles, but do not actually stretch the skin. Fasten the skin from the hind legs to the stretcher with clamp clothespins. Straighten out the folds in the neck skin. Lift up the skin on the front legs so it will not come in contact with the pelt and will dry more readily, and then hang the skin up for drying. No salt or other preservative should be used in preparing the pelts for marketing.

MEAT

After skinning the rabbit, make a slit in the abdominal wall of the carcass along the midline of the belly, cutting from the breastbone to the tail. Remove the bladder whole and take out the

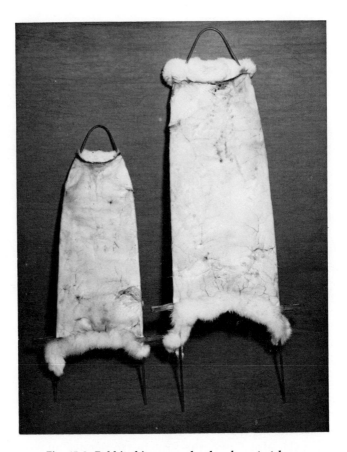

Fig. 15-3. Rabbit skins properly placed on stretchers.

entrails. Pinch or cut the gall bladder away from the liver and leave the heart, liver, and kidneys intact.

The carcass will draw out of shape if left suspended on the hook; for it to have a more blocky and attractive appearance it should be shaped up in a wire tray and chilled for 10 to 12 hours before being cut up.

Particular care must be taken to prevent hairs from getting on the carcass, for in addition to being very difficult to remove, they detract from the appearance. Rinsing in cold water will remove the hairs and blood and cleanse the carcass, but it should not be left in the water for more than 15 minutes because prolonged soaking causes the meat to absorb water; although it blanches the meat, this is not necessary, does not make it more desirable, and is considered an adulteration. If small blood clots have formed around the neck, they can usually be removed by brushing.

All work in connection with rabbit carcasses should be done in a sanitary manner. If the rabbit meat is to be marketed in cities where health regulations regarding the inspection of slaughtering plants and meat are in effect, or if the meat is to be moved into trade channels where city, county, state, or other inspection is required, the proper health authorities should be contacted for detailed information relative to such inspection.

SKINS

Curing

Hang the skins up to dry where they will be protected from sun, flies, and mice. The following day examine them to see that the edges are drying flat and that the skin on the front legs is straightened out. Remove any patches of fat, for it will cause the skin to burn and lower the value of the pelt. During periods of low temperature, some artificial heat will be required to dry out the

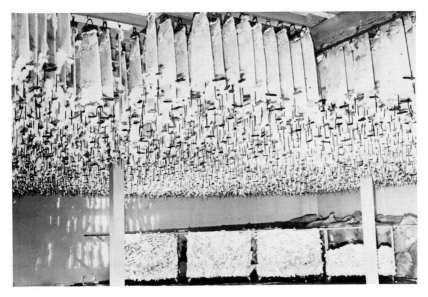

Fig. 15-4. Pelts being dried, and bins of graded dried pelts, in a large slaughtering plant. (Courtesy of H. F. Pelphrey & Son)

skins. This is accomplished in large slaughtering plants (Fig. 15-4) by circulation of warm air through the pelt-curing room.

Tanning Skins for Home Use

Skins that are to be sold should not be tanned before shipment, because fur buyers prefer them in the raw state. If intended for home use, however, the skins may be tanned by the methods described below. They should not be expected to compare favorably in appearance and pliability with products of a tannery or factory equipped with modern machinery and operated by experienced workers.

The first step in tanning is to get the skin thoroughly softened, clean, and free from flesh and grease. If it is cased or whole, slit the skin down the middle of the belly and soak it in clean, cool water. Change the water several times. When the skin is soft, lay it over a pole or board and work over the skin side with a coarse file or dull knife, breaking up and removing the adhering tissue, flesh, and fat, at the same time working the grease out of the skin. It is useless to start tanning until all the tissue and fat have been removed and the skin has been made uniformly soft and pliable.

The thickness and condition of the pelt determine the length of time a skin must be soaked. Some skins require two or three hours and others longer. A skin should be soaked until it is soft, but it should not remain wet longer than necessary, as the hair may start to slip. When it has been thus treated and is somewhat softened, work it in lukewarm water containing 1 ounce of soda or borax to the gallon. Soap added to the water is also helpful in cutting the grease and softening and cleansing the skin. After rinsing the skin thoroughly in lukewarm water, squeeze out the water but do not wring the pelt. Finally work the skin in gasoline, which should remove the last particles of dirt and grease. It is then ready for tanning.

There are several methods for tanning rabbit skins. Directions for using two of the more successful methods—the salt-acid and salt-alum processes—are given below.

Salt-Acid Process

The salt-acid formula calls for a solution made of 1 pound of common salt and ½ ounce of concentrated sulfuric acid to each gallon of water. Dissolve the salt in the water and carefully pour in the acid while stirring. This tanning liquor should be made and used in glass or earthen jars or wooden vessels, never in metal containers of any kind. When pouring in the acid, do not inhale the fumes given off. Be careful also not to get any of the strong acid on the skin or clothing. As soon as the salt-acid solution has cooled, it is ready for use.

Put the cleaned, softened skin in the solution so that it is entirely covered. Leave it in for one to three days, stirring it frequently, then remove it and rinse it in clean, cool water. Then work the skin for about 10 minutes in a solution of 1 ounce of borax to 1 gallon of water. Rinse again in clean water and squeeze (but do not wring) as dry as possible. Work the skin a few minutes in the hands by rubbing and pulling; then tack it out flat, flesh side up, and apply a thin coating of grease or oil and let it dry. Fresh butter, neat's-foot oil, or olive oil will be good for this purpose.

When the pelt is nearly dry but still damp, begin to work it with the hands, stretching it in all directions, working the flesh side over the edge of a board, and pulling it back and forth as if shining shoes with a cloth. If the skin is rough, you may smooth it by working it over a sandpaper block, which also helps to make it soft and pliable. Much of the success in producing a soft, pliable skin depends upon this repeated working, which must be done while the skin is drying out and not after it is dry. If the skin is not soft enough when dry, it should be dampened and worked again as before. If it is still greasy, it may be given a hasty bath in gasoline. A final cleaning, accomplished by working the skin in warm, dry hardwood sawdust, is beneficial and will add to the luster of the fur.

Salt-Alum Process

The salt-alum formula calls for 1 pound of ammonia alum (ammonium aluminum sulfate) or potash alum (potassium aluminum sulfate) dissolved in 1 gallon of water; and 4 ounces of washing soda (crystallized sodium carbonate) and 8 ounces of common salt dissolved together in ½ gallon of water. Pour the soda-salt solution slowly into the alum solution while stirring vigorously. Mix the combined solution, as used, with sufficient flour to make a thin paste, first mixing the flour with a little water to prevent lumps.

After cleaning and softening the skin as previously described, tack it out smoothly, flesh side up, on a board; then coat it about ⅛ inch thick with the tanning paste and protect it with paper or sacking laid on lightly so as not to come in close contact with the paste. The next day scrape off most of the paste and give another coating. At one-day intervals repeat this application two or three times, depending upon the thickness of the skin. Only thick skins from mature bucks will need as many as three applications. Leave the last coating on for three or four days. Finally, scrape off the paste, work the skin in borax water, rinse and squeeze it, and then stretch and work it over a board in the manner described for the salt-acid process.

The salt-alum process is widely used and is considered slightly better than the salt-acid tannage, although alum-tanned skins often come out stiff and hard and require much working to make them soft and pliable.

16

Rabbit Meat and Its Preparation for the Table

Rabbit meat is tasty and nutritious. For the rabbit industry to expand and prosper, the fine qualities of rabbit meat must be appreciated by an increasing number of consumers. An essential component of the development of the industry is promotion and marketing.

NUTRITIONAL PROPERTIES OF RABBIT MEAT

Rabbit meat is high in protein and low in fat. It has a low content of saturated fatty acids. It has a low cholesterol content and a low sodium content. Thus it is a highly nutritious meat and is suitable for special diets, such as those for heart disease patients, diets for the aged, low sodium diets, weight reduction diets, etc.

Rao et al. (1979) have published an extensive compilation of data on the composition of rabbit meat. The values are averages of the four major cuts (arms, ribs, loin, legs). Values for nutrients significant in human nutrition are shown in Table 16-1.

COOKING RABBIT MEAT

Rabbit meat is available in many supermarkets, in both fresh and frozen form. It is usually cut into serving portions and pack-

Table 16-1. Nutrient Composition of Rabbit Meat

Nutrient	Amount of Nutrient	Nutrient	Amount of Nutrient
Crude protein (%)	18.5[1]	*Minerals*[2]	
Fat (%)	7.4[1]	Zinc (mg/kg)	54
Water (%)	71[1]	Sodium (mg/kg)	393
Ash (%)	0.64[1]	Potassium (g/kg)	2
Unsaturated fatty acids		Calcium (mg/kg)	130
(% of total fatty acids)	63	Magnesium (mg/kg)	145
Cholesterol (mg/100 g)	136[2]	Iron (mg/kg)	29
Vitamins[2]		*Amino acids*[3]	
Thiamine (mg/100 g)	0.11	Leucine	8.6
Riboflavin (mg/100 g)	0.37	Lysine	8.7
Niacin (mg/kg)	21.2	Histidine	2.4
Pyridoxine (mg/kg)	0.27	Arginine	4.8
Pantothenic acid (mg/kg)	0.10	Threonine	5.1
Vitamin B_{12} (μg/kg)	14.9	Valine	4.6
Folic acid (μg/kg)	40.6	Methionine	2.6
Biotin (μg/kg)	2.8	Isoleucine	4.0
		Phenylalanine	3.2

[1]Wet weight basis.
[2]Dry weight basis.
[3]Amino acids expressed as percentage of protein.
Adapted from Rao, D. R., et al., "Nutritive Value of Rabbit Meat," *The Domestic Rabbit: Potentials, Problems, and Current Research* (Corvallis: Oregon State University Rabbit Research Center, 1979), pp. 53–59.

aged. In some areas, especially in ethnic markets, it may be sold in the whole carcass form.

Fryer rabbits are usually 8–10 weeks of age, and can be cooked in any way that broiler chickens are cooked. In fact, rabbit can be substituted directly for chicken in recipes. Stewers are older animals (above 6 pounds live weight) which should be cooked longer and more slowly in a covered pan.

Promotional activities to increase the acceptance of rabbit meat in the marketplace are needed. For example, the use of rabbit meat for barbecuing could be promoted. Barbecued rabbit is especially delicious. With the widespread popularity of outdoor barbecues, increased promotional emphasis could be given in rabbit marketing programs to develop this large potential market. Promotional activities, such as serving barbecued rabbit at state and local fairs, civic events, etc., should be considered by rabbit clubs and associations as a means of introducing new consumers to rabbit meat.

Fig. 16-1. Attractively prepared fried rabbit. (Courtesy of USDA)

BAKED RABBIT HASH

2 cups finely chopped cooked rabbit
    meat
2 cups finely chopped raw potatoes
2 tablespoons chopped green pepper
¾ cup finely chopped onion
1½ teaspoons salt

Pepper to taste
½ cup rabbit broth (or water with 1
    chicken bouillon cube)
¼ cup fine dry crumbs mixed with
    butter or margarine

    Mix all ingredients except the crumbs. Pile lightly into a greased baking dish or pan. Cover and bake at 350°F (moderate oven) about 40 minutes.

    Remove cover and sprinkle crumbs over the hash. Bake uncovered 20 minutes longer to brown.

    Four servings, 1 cup each.

BRAISED RABBIT WITH GRAVY

Young rabbit (2 to 2½ pounds ready-
    to-cook), cut in serving pieces
Flour, salt, pepper
3 tablespoons cooking fat or oil

¼ cup hot water
2 cups milk
2 tablespoons flour

Roll rabbit in mixture of flour, salt, and pepper. Heat fat or oil in a heavy fry pan and brown the rabbit slowly, turning to brown on all sides. Add water and cover pan tightly.

Reduce heat and cook slowly until meat is tender (about 1 hour), adding a little more water if needed. Uncover and cook 5 minutes longer to recrisp surface. Remove rabbit from pan and keep it hot.

Remove fat from pan and pour back 2 tablespoonfuls. Stir in the 2 tablespoons flour and cook until mixture bubbles. Add milk slowly, stirring constantly. Cook until thick, stirring occasionally, then cook a little longer. Add salt and pepper if needed.

Four servings.

To braise a large rabbit (about 4 pounds), use ⅓ cup fat or oil for browning and ⅓ cup water. Cook about 1½ hours, or until tender. Make gravy with 3 tablespoons flour, 3 tablespoons fat, and 3 cups milk.

Eight servings.

BREADED RABBIT CUTLETS

Hind rabbit legs
Cracker or bread crumbs
1 egg, beaten with 2 tablespoons water

Lawry's seasoned salt
Pepper to taste
Salad oil

Carefully bone rabbit legs. Place each piece of meat between two pieces of plastic wrap and pound gently with the edge of a saucer or tenderizer tool, until entire piece is the same thickness—about ½ inch. Remove plastic wrap. Sprinkle with desired amount of salt and pepper, dip in egg, and then coat both sides with crumbs. Place salad oil in skillet over medium heat. Brown rabbit on each side, about 7 to 10 minutes to a side.

BREAKFAST SAUSAGE

2¼ pounds fresh boneless rabbit, cut
  into strips or chunks
¾ pound fresh pork fat
2½ teaspoons rubbed sage
2 teaspoons salt
2 teaspoons pepper

½ teaspoon marjoram
¼ teaspoon each—allspice, nutmeg,
  dry mustard
Pinch of cayenne
¼ cup warm water

Chill rabbit and pork fat for easier grinding. Grind rabbit and pork fat together, using fine hole disc of meat grinder. Mix spices with warm water; then add to meat. Mix with hands until thoroughly blended. Refrigerate up to 12 hours to allow flavors to develop. Shape into patties or rolls for slicing. Cook same as pork sausage. Freezes well up to 3 months.

BROWNED RABBIT

Stewed rabbit (about 4 pounds ready-
  to-cook—see Stewed Rabbit recipe)
Flour, salt, pepper

⅓ cup cooking fat or oil
3 tablespoons flour
3 cups rabbit broth (or broth plus milk)

Remove rabbit from broth and save broth for gravy. Drain rabbit and roll it in mixture of flour, salt, and pepper.

Heat the fat and brown the rabbit, turning to brown on all sides and making the outside crisp. Browning will take 20 to 30 minutes. Remove rabbit from pan and keep it hot.

Remove fat from pan and pour back 3 tablespoonfuls. Stir in the 3 tablespoons flour and cook until the mixture bubbles. Add broth gradually and cook over low heat until thick and smooth, stirring occasionally. Cook a little longer and season to taste.

Eight servings.

CANNED RABBIT

Cut rabbit into equal sized pieces and sprinkle lightly with salt. Using a tiny bit of oil in a heavy skillet (several skillets can be going at one time), fry each piece until golden brown. Remove browned pieces to a large pan and place in oven at 300°F, keeping all pieces hot until ready to pack jars. Pack into hot jars, leaving 1 inch headspace. Add ½ teaspoon salt or chicken bouillon per quart. Add 2 cups water to drippings in skillet, bring to a boil, scrape all browned particles to dissolve. Divide evenly and pour over rabbit in quart jars. Finish filling jars with boiling water, leaving 1 inch headspace. Make *certain* rims of jars are wiped clean; then adjust lids. Process quarts 1¼ hours at 10 pounds pressure.

CANNED RABBIT AND DUMPLINGS

Place contents of one quart of canned rabbit in a 3-quart pan on top of stove. Save out and put into a smaller pan as much as possible of the jellied meat broth from around the rabbit. Set aside. Add to the rabbit in large pan—

1 small chopped onion	½ teaspoon rosemary (optional)
½ cup chopped celery	1 teaspoon chicken bouillon
¼ cup chopped parsley	¼ teaspoon pepper
1 crushed bay leaf	

Now add enough water to bring up to the level of the top of the rabbit. Bring to a boil. Reduce heat to a strong simmer; place dumplings on top.

Dumplings

Mix 2 cups Bisquick baking mix and ⅔ cup milk until soft dough forms. Drop by tablespoonfuls into boiling stew. Cook uncovered over low heat 10 minutes. Cover and cook an additional 10 minutes.

Remove dumplings to a warmed serving dish. Add jellied meat broth, previously set aside, to the rabbit and remaining juices in bottom of pan. Bring to a boil, thicken slightly if necessary, and serve as gravy over the hot dumplings.

CHINESE BROILED RABBIT

½ cup finely chopped onion
¼ cup butter
1 cup (8-ounce can) tomato sauce
¾ cup pineapple juice
2 tablespoons lemon juice
2 tablespoons brown sugar, firmly
packed

1 teaspoon salt
½ teaspoon dry mustard
¼ teaspoon seasoned salt
¼ teaspoon pepper
1 rabbit (2 to 2½ pounds), cut in serving pieces
Hot mustard sauce (see following recipe)

Cook onion in butter until tender. Mix in tomato sauce, pineapple juice, lemon juice, brown sugar, and seasonings. Cook over low heat 15 to 20 minutes to blend flavors. Pour over rabbit. Let stand 1½ to 2 hours. Place rabbit pieces, meat side up, on rack in broiler pan 7 to 9 inches from heat. Broil 25 to 30 minutes. Turn. Broil 20 to 25 minutes longer, or until rabbit is tender. Baste every 8 to 10 minutes with sauce. Salt before serving. Serve with hot mustard sauce.

Three to four servings.

Hot Mustard Sauce

2 tablespoons dry mustard
½ teaspoon salt
2 teaspoons salad oil

1 teaspoon cornstarch
6 tablespoons water
Turmeric

Mix mustard, salt, and salad oil. Combine cornstarch and water. Bring to boil. Heat and stir until thickened and clear. Gradually add to mustard mixture. Mix well. Add turmeric if a deeper color is desired. Yield: ½ cup.

CREAMED RABBIT

3½ tablespoons butter or margarine
3½ tablespoons flour
2½ cups milk (or milk plus rabbit broth)
Salt and pepper to taste

2½ cups coarsely cut cooked rabbit meat
2 teaspoons lemon juice
1 teaspoon grated onion
1 hard-boiled egg, finely chopped

Melt butter or margarine and blend in the flour. Add milk gradually and cook over very low heat, stirring frequently, until smooth and thick. Add salt and pepper.

Add rabbit meat and heat thoroughly, stirring occasionally.

Stir in lemon juice and onion. Sprinkle egg over the top.

Four servings, ⅔ cup each.

CREOLE RABBIT

1 rabbit (about 3 pounds ready-to-cook), cut in serving pieces
¼ cup milk

Flour, salt, pepper
3 tablespoons cooking fat or oil
Creole sauce (see following recipe)

Dip rabbit in milk and roll it in mixture of flour, salt, and pepper.

Heat fat or oil and brown rabbit lightly on all sides. Pour sauce over rabbit; cover pan.

Bake at 325°F (slow oven) 1½ hours, or until meat is tender. Uncover and bake 30 minutes longer to brown top.

Six servings.

Creole Sauce

2 medium onions, sliced
1 clove garlic, finely chopped
1 tablespoon chopped parsley
3 tablespoons butter, margarine, or oil

3½ cups tomato juice (No. 2½ can)
¼ teaspoon Worcestershire sauce
Salt and pepper to taste

Cook onions, garlic, and parsley in the butter, margarine, or oil until onion is golden brown. Add other ingredients except salt and pepper and cook gently for 15 minutes. Season to taste.

CURRIED RABBIT

2 cups rabbit broth
¼ cup finely chopped onion
1 clove garlic, cut in half
1 teaspoon curry powder
¼ cup milk

⅓ cup sifted flour
2 cups coarsely cut cooked rabbit meat
Salt and pepper to taste
1½ cups hot cooked rice (½ cup raw)

Boil broth, onion, garlic, and curry powder in a covered pan for 20 minutes. Remove garlic.

Stir the milk into the flour. Add a few tablespoons of the hot broth, and stir mixture into the rest of the broth. Cook over low heat until thick and smooth; stir frequently.

Add the rabbit meat and salt and pepper. Heat thoroughly and serve over rice.

Four servings, 1 cup each.

FRIED RABBIT

Small young rabbit (1½ to 2 pounds ready-to-cook), cut in serving pieces

Flour, salt, pepper
Cooking fat or oil

Roll rabbit in mixture of flour, salt, and pepper. Heat fat or oil about ¼-inch deep in a heavy fry pan large enough to hold the pieces without crowding.

Use moderate heat for frying. Put in the large, meaty pieces of rabbit first and cook about 10 minutes before adding the smaller pieces and giblets. Turn the pieces often for even cooking, and cook until well browned and tender (30 to 35 minutes total time).

Three to four servings.

HASSENPFEFFER

½ cup vinegar
2 cups water
2 teaspoons salt
¼ teaspoon pepper
½ teaspoon whole cloves
2 teaspoons sugar
4 bay leaves

1 medium onion, sliced
Small rabbit (about 2½ pounds ready-
  to-cook), cut in serving pieces
Flour
3 tablespoons fat
2 teaspoons Worcestershire sauce
3 tablespoons flour

Make pickling mixture by combining the vinegar, water, salt, pepper, cloves, sugar, bay leaves, and onion in glass or enamelware bowl.

Add pieces of rabbit and sliced giblets, and cover the bowl. Let stand in refrigerator 8 to 12 hours, turning the pieces occasionally so that they will absorb the flavor evenly.

Remove the rabbit pieces. Save liquid and onions but discard bay leaves and cloves.

Roll the rabbit in flour. Heat fat in a heavy pan and brown the rabbit in it, turning to brown all sides.

Pour the pickling mixture over the rabbit. Cover pan and cook over low heat about 1 hour, or until rabbit is tender.

Take rabbit from pan and keep it hot. Add Worcestershire sauce to the liquid. Mix the 3 tablespoons flour with a little cold water, add a few tablespoons of hot liquid to it, and pour the mixture back into the pan. Stir and cook until the sauce is thick and smooth; then cook a little longer. Pour sauce over rabbit.

Four servings.

To use a large rabbit (about 4 to 5 pounds ready-to-cook), double the amounts of ingredients for the pickling mixture. It is important to have enough to flavor all the meat. Use ⅓ cup fat to brown the rabbit and ⅓ cup flour to thicken the sauce. It may be necessary to skim off part of the fat before thickening the sauce.

Eight to ten servings.

ITALIAN SAUSAGE

Italian sausage is most useful to have on hand. It can flavor spaghetti sauce or be used in quiche, scrambled in eggs, or added to meat loaf. Italian sausage can be sweet (mild) or hot. This recipe is for medium hot. For a mild variety, omit crushed red pepper.

3 pounds boneless rabbit, cut into
  cubes or strips—well chilled
1 pound fresh pork fat, cut same
½ cup fresh parsley, chopped fine
2 tablespoons finely chopped garlic
2 tablespoons salt
2 teaspoons ground pepper

2 teaspoons crushed fennel seed
2 teaspoons crushed red pepper
1 teaspoon ground thyme
4 crumbled bay leaves
½ teaspoon allspice
¼ teaspoon nutmeg

Using the large hole disc of meat grinder, grind rabbit and pork fat. Place meat in large bowl with remaining ingredients. Mix with hands until thoroughly blended. Shape into rolls or patties. Can be refrigerated up to 3 days, or frozen.

LEMON BARBECUED RABBIT

1 rabbit, cut in serving pieces
Lemon sauce (see following recipe)
¾ cup and 2 teaspoons flour
2 teaspoons salt

¼ teaspoon pepper
⅓ cup butter
1 teaspoon kitchen bouquet
2 tablespoons sugar

Marinate rabbit in lemon sauce 2 hours. Remove pieces and dry slightly. Combine ¾ cup flour, salt, and pepper. Roll rabbit in flour mixture. Brown well in butter. Combine lemon sauce and kitchen bouquet. Pour over rabbit. Cover and cook over low heat 45 minutes, or until tender. Remove rabbit pieces to hot platter. Combine 2 teaspoons flour with a little cold water. Add to sauce with sugar. Heat and stir to boiling. Serve over rabbit.

Four servings.

Lemon Sauce

1 clove garlic
2½ teaspoons salt
⅓ cup salad oil
½ cup lemon juice

¾ cup water
¼ cup finely chopped onion
1 teaspoon black pepper
1 teaspoon ground thyme

Crush garlic with salt. Mix in remaining ingredients. Let stand overnight.

Note: This sauce has a very distinct lemon flavor. For milder flavor, reduce lemon juice to ¼ cup.

OVEN FRIED RABBIT LEGS

Use front legs saved when boning rabbits for sausage. Preheat oven to 375°F. Use a 13 × 9–inch pan for 4 to 6 servings, or oven broiler pan for a larger group. Coat bottom of pan with a thin layer of salad oil. Salt and pepper legs as desired. (Lawry's seasoned salt is good.) Place legs in pan in a single layer, turning each one over so both sides are coated with oil. Put in 375°F oven for 45 to 60 minutes—until browned and crisp. Also can be basted with barbecue sauce the last 12 to 15 minutes if desired.

OVEN RICE AND RABBIT CASSEROLE

2 tablespoons salad oil
1 rabbit, cut up
2 cups long grain white rice, raw
3 chicken bouillon cubes dissolved in 5
    cups hot water
1 clove garlic, minced
½ cup chopped onion

½ cup chopped celery
¼ cup chopped parsley
1 crumbled bay leaf
½ teaspoon rosemary
1½ teaspoons salt
¼ teaspoon pepper

Brown rabbit in 1 tablespoon salad oil in Dutch oven–type pot. Remove rabbit. Add 1 tablespoon salad oil and rice. Toast rice in oil, stirring frequently until light brown. Add all remaining ingredients, adding browned rabbit last. Cover tightly, put in preheated 350°F oven, and cook 1 hour. Check occasionally to make certain rice has enough liquid. Adjust by adding hot water if necessary.

Six to eight servings.

RABBIT À LA KING

⅓ cup chopped celery
3 tablespoons finely chopped onion
3 tablespoons finely chopped green pepper
3 tablespoons sliced mushrooms
⅓ cup water

½ cup butter or margarine
¼ cup sifted flour
2½ cups milk (part rabbit broth may be used)
Salt and pepper to taste
2 cups coarsely cut cooked rabbit meat

Cook vegetables and mushrooms gently in the water in a covered pan until just tender (about 20 minutes). Drain, and save the liquid.

Melt butter or margarine; blend in the flour. Add cooking liquid to milk and pour gradually into fat-flour mixture, stirring frequently, until thick and smooth. Season with salt and pepper.

Add vegetables, mushrooms, and rabbit meat to the sauce and heat thoroughly.

Four servings, ¾ cup each.

RABBIT CHOP SUEY

2 cups coarsely cut cooked rabbit meat
¼ cup sliced mushrooms
2 tablespoons butter or margarine
1 cup thinly sliced celery
1 small carrot, cut in thin strips
1 medium onion, thinly sliced
1½ cups rabbit broth (or water with 3 chicken bouillon cubes)

2 cups canned bean sprouts, with liquid
3 tablespoons cornstarch
3 tablespoons soy sauce
Salt and pepper to taste
1½ cups hot cooked rice (½ cup raw)

Cook rabbit meat and mushrooms in the fat over low heat a few minutes, until lightly browned. Add celery, carrot, onion, and broth.

Cover the pan and boil gently 10 to 15 minutes, or until vegetables are tender. Add the bean sprouts and liquid, and heat to boiling.

Mix the cornstarch and soy sauce; add gradually to the boiling mixture, stirring constantly. Cook 2 minutes, or until slightly thickened; add salt and pepper. Serve over rice.

Six servings, about 1 cup each.

RABBIT FRICASSEE WITH VEGETABLES

1 rabbit (about 3 pounds ready-to-cook), cut in serving pieces
Flour, salt, pepper
⅓ cup cooking fat or oil
2 cups hot water

4 cups raw vegetables—peas and coarsely chopped carrots, onions, and celery
1 teaspoon salt
¼ cup sifted flour

Roll rabbit in mixture of flour, salt, and pepper.

Heat fat or oil and brown the rabbit slowly, turning often. Add water and cover pan.

Cook slowly on top of range about 1 hour, or until rabbit is almost tender. Add water if needed during cooking. Add vegetables and salt, and cook about 20 minutes longer, or until vegetables are done.

Or, after browning, bake the rabbit at 325°F (slow oven) about 1½ hours, add vegetables, and bake about 30 minutes longer.

Mix the ¼ cup flour with a little cold water, add a few tablespoons of hot liquid from the pan, and stir the mixture into the liquid in pan. Cook 15 minutes longer, or until sauce is smooth and thick.

Eight servings.

To fricassee a smaller rabbit (about 2 pounds ready-to-cook), use ¼ cup fat or oil for browning, and half the quantity of the other ingredients in the recipe above. Cooking time on top of range before adding vegetables is about 30 minutes; in oven, about 45 minutes.

Four servings.

RABBIT-HAM CROQUETTES

2 tablespoons butter or margarine	⅔ cup ground cooked ham
2½ tablespoons flour	1 teaspoon chopped parsley
⅛ teaspoon dry mustard	1 teaspoon chopped green pepper
¾ cup milk	Beaten egg
1 teaspoon onion juice or grated onion	Fine dry crumbs
1⅓ cups chopped cooked rabbit meat	Fat or oil for deep-frying

Melt butter or margarine and stir in the flour and mustard. Cook until mixture bubbles.

Add the milk gradually, stirring constantly. Add onion and cook over low heat until thick and smooth, stirring occasionally.

Blend the meat, parsley, and green pepper into the sauce. Cool. If the mixture is very soft, chill it until it is firm enough to handle easily.

Shape into 8 croquettes. Dip them in the egg and roll them in the crumbs.

Fry in deep fat at 350°F about 4 minutes, or until golden brown.

Four servings.

RABBIT IN BARBECUE SAUCE

1 rabbit (about 3 pounds ready-to-cook), cut in serving pieces	3 tablespoons cooking fat or oil
Flour, salt, pepper	Barbecue sauce (see following recipe)

Roll rabbit in mixture of flour, salt, and pepper. Heat the fat and brown rabbit on all sides over moderate heat (about 20 minutes). Pour sauce over rabbit; cover pan.

Bake at 325°F (slow oven) about 45 minutes, or until meat is tender. Uncover pan and place under broiler. Broil 15 minutes, or until meat is brown.

Six servings.

Barbecue Sauce

2 tablespoons brown sugar
1 tablespoon paprika
1 teaspoon salt
1 teaspoon dry mustard
¼ teaspoon chili powder
Few grains cayenne pepper

2 tablespoons Worcestershire sauce
1 cup tomato juice
¼ cup chili sauce or catsup
¼ cup vinegar
½ cup chopped onion

Combine ingredients and cook over low heat 15 minutes.

RABBIT LIVER PÂTÉ

3 slices bacon
3 rabbit livers, cubed
¼ cup margarine
½ cup chopped onion
2 tablespoons chopped parsley

1 clove garlic, finely minced
¼ teaspoon ground thyme
¼ teaspoon dry mustard
Dash of pepper
½ teaspoon salt—or to taste

Using heavy skillet, fry bacon to crisp stage. Remove bacon and add liver cubes. Fry until just barely done. Remove liver and add to same skillet margarine, onion, parsley, and garlic. Sauté until onion is transparent and golden in color. Cool cooked ingredients at least 5 minutes. Place in blender or food processor with all the scrapings from skillet—plus spices. Blend until smooth. Place in refrigerator and allow flavors to develop several hours before serving.

RABBIT LOGS

3¾ pounds boned rabbit meat
1¼ pounds beef suet
5 slightly rounded teaspoons Morton's
   Tender Quick Curing Salt
2½ teaspoons whole mustard seed

2½ teaspoons ground pepper—
   coarsely ground preferable
2 teaspoons hickory smoke salt
2 teaspoons garlic powder (or 5 cloves
   fresh garlic, pressed)

Put rabbit and beef suet through meat grinder, using a fine blade. Mix salt and spices together thoroughly with meat. Refrigerate until next day. Mix well again and return to refrigerator. On third day, form into 5 salami-type rolls. Put on broiler rack over broiler pan. Place in oven on lowest rack. Cook for 8 hours at 170°F, turning over every 2 hours. Makes excellent sandwich meat and freezes well.

RABBIT 'N' ONIONS

12 small white onions
2 cups cider
1 tablespoon vinegar
½ cup and 3 tablespoons flour
2½ teaspoons salt
1 teaspoon celery salt
2 teaspoons paprika

½ teaspoon pepper
1 rabbit (2 to 2½ pounds), cut in serving pieces
½ cup butter
¼ cup chopped green pepper
⅛ teaspoon garlic powder
½ cup slivered ripe olives

Cook onions in cider and vinegar 30 to 40 minutes, or until tender. Combine ½ cup flour, salt, celery salt, paprika, and pepper. Roll rabbit pieces in flour mixture. Brown well in butter. Remove to a large saucepan or casserole. Cook green pepper and garlic powder in butter until tender. Add to rabbit with olives, onions, and cider. Cover and cook over low heat 40 minutes, or until rabbit is tender. Remove rabbit pieces and keep hot. Combine 3 tablespoons flour with a little cold water to form a smooth paste. Blend into pan liquid. Heat and stir until boiling and thickened. Serve over rabbit.

Three to four servings.

RABBIT PAPRIKA

1 cup finely chopped onion	1 teaspoon pepper
½ cup butter	1 tablespoon lemon juice
2 tablespoons red paprika	1 teaspoon caraway seeds
1 rabbit (2 to 2½ pounds), cut in serving pieces	¼ cup water
	2 cups sour cream
4 teaspoons salt	3 tablespoons flour

Cook onion in butter until tender. Blend in 1 tablespoon paprika. Rub rabbit with salt and pepper. Brown. Add lemon juice, caraway seeds, and water. Cook over low heat 40 minutes, or until tender. Remove rabbit and keep hot. Blend sour cream, flour, and 1 tablespoon paprika together thoroughly. Slowly mix into pan drippings. Heat and stir just to boiling. Serve over rabbit.

Three to four servings.

RABBIT PIE

¼ cup butter or margarine	Salt and pepper to taste
¼ cup chopped onion	3 cups coarsely cut cooked rabbit meat
½ cup chopped green pepper	Pastry (see following recipe)
¼ cup sifted flour	
2 cups rabbit broth (or water with 4 chicken bouillon cubes)	

Heat butter or margarine in a large fry pan. Add onion and green pepper, and cook about 5 minutes over low heat.

Blend in the flour and cook until the mixture bubbles. Pour in the broth gradually, stirring constantly. Cook until thick and smooth, stirring frequently. Add salt and pepper.

Add meat to the sauce and heat thoroughly. Pour mixture into a shallow baking dish or pan.

Roll out the pastry and cut slits for steam to escape. Fit to top of dish or pan, crimping the edges of the crust.

Bake the pie at 425°F (hot oven) 15 to 20 minutes, or until crust browns and sauce bubbles.

For variety, use 1 cup of cooked diced vegetables (potatoes, carrots, celery) with 2 cups of rabbit meat. Make the topping of tiny baking powder biscuits.

Four to six servings.

Pastry

1 cup sifted flour
½ teaspoon salt

⅓ cup shortening
About 2 tablespoons cold water

Sift flour and salt together and cut in the shortening. Mix in just enough water to hold ingredients together.

RABBIT SALAD

2 cups coarsely cut cooked rabbit meat
¼ cup chopped sweet pickle
½ cup chopped celery
1 tablespoon chopped onion
½ cup diced cooked potatoes

½ teaspoon salt
1 tablespoon liquid from sweet pickles
½ tablespoon lemon juice
¼ cup mayonnaise or other thick salad
    dressing

Mix first six ingredients lightly but thoroughly. Blend pickle liquid and lemon juice into dressing, and mix with the other ingredients. Chill for an hour to blend flavors.

Four servings, ¾ cup each.

RABBIT SALAD LOAF

1 envelope unflavored gelatin (1 table-
    spoon)
¼ cup cold water
1⅔ cups hot rabbit broth (or water
    with 4 chicken bouillon cubes)
Salt to taste
1 teaspoon grated onion or onion juice

1½ tablespoons vinegar or lemon juice
1 hard-boiled egg, sliced
6 stuffed olives, sliced
1½ cups diced cooked rabbit
⅓ cup cooked peas
3 tablespoons finely chopped celery

Soften the gelatin in the cold water a few minutes and dissolve in the hot broth. Add salt, onion, and lemon juice.

Pour a layer of the gelatin mixture ¼ inch deep in the bottom of an oiled 3- or 4-cup loaf pan or mold, and cool until firm. Let the rest of the gelatin mixture thicken but not set.

Press a design of the sliced egg and olives lightly into the firm gelatin in the pan.

Add the rabbit, peas, and celery to the thickened gelatin-broth mixture, and pour it carefully over the sliced egg and olives. Chill until firm. Unmold and slice for serving.

Four servings, about ⅔ cup each.

RABBIT SANDWICH SPREAD

1 cup finely chopped cooked rabbit
    meat

¼ cup finely chopped sweet pickle or
    pickle relish

2 tablespoons finely chopped onion
2 tablespoons finely chopped green
  pepper
¼ cup finely chopped celery

⅓ cup mayonnaise or other thick salad
  dressing
Salt to taste

Mix all ingredients well. Keep cold and use within a week.
Makes 1½ cups, enough for 6 sandwiches, ¼ cup each.

RABBIT WITH DUMPLINGS

Stewed rabbit (about 4 pounds ready-
  to-cook—see Stewed Rabbit recipe)
4 cups rabbit broth
⅓ cup fat (skimmed from broth, plus
  butter or margarine if needed)

⅓ cup sifted flour
Salt and pepper to taste
Dumpling mixture (see following recipe)

If rabbit and broth are cold, heat them together until meat is hot.
Blend fat and flour, and stir in several tablespoons of the hot broth. Pour the mixture gradually into the rest of the broth, stirring constantly. Cook until thickened. Season with salt and pepper. Drop dumpling mixture by spoonfuls on the pieces of rabbit in the boiling gravy. Space so that dumplings will not run together in cooking.
Cover pan tightly and cook 15 minutes without lifting the cover.
Eight servings.

Dumpling Mixture

¾ cup sifted flour
2 teaspoons baking powder
½ teaspoon salt

1 egg, beaten
⅓ cup milk

Sift flour, baking powder, and salt together. Combine egg and milk and add to dry ingredients, mixing just enough to moisten.

RAGOUT OF RABBIT

½ cup and 3 tablespoons flour
1 tablespoon salt
¾ teaspoon seasoned salt
½ teaspoon pepper
1½ teaspoons paprika
1 rabbit (2 to 2½ pounds), cut in serving pieces
½ cup milk
⅓ cup butter

¾ cup finely chopped onions
1 teaspoon ground caraway
½ cup white wine
1 cup chicken bouillon
1½ cups sliced carrots
1 package (10 ounces) frozen green
  peas
½ cup sliced green olives

Combine ½ cup flour, salt, seasoned salt, pepper, and paprika. Dip rabbit pieces in milk, then in flour mixture. Brown well in butter. Remove rabbit to a casserole or heavy saucepan. Cook onions in butter until tender. Add to rabbit with caraway, wine, and bouillon. Cover and cook over low heat 10 to 15 minutes. Add carrots, peas, and olives. Cook 15 minutes longer, or until vegetables are tender.

Remove rabbit and keep warm. Combine 3 tablespoons flour with a little cold water to form a smooth paste. Stir into gravy. Heat and stir until boiling and thickened. Serve over rabbit.

Three to four servings.

ROTISSERIE RABBIT

Preheat rotisserie oven, or use a barbecue unit with charcoal. Sprinkle inside of rabbit with salt and pepper; skewer rabbit lengthwise securely with spit rod, balancing carefully. Set timer for 1 hour and 50 minutes. Baste as rabbit turns with a mixture of 1 cup barbecue sauce, ¼ cup salad oil, ½ teaspoon hickory smoke salt, and a pinch of cayenne pepper. Baste every 15 minutes.

ROYAL RABBIT SCALLOP

1 rabbit (2 to 2½ pounds)
2 stalks celery
1 medium onion, quartered
1 bay leaf
3 peppercorns, slightly crushed
1½ teaspoons and 2¼ teaspoons salt
3 medium potatoes
1½ cups coarsely chopped onion
¼ cup finely chopped celery leaves

¼ cup and 6 tablespoons melted butter
2 cups (15-ounce can) cut green beans, drained
3 tablespoons chopped parsley
¼ cup diced pimiento
6 tablespoons flour
¾ teaspoon ground rosemary
⅜ teaspoon pepper

Cover rabbit, celery, onion, bay leaf, peppercorns, and 1½ teaspoons salt with water. Heat to boiling. Cover and cook over low heat 1 hour and 15 minutes, or until rabbit is tender. Add potatoes. Cook 20 to 25 minutes longer. Strain broth and save 1¾ cups. Cut meat into small pieces. Heat oven to moderate (350°F). Butter a 2-quart casserole. Cook onion and celery leaves in ¼ cup butter until tender. Peel and thinly slice potatoes. Layer rabbit, green beans, and potatoes in casserole. Sprinkle ½ of the onion mixture and ⅓ of the parsley and pimiento on top of each of the bottom two layers. Blend flour, rosemary, pepper, and 2¼ teaspoons salt with 6 tablespoons butter. Gradually stir in saved broth. Heat and stir until thickened and boiling. Pour over casserole. Sprinkle with remaining parsley and pimiento. Cover and bake 30 minutes. Uncover and bake 10 minutes longer, or until bubbly.

Six servings.

SMOKED RABBIT

Make brine for marinating—enough for 4 rabbits.

1 gallon water
1½ cups uniodized salt
4 cloves garlic, pressed or finely chopped

1 small, finely chopped onion
½ cup brown sugar
¼ cup soy sauce

Mix all ingredients, making certain salt is completely dissolved. Place brine in large pan (don't use aluminum) or crock. An enameled water bath canner pot works well. Add rabbits, cover with brine, and weight to keep rabbits completely covered. A large plate over the rabbits with a gallon jar filled with water makes a fine weight. Marinate 8 to 10 hours. Remove from brine and allow to drain dry for about 2½ hours, or until outside looks dry. Place in smoker and smoke according to manufacturer's directions. Cut the 4 rabbits in half crosswise, flatten as much as possible, and smoke for 8 hours, with low heat. When finished there should be no pink coloring around the bone.

STEWED RABBIT

1 rabbit (about 4 pounds ready-to-cook), cut in serving pieces

1½ teaspoons salt
Hot water

Put rabbit into pan large enough to hold the pieces without crowding. Add salt and enough water to half cover the rabbit.

Cover pan and cook over low heat about 1½ hours, or until meat is very tender. Add more water during cooking if needed.

Serve hot with gravy made by thickening the broth and seasoning as desired, or use meat and broth in other recipes.

If not used at once, cool the meat and broth quickly by setting the pan in cold water, and storing in the refrigerator. Meat stored in the broth may be somewhat juicier than meat stored separately.

Eight servings.

SWEET-SOUR RABBIT

Small rabbit (about 2½ pounds ready-to-cook), cut in serving pieces
Flour, salt, pepper
2 tablespoons cooking fat or oil
1 cup pineapple juice
¼ cup vinegar
½ teaspoon salt

1 cup pineapple pieces
1 medium green pepper, cut in thin half slices
1½ tablespoons cornstarch
¼ cup sugar
½ cup water

Roll rabbit in mixture of flour, salt, and pepper.

Heat fat or oil in a heavy pan, and brown the rabbit over moderate heat, turning to brown on all sides.

Add pineapple juice, vinegar, and salt. Cover pan; cook over low heat 40 minutes, or until meat is tender. Add pineapple and green pepper; cook a few minutes longer.

Mix cornstarch and sugar and stir in the water. Stir this mixture gradually into liquid in the pan and cook slowly about 5 minutes.

Six servings.

VEGETABLE SOUP WITH RABBIT STOCK

3 quarts rabbit stock—made after boning rabbits for sausage
1 quart canned whole tomatoes
1 cup potato chunks

1 diced onion
2 large bay leaves
6 whole allspice
1 teaspoon oregano

2 cups other desired vegetables   ½ teaspoon pepper
½ cup green pepper   Salt to taste

Combine all ingredients and cook at simmer at least 1½ hours on top of stove, or place all in crock pot for 6 to 8 hours. This recipe can be doubled or tripled, then canned to provide a handy convenience food.

RABBIT RECIPES FOR QUANTITY SERVICE

The meat of the domestic rabbit is white, resembling chicken in texture, with little fat. It is sweet and adapts easily to many attractive, palatable dishes. The bones are light in weight in proportion to the size of the animal.

Cooking covered, with some moisture added, gives the best flavor and texture. When boiled rabbit remains in the broth overnight, there is a slight gain in weight. As purchased, the ready-to-cook rabbit usually has the kidneys attached. These, together with the liver, which is sometimes included, may be cooked separately and served as an entree.

Boiled Rabbit

1. Place washed ready-to-cook rabbit in a stock pot or steam jacketed kettle.

2. Cover with hot water and boil gently until tender. The cooking time for a young 2¾-pound rabbit will be about 1½ hours, and for a mature 4-pound rabbit, about 2½ hours.

3. When rabbit is tender, remove from the broth. Cool rabbit and broth quickly. Strip meat from the bones. If rabbit is not to be used until the next day, return the meat to the cooled broth and refrigerate.

The boiled rabbit meat may be sliced for cold meat platters or used in salads, sandwiches, or croquettes. The broth has a delicate flavor served as bouillon; it also makes a flavorful base for noodle or vegetable soup.

Fried Rabbit

Young tender rabbit may be pan-fried. The pieces of meat are floured, seasoned with salt and pepper, and cooked slowly, uncovered, in fat 1 inch deep in a frying pan, until golden brown on both sides. One hour altogether is usually required, half of the time for cooking and browning each side.

RABBIT CREOLE

Portion, ¼ cup sauce, 4 ounces rabbit

Ingredients	25 Portions	50 Portions	100 Portions
Sauce			
Sliced onion	1 pound (3 cups)	2 pounds (1½ quarts)	4 pounds (3 quarts)
Finely chopped garlic	½ ounce (8 cloves)	1 ounce (16 cloves)	2 ounces (32 cloves)
Chopped parsley	¼ cup	½ cup	1 cup
Butter or margarine	4 ounces (½ cup)	8 ounces (1 cup)	1 pound (2 cups)
Tomato juice	3½ quarts	1¾ gallons	3½ gallons
Worcestershire sauce	1 teaspoon	2 teaspoons	4 teaspoons
Salt	½ teaspoon	1 teaspoon	2 teaspoons
Rabbit			
Young rabbit (about 4-ounce pieces)	25	50	100
Milk	1 cup	2 cups	1 quart
Sifted all-purpose flour	6 ounces (1½ cups)	12 ounces (3 cups)	1 pound 8 ounces (1½ quarts)
Salt	4 teaspoons	8 teaspoons	5 tablespoons
Pepper	½ teaspoon	1 teaspoon	2 teaspoons
Vegetable shortening or lard	4 ounces (½ cup)	8 ounces (1 cup)	1 pound (2 cups)
Steam table pans 16½ by 10½ inches	2	4	8

Sauce:
    1. Sauté onion, garlic, and parsley in butter or margarine until golden brown.
    2. Add tomato juice, Worcestershire sauce, and salt. Simmer 15 minutes.

Rabbit:
    1. Dip rabbit in milk and then in flour, salt, and pepper which have been sifted together.
    2. Brown rabbit in shortening or lard. Place pieces in baking pans, and add the sauce (1½ quarts per pan).
    3. Cover and bake at 375°F (moderate) for 1½ hours, or until tender. Uncover and bake 30 minutes longer to brown.

CURRIED RABBIT

Portion, ½ cup (4½ ounces) rabbit, ¼ cup rice

Ingredients	28 Portions	56 Portions	112 Portions
Rabbit broth	2½ quarts	1¼ gallons	2½ gallons
Coarsely chopped onion	6 ounces (1 cup)	12 ounces (2 cups)	1 pound 8 ounces (1 quart)
Finely chopped garlic	2 cloves	4 cloves	8 cloves
Curry powder	1½ tablespoons	3 tablespoons	⅓ cup
Sifted all-purpose flour	3 ounces (¾ cup)	6 ounces (1½ cups)	12 ounces (3 cups)
Milk	1 cup	2 cups	1 quart
Eggs, slightly beaten	2	4	8
Salt	½ teaspoon	1 teaspoon	2 teaspoons
Diced cooked rabbit	3 pounds 8 ounces (2¾ quarts)	7 pounds (5½ quarts)	14 pounds (2¾ gallons)
Hot cooked rice	1¾ quarts	3½ quarts	1¾ gallons

1. Combine the broth, onion, garlic, and curry powder. Boil for 20 minutes. Strain.

2. Blend flour, milk, eggs, and salt. Add ½ of broth to this mixture, stirring constantly. Return to the remaining broth. Cook until thickened, stirring constantly.

3. Combine rabbit with the curry mixture. Reheat.

4. Serve over cooked rice.

FRICASSEED RABBIT

Portion, 4 ounces rabbit, ¼ cup gravy

Ingredients	25 Portions	50 Portions	100 Portions
Rabbit			
Rabbit (about 4-ounce pieces)	11 pounds	22 pounds	44 pounds
Flour	6 ounces (1½ cups)	12 ounces (3 cups)	1 pound 8 ounces (1½ quarts)
Salt	1 tablespoon	1 ounce (2 tablespoons)	2 ounces (¼ cup)
Pepper	¼ teaspoon	½ teaspoon	1 teaspoon
Carrots, whole	12 ounces	1 pound 8 ounces	3 pounds
Celery stalks, with leaves	4 ounces	8 ounces	1 pound
Onions, quartered	6 ounces	12 ounces	1 pound 8 ounces
Vegetable shortening or lard	2 ounces (¼ cup)	4 ounces (½ cup)	8 ounces (1 cup)
Water	1½ quarts	3 quarts	1½ gallons
Gravy			
Drippings	½ cup	1 cup	2 cups
Sifted all-purpose flour	2 ounces (½ cup)	4 ounces (1 cup)	8 ounces (2 cups)
Salt	1 teaspoon	2 teaspoons	1 tablespoon
Water	1¾ quarts	3 quarts	1½ gallons

Rabbit:
1. Roll the rabbit in flour, salt, and pepper, which have been sifted together.
2. Place the vegetables in a roasting pan.
3. Cover the vegetables with the rabbit.
4. Dot rabbit with shortening or lard.
5. Add the water, cover and bake 25 minutes longer, or until brown.

Gravy:
1. Combine drippings, flour, and salt in saucepan.
2. Gradually add water and cook, stirring constantly, until thickened.

RABBIT SALAD

Portion, ½ cup (3½ ounces)

Ingredients	25 Portions	50 Portions	100 Portions
Diced cooked domestic rabbit	2 pounds 8 ounces (2 quarts)	5 pounds (1 gallon)	10 pounds (2 gallons)
Chopped sweet pickle	10 ounces (2 cups)	1 pound 8 ounces (1 quart)	2 pounds 10 ounces (2 quarts)
Chopped celery	9 ounces (2¼ cups)	1 pound 2 ounces (4½ cups)	2 pounds 4 ounces (2¼ quarts)
Chopped onion	2 ounces (⅓ cup)	4 ounces (⅔ cup)	8 ounces (1⅓ cups)
Cooked rice	14 ounces (1¾ cups)	1 pound 12 ounces (3½ cups)	3 pounds 8 ounces (1¾ quarts)
Pickle juice	⅓ cup	⅔ cup	1⅓ cups
Mayonnaise	1 cup	2¼ cups	4½ cups
Salt	2 teaspoons	4 teaspoons	8 teaspoons
Lemon juice	2¼ tablespoons	4½ tablespoons	⅔ cup
Prepared mustard	¾ teaspoon	1¼ teaspoons	2½ teaspoons

1. Combine all ingredients and mix well. Chill.
2. Portion with No. 8 scoop on lettuce leaf and garnish with pimiento.

Glossary

Anterior presentation—Normal birth. Front feet and head presented first.

Antibiotics—Compounds used as feed supplements and for combatting disease. Produced by molds; inhibit the growth of bacteria.

Antisera—Sera (serums) that contain specific antibodies.

Artificial insemination—Artificial introduction of semen into the reproductive tract of the female.

Balanced ration—A ration that has the proper proportions of individual ingredients to provide for growth, production, and reproduction.

Barren period—The period during which a rabbit does not conceive.

Breach presentation—Normal birth. Hind feet and rump presented first.

Break pressure tank—A tank with a float valve, used with an automatic watering system.

Buck—A mature male rabbit used for breeding.

Butcher run—Unsorted and ungraded rabbits purchased for slaughter.

Cannibalism—The practice of a doe eating her own young.

Carcass yield—Dressing percent. Obtained by dividing the weight of the dressed carcass by the weight of the live rabbit.

Carrier—An animal carrying a gene for a specific characteristic that may be transmitted to offspring, although it may or may not be apparent in successive generations. Also, an animal with a subclinical level of disease; it may not show signs of disease, but can infect others (e.g., a carrier of *Pasteurella*).

Cecum—The blind gut at the head of the large intestine.

Chromosomes—The microscopic rod-shaped bodies in the egg and sperm cells that carry the hereditary factors (genes).

Conception—The union of ovum and sperm.

Concentrates—Grains, milled products, and supplements of protein, vitamins, and minerals in the ration.

Contagious disease—A disease that spreads from one individual to another. Catching.

Coprophagy—The practice of rabbits consuming some of the droppings (soft, night pellets) directly from the anus.

Developing period—The time from weaning until starting in production.

Dewlap—The pendulous fold of skin under a rabbit's neck.

Doe—A mature female rabbit used for breeding.

Dominant characteristic—A characteristic of one parent (normal coat, white fat, etc.) that, when transmitted to offspring, masks a recessive characteristic.

Dressing percent—Same as **Carcass yield.**

Embryo—The developing rabbit from the time the fertilized egg is implanted in the uterus until the time the doe kindles.

Estrus cycle or "heat period"—The recurring 14- to 16-day cycle when a doe is more apt to conceive.

False pregnancy—Same as **Pseudopregnancy.**

Felting—The manufacturing of felts from furs of rabbits and other animals.

Fetus—Same as **Embryo.**

Finish—The desired condition of flesh and coat for market or show rabbits.

Fly back—The prompt and even flowing back of the fur when it is stroked from the tail toward the head of the animal.

Follicles—Small enlargements on the surface of the ovary, containing egg cells.

Fostering—Using a doe other than the dam to nurse and develop young.

Fryer—A rabbit kept for meat consumption before the age of 12 weeks.

Full feeding—Supplying a rabbit each day with all the feed it will consume.

Furrier—One who dresses furs or makes or sells fur garments.

Gene—A small part of chromosome. The determiner of a hereditary factor.

Gestation period—The time from mating of the doe to kindling.

Gram—A unit of weight. One pound equals 453.6 grams.

Glossy coat—Smooth, bright, lustrous fur.

Grooming—Removing foreign material or loose fibers from the coat of a rabbit by brushing or rubbing its coat with the hands, proceeding from the head toward the tail.

Hand-feeding—Giving a rabbit the required amount of feed each day.

Heredity—Characteristics inherited from ancestors.

Hopper-feeding—Making available to a rabbit a sufficient quantity of feed for several days so the animal may eat as often as it wishes and not be limited to a certain amount.

Hybrid—The offspring of parents of different breeds, varieties, species, or genera.

Impaction—Lodgment of undigested food in the digestive tract.

Inbreeding—Mating closely related animals.

Infectious disease—A disease caused by germs. May or may not be contagious.

Juniors—Developing young from time of weaning until old enough to go into production.

Kindling—Same as **Parturition.**

Kitling (kit)—A young rabbit from birth to weaning.

Lactation—The secretion of milk.

Limit feeding—Restricting a rabbit's feed intake to an arbitrary level.

Linebreeding—The breeding or mating of successive generations. The animals are not as closely related as with inbreeding.

Litter—A number of young born to a doe at one time.

Maintain—To keep an adult rabbit in good condition without gaining or losing weight.

Malocclusion—A deviation from the proper closing or meeting of the teeth.

Manger—A container for holding hays and roughages.

Mature—Fully developed, adult.

Mesentery—Supporting membranes of the intestines.

Milligram—A unit of weight. One gram equals 1000 milligrams.

Miss—Same as **Pass.**

Nick—A mating which produces offspring that are superior to either parent.

Palpate—To feel for developing young in the uterus through the abdominal wall.

Parturition—Kindling. Act of giving birth.

Pass—Failure to conceive and produce young, an infertile mating (a miss).

Pedigree—A record of ancestors.

Peritoneum—The transparent membrane that lines the abdominal cavity.

Posing—Placing the rabbit in the most advantageous posture for show.

Predator—A pillaging or destructive animal that kills, maims, or stresses rabbits.

Prepotency—An exceptional capacity to transmit certain characteristics to offspring.

Prime coat—A mature, glossy coat with good "fly back" and free of loose fur or patches of ingrowing fur.

Prolific—Fertile, reproducing freely.

Protein—A combination of amino acids. Essential in the diet.

Pseudopregnancy—A 17-day period during which a doe may not conceive. May be caused by sterile mating or by other sexual stimulation. The doe experiences physical symptoms and changes in hormonal balance simulating those in pregnancy.

Purebred—A recognized breed kept pure for generations.

Rabbitry—A place where domestic rabbits are kept; also, a rabbit raising enterprise.

Random mating—Mating within a selected group with no attention paid to a definite mating system.

Recessive characteristic—A characteristic of one parent (woolly coat, yellow fat, etc.) that, when transmitted to offspring, is subordinate to the dominant characteristic of the other parent.

Registration—The official record of a rabbit that has been approved by a licensed registrar.

Restrained mating—Forced mating in which a person holds the doe.

Retarded wool growth—The slower than normal growth of wool on areas of the body of an Angora rabbit.

Roughage—Hay, grass, etc.

Settle—To conceive.

Sexing—Determining the sex of a rabbit.

Sheen—Shining. *See* **Glossy coat.**

Specialty club—A rabbit club that specializes in matters pertaining to one breed.

Standard—The characteristic for a breed of rabbits as set up and approved by a registering organization.

Sterile—Barren or infertile.

Succulent feed—Fresh, green, growing plants containing a large amount of moisture.

Suckling period—The time from birth to weaning.

Tan—To make into leather.

Tattoo—To make a permanent identification mark in the ear of a rabbit by using a perforating instrument and rubbing India ink into the perforations.

Thermostat—An instrument for automatically controlling the turning on and off of water sprinklers.

Toxic—Poisonous.

Vulva—The external opening of the female genital organs.

Warrens—Outside pens in which groups or colonies of rabbits may be kept.

Weaner (weanling)—A newly weaned rabbit, regardless of intended future use.

Weaning—Removing the young from the doe's cage for developing or marketing.

Wool—The coat of the Angora rabbit.

Wool block—An indigestible mass of wool swallowed by a rabbit.

Woolliness—A recessive characteristic transmitted to offspring, producing a hair coat which resembles wool.

Yellow fat—A recessive characteristic intensified in susceptible offspring by the feeding of green feeds.

Xanthophyll—A yellow compound found in plants, conducive to the development of yellow fat in susceptible animals.

Index

A

Abortion, 113
Abscesses, 174
Acid detergent fiber, 123–124
Ad libitum feeding, 149
Aflatoxin, 143
Age to breed, 62
Albinism, 220, 239
Alfalfa hay, 178
Alfalfa meal, 102, 103, 111, 120, 131, 160
Alleles, 216
Amaranthus, 137
Amino acids, 100
Amino acids, essential, 100
Amylase, 120
Angora wool, 269, 279
Angora wool, grades of, 297
Angora wool, grooming, 282
Antibiotics, 144
Artificial insemination, 66
Artificial milk, 152
Aspergillus flavus, 143, 157
Atherosclerosis, 102
Australia, rabbits in, 2, 5
Avidin, 115

B

Backyard rabbit production, 4, 6, 13, 18
Barley, 139
Beans, 157
Bedding, for nest boxes, 52
Beet pulp, 140
Bentonite, 145
Big head disease, 189
Biotin, 114

Blood clotting, 113
Blood meal, 144
Bomb calorimeter, 124
Books on rabbit production, 15
Bordetella bronchisepticum, 172
Breeding records, 249, 250
Breeding schedule, 62
Breeds, 26, 35
Breeds, genotypes of, 221
Brewers grains, 140
Broken back, 191
Buck cages, 41
Bucks, number of, 62
Buckteeth, 185
Building, 37, 43
Butchering, 289

C

Cage cards, 90
Cages, 37, 39
Cages, European-style, 39
Cages, quonset-style, 39
Caked breast, 182
Calcium, 103
Calcium, in urine, 87, 194
Calorie, 124
Cancer, 160
Cannibalism, 210
Canola meal, 143
Capacitation, 204, 207
Carbohydrate digestion, 120
Carbohydrate overload, 97, 101, 120, 139
Carbohydrates, 101
Carcass, dressing percent, 273
Carotene, 111